ABOUT THIS PUBLICATION

FOR SERVICE ASSISTANCE

Customer Service
1.704.898.0770

North Carolina General Statues is published by The Muliti-Media Group of Greater Charlotte in Charlotte, North Carolina. Copyright 2015 by the Multi-Media Group of Greater Charlotte. This book or parts thereof may not be reproduced in any form, stored in a retrieval system, or transmitted in any form by any means—electronic, mechanical, photocopy, recording or otherwise—without prior written permission of the publisher, except as provided by United States of America copyright law.

The records required by U.S. Code 2257(a) through (c) and the pertinent regulations 28 C.F.R. Cli. 1, Part 75 with respect to this publication and all materials associated with such records are maintained by The Multi-Media Group of Greater Charlotte, Publisher and available for review by Attorney General.

www.visionbooks.org

Copyright © 2015 by MMGGC
All rights reserved!

TID: 5064346
ISBN (10) digit: 1502935627
ISBN (13) digit: 978-1502935625

123-4-56789-01239-Paperback
123-4-56789-01239-Hardback

First Edition

090520140547

Printed in the United States of America

2015 EDITION

North Carolina Criminal Law And Procedure-Pamphlet # 54

Printed In conjunction with the Administration of the Courts

North Carolina Criminal Law and Procedure
Pamphlet Reference Guide

Chapters	Pamphlet
Chapter 1 Civil Procedure	1
Chapter 1 Civil Procedure (Continue)	2
Chapter 1A Rules of Civil Procedure	2
Chapter 1B Contribution.	2
Chapter 1C Enforcement of Judgments.	2
Chapter 1D Punitive Damages.	2
Chapter 1E Eastern Band of Cherokee Indians.	2
Chapter 1F North Carolina Uniform Interstate Depositions and Discovery Act.	2
Chapter 2 - Clerk of Superior Court [Repealed and Transferred.]	3
Chapter 3 - Commissioners of Affidavits and Deeds [Repealed.]	3
Chapter 4 - Common Law	3
Chapter 5 - Contempt [Repealed.]	3
Chapter 5A - Contempt	3
Chapter 6 - Liability for Court Costs	3
Chapter 7 - Courts [Repealed and Transferred.]	3
Chapter 7A – Judicial Department	3
Chapter 7A – Continuation (Judicial Department)	4
Chapter 7A – Continuation (Judicial Department)	5
Chapter 7B - Juvenile Code	5
Chapter 8 - Evidence	6
Chapter 8A - Interpreters for Deaf Persons [Recodified.]	6
Chapter 8B - Interpreters for Deaf Persons	6
Chapter 8C - Evidence Code	6
Chapter 9 - Jurors	6
Chapter 10 - Notaries [Repealed.]	6
Chapter 10A - Notaries [Recodified.]	6
Chapter 10B - Notaries	6
Chapter 11 - Oaths	6
Chapter 12 - Statutory Construction	6
Chapter 13 - Citizenship Restored	6
Chapter 14 - Criminal Law	7
Chapter 14 –Criminal Law (Continuation)	8
Chapter 15 - Criminal Procedure	9
Chapter 15A - Criminal Procedure Act (Continuation)	10
Chapter 15A - Criminal Procedure Act (Continuation)	11
Chapter 15B - Victims Compensation	11
Chapter 15C - Address Confidentiality Program	11
Chapter 16 - Gaming Contracts and Futures	11
Chapter 17 - Habeas Corpus	11

Chapter 17A - Law-Enforcement Officers [Recodified.]	11
Chapter 17B - North Carolina Criminal Justice Education and Training System [Recodified.] Chapter 17C - North Carolina Criminal Justice Education and Training Standards Commission	11 11
Chapter 17D - North Carolina Justice Academy	11
Chapter 17E - North Carolina Sheriffs' Education and Training Standards Commission	11
Chapter 18 - Regulation of Intoxicating Liquors [Repealed.]	12
Chapter 18A - Regulation of Intoxicating Liquors [Repealed.]	12
Chapter 18B - Regulation of Alcoholic Beverages	12
Chapter 18C - North Carolina State Lottery	12
Chapter 19 - Offenses against Public Morals	12
Chapter 19A - Protection of Animals	12
Chapter 20 - Motor Vehicles	13
Chapter 20 - Motor Vehicles (Continuation)	14
Chapter 20 - Motor Vehicles (Continuation)	15
Chapter 20 - Motor Vehicles (Continuation)	16
Chapter 21 - Bills of Lading	17
Chapter 22 - Contracts Requiring Writing	17
Chapter 22A - Signatures	17
Chapter 22B - Contracts Against Public Policy	17
Chapter 22C - Payments to Subcontractors	17
Chapter 23 - Debtor and Creditor	17
Chapter 24 – Interest	17
Chapter 25 – Uniform Commercial Code	18
Chapter 25 – Uniform Commercial Code (Continuation)	19
Chapter 25A – Retail Installment Sales Act	20
Chapter 25B - Credit	20
Chapter 25C - Sales of Artwork	20
Chapter 26 - Suretyship	20
Chapter 27 - Warehouse Receipts [Repealed.]	20
Chapter 28 - Administration [Repealed.]	20
Chapter 28A - Administration of Decedents' Estates	20
Chapter 28B - Estates of Absentees in Military Service	20
Chapter 28C - Estates of Missing Persons	20
Chapter 29 - Intestate Succession	21
Chapter 30 - Surviving Spouses	21
Chapter 31 - Wills	21
Chapter 31A - Acts Barring Property Rights	21
Chapter 31B - Renunciation of Property and Renunciation of Fiduciary Powers Act	21
Chapter 31C - Uniform Disposition of Community Property Rights at Death Act	21
Chapter 32 - Fiduciaries	21
Chapter 32A - Powers of Attorney	21
Chapter 33 - Guardian and Ward [Repealed and Recodified.]	21

Chapter 33A - North Carolina Uniform Transfers to Minors Act	21
Chapter 33B - North Carolina Uniform Custodial Trust Act	21
Chapter 34 - Veterans' Guardianship Act	22
Chapter 35 - Sterilization Procedures	22
Chapter 35A - Incompetency and Guardianship	22
Chapter 36 - Trusts and Trustees [Repealed.]	22
Chapter 36A - Trusts and Trustees	22
Chapter 36B - Uniform Management of Institutional Funds Act [Repealed.]	22
Chapter 36C - North Carolina Uniform Trust Code	22
Chapter 36D - North Carolina Community Third Party Trusts, Pooled Trusts	23
Chapter 36E - Uniform Prudent Management of Institutional Funds Act	23
Chapter 37 - Allocation of Principal and Income [Repealed.]	23
Chapter 37A - Uniform Principal and Income Act	23
Chapter 38 - Boundaries	23
Chapter 38A - Landowner Liability	23
Chapter 39 - Conveyances	23
Chapter 39A - Transfer Fee Covenants Prohibited	23
Chapter 40 - Eminent Domain [Repealed.]	23
Chapter 40A - Eminent Domain	23
Chapter 41 - Estates	23
Chapter 41A - State Fair Housing Act	23
Chapter 42 - Landlord and Tenant	23
Chapter 42A - Vacation Rental Act	23
Chapter 43 - Land Registration	23
Chapter 44 - Liens	24
Chapter 44A - Statutory Liens and Charges	24
Chapter 45 - Mortgages and Deeds of Trust	24
Chapter 45A - Good Funds Settlement Act	24
Chapter 46 - Partition	24
Chapter 47 - Probate and Registration	25
Chapter 47A - Unit Ownership	25
Chapter 47B - Real Property Marketable Title Act	25
Chapter 47C - North Carolina Condominium Act	25
Chapter 47D - Notice of Settlement Act [Expired.]	25
Chapter 47E - Residential Property Disclosure Act	25
Chapter 47F - North Carolina Planned Community Act	25
Chapter 47G - Option to Purchase Contracts	25
Chapter 47H - Contracts for Deed	25
Chapter 48 - Adoptions +	26
Chapter 48A - Minors	26
Chapter 49 - Bastardy	26
Chapter 49A - Rights of Children	26
Chapter 50 - Divorce and Alimony	26
Chapter 50A - Uniform Child-Custody Jurisdiction and	

Enforcement Act	26
Chapter 50B - Domestic Violence	26
Chapter 50C - Civil No-Contact Orders	26
Chapter 51 - Marriage	26
Chapter 52 - Powers and Liabilities of Married Persons	27
Chapter 52A - Uniform Reciprocal Enforcement of Support Act [Repealed.]	27
Chapter 52B - Uniform Premarital Agreement Act	27
Chapter 52C - Uniform Interstate Family Support Act	27
Chapter 53 - Banks	27
Chapter 53A - Business Development Corporations and North Carolina Capital Resource Corporations	28
Chapter 53B - Financial Privacy Act	28
Chapter 54 - Cooperative Organizations	28
Chapter 54A - Capital Stock Savings and Loan Associations [Repealed.]	28
Chapter 54B - Savings and Loan Associations	29
Chapter 54C - Savings Banks	29
Chapter 55 - North Carolina Business Corporation Act	30
Chapter 55A - North Carolina Nonprofit Corporation Act	31
Chapter 55B - Professional Corporation Act	31
Chapter 55C - Foreign Trade Zones	31
Chapter 55D - Filings, Names, and Registered Agents for Corporations, Nonprofit Corporations, and Partnerships	31
Chapter 56 - Electric, Telegraph and Power Companies [Repealed.]	31
Chapter 57 - Hospital, Medical and Dental Service Corporations [Recodified.]	31
Chapter 57A - Health Maintenance Organization Act [Recodified.]	31
Chapter 57B - Health Maintenance Organization Act [Recodified.]	31
Chapter 57C - North Carolina Limited Liability Company Act.	31
Chapter 58 - Insurance.	32
Chapter 58 - Insurance (Continuation)	33
Chapter 58 - Insurance (Continuation)	34
Chapter 58 - Insurance (Continuation)	35
Chapter 58 - Insurance (Continuation)	36
Chapter 58 - Insurance (Continuation)	37
Chapter 58 - Insurance (Continuation)	38
Chapter 58A - North Carolina Health Insurance Trust Commission [Recodified.]	38
Chapter 59 - Partnership.	39
Chapter 59B - Uniform Unincorporated Nonprofit Association Act.	39
Chapter 60 - Railroads and Other Carriers [Repealed and Transferred.]	39
Chapter 61 - Religious Societies	39
Chapter 62 - Public Utilities	39

Chapter 62 - Public Utilities (Continuation)	40
Chapter 62A - Public Safety Telephone Service And Wireless Telephone Service	40
Chapter 63 - Aeronautics	40
Chapter 63A - North Carolina Global TransPark Authority	40
Chapter 64 - Aliens	40
Chapter 65 – Cemeteries	40
Chapter 66 - Commerce and Business	41
Chapter 67 - Dogs	41
Chapter 68 - Fences and Stock Law	41
Chapter 69 - Fire Protection	41
Chapter 70 - Indian Antiquities, Archaeological Resources and Unmarked Human Skeletal Remains Protection	42
Chapter 71 - Indians [Repealed.]	42
Chapter 71A - Indians	42
Chapter 72 - Inns, Hotels and Restaurants	42
Chapter 73 - Mills	42
Chapter 74 - Mines and Quarries	42
Chapter 74A - Company Police [Repealed.]	42
Chapter 74B - Private Protective Services Act [Repealed.]	42
Chapter 74C - Private Protective Services	42
Chapter 74D - Alarm Systems	42
Chapter 74E - Company Police Act	42
Chapter 74F - Locksmith Licensing Act	42
Chapter 74G - Campus Police Act	42
Chapter 75 - Monopolies, Trusts and Consumer Protection	42
Chapter 75A - Boating and Water Safety	43
Chapter 75B - Discrimination in Business	43
Chapter 75C - Motion Picture Fair Competition Act	43
Chapter 75D - Racketeer Influenced and Corrupt Organizations	43
Chapter 75E - Unlawful Activities in Connection With Certain Corporate Transactions	43
Chapter 76 - Navigation	43
Chapter 76A - Navigation and Pilotage Commissions	43
Chapter 77 - Rivers, Creeks, and Coastal Waters	43
Chapter 78 - Securities Law [Repealed.]	43
Chapter 78A - North Carolina Securities Act	43
Chapter 78B - Tender Offer Disclosure Act [Repealed.]	43
Chapter 78C - Investment Advisers	43
Chapter 78D - Commodities Act	43
Chapter 79 - Strays [Repealed.]	43
Chapter 80 - Trademarks, Brands, etc.	44
Chapter 81 - Weights and Measures [Recodified.]	44
Chapter 81A - Weights and Measures Act of 1975.	44
Chapter 82 - Wrecks [Repealed.]	44
Chapter 83 - Architects [Recodified.]	44

Chapter 83A - Architects	44
Chapter 84 - Attorneys-at-Law	44
Chapter 84A - Foreign Legal Consultants	44
Chapter 85 - Auctions and Auctioneers [Repealed.]	44
Chapter 85A - Bail Bondsmen and Runners [Recodified.]	44
Chapter 85B - Auctions and Auctioneers	44
Chapter 85C - Bail Bondsmen and Runners [Recodified.]	44
Chapter 86 - Barbers [Recodified.]	44
Chapter 86A - Barbers	44
Chapter 87 - Contractors	44
Chapter 88 - Cosmetic Art [Repealed.]	44
Chapter 88A - Electrolysis Practice Act	44
Chapter 88B - Cosmetic Art	45
Chapter 89 - Engineering and Land Surveying [Recodified.]	45
Chapter 89A - Landscape Architects	45
Chapter 89B - Foresters	45
Chapter 89C - Engineering and Land Surveying	45
Chapter 89D - Landscape Contractors	45
Chapter 89E - Geologists Licensing Act	45
Chapter 89F - North Carolina Soil Scientist Licensing Act	45
Chapter 89G - Irrigation Contractors	45
Chapter 90 - Medicine and Allied Occupations	45
Chapter 90 - Medicine and Allied Occupations (Continuation)	46
Chapter 90 - Medicine and Allied Occupations (Continuation)	47
Chapter 90 - Medicine and Allied Occupations (Continuation)	48
Chapter 90A - Sanitarians and Water and Wastewater Treatment Facility Operators	48
Chapter 90B - Social Worker Certification and Licensure Act	48
Chapter 90C - North Carolina Recreational Therapy Licensure Act	48
Chapter 90D - Interpreters and Transliterators	48
Chapter 91 - Pawnbrokers [Repealed.]	48
Chapter 91A - Pawnbrokers Modernization Act of 1989	48
Chapter 92 - Photographers [Deleted.]	48
Chapter 93 - Certified Public Accountants	48
Chapter 93A - Real Estate License Law	49
Chapter 93B - Occupational Licensing Boards	49
Chapter 93C - Watchmakers [Repealed.]	49
Chapter 93D - North Carolina State Hearing Aid Dealers and Fitters Board.	49
Chapter 93E - North Carolina Appraisers Act	49
Chapter 94 - Apprenticeship	49
Chapter 95 - Department of Labor and Labor Regulations	49
Chapter 95 - Department of Labor and Labor Regulations (Continuation)	50
Chapter 96 - Employment Security	50
Chapter 97 - Workers' Compensation Act	50
Chapter 97 - Workers' Compensation Act (Continuation)	51

Chapter 98 - Burnt and Lost Records	51
Chapter 99 - Libel and Slander	51
Chapter 99A - Civil Remedies for Criminal Actions	51
Chapter 99B - Products Liability	51
Chapter 99C - Actions Relating to Winter Sports Safety and Accidents	51
Chapter 99D - Civil Rights	51
Chapter 99E - Special Liability Provisions	51
Chapter 100 - Monuments, Memorials and Parks	51
Chapter 101 - Names of Persons	51
Chapter 102 - Official Survey Base	51
Chapter 103 - Sundays, Holidays and Special Days	51
Chapter 104 - United States Lands	51
Chapter 104A - Degrees of Kinship	51
Chapter 104B - Hurricanes or Other Acts of Nature	51
Chapter 104C - Atomic Energy, Radioactivity and Ionizing Radiation [Repealed and Recodified.]	51
Chapter 104D - Southern States Energy Compact	51
Chapter 104E - North Carolina Radiation Protection Act	51
Chapter 104F - Southeast Interstate Low-Level Radioactive Waste Management Compact [Repealed]	51
Chapter 104G - North Carolina Low-Level Radioactive Waste Management Authority Act of 1987 [Repealed]	51
Chapter 105 - Taxation	51
Chapter 105 - Taxation (Continuation)	52
Chapter 105 - Taxation (Continuation)	53
Chapter 105 - Taxation (Continuation)	54
Chapter 105A - Setoff Debt Collection Act	55
Chapter 105B - Defaulted Student Loan Recovery Act	55
Chapter 106 - Agriculture	55
Chapter 106 - Agriculture (Continue)	56
Chapter 106 - Agriculture (Continue)	57
Chapter 107 - Agricultural Development Districts [Repealed.]	57
Chapter 108 - Social Services [Repealed and Recodified.]	57
Chapter 108A - Social Services	57
Chapter 108B - Community Action Programs	58
Chapter 108C Medicaid and Health Choice Provider Requirements.	58
Chapter 108D Medicaid Managed Care for Behavioral Health Services.	58
Chapter 109 - Bonds [Recodified.]	58
Chapter 110 - Child Welfare	58
Chapter 111 - Aid to the Blind	58
Chapter 112 - Confederate Homes and Pensions [Repealed.]	58
Chapter 113 - Conservation and Development	58
Chapter 113 - Conservation and Development (Continuation)	59

Chapter 113A - Pollution Control and Environment	59
Chapter 113A - Pollution Control and Environment (Continuation)	60
Chapter 113B - North Carolina Energy Policy Act of 1975	60
Chapter 114 - Department of Justice	60
Chapter 115 - Elementary and Secondary Education [Repealed.]	60
Chapter 115A - Community Colleges, Technical Institutes, and Industrial Education Centers [Repealed.]	60
Chapter 115B - Tuition and Fee Waivers	60
Chapter 115C - Elementary and Secondary Education	60
Chapter 115C - Elementary and Secondary Education (Continuation)	61
Chapter 115C - Elementary and Secondary Education (Continuation)	62
Chapter 115C - Elementary and Secondary Education (Continuation)	63
Chapter 115D - Community Colleges	63
Chapter 115E - Private Educational Facilities Finance Act [Recodified]	63
Chapter 116 - Higher Education	63
Chapter 116 - Higher Education (Continuation)	63
Chapter 116A - Escheats and Abandoned Property [Repealed.]	64
Chapter 116B - Escheats and Abandoned Property	64
Chapter 116C - Continuum of Education Programs	64
Chapter 116D - Higher Education Bonds	64
Chapter 117 - Electrification	64
Chapter 118 - Firemen's and Rescue Squad Workers' Relief and Pension Funds [Recodified.]	64
Chapter 118A - Firemen's Death Benefit Act [Repealed.]	64
Chapter 118B - Members of a Rescue Squad Death Benefit Act [Repealed.]	64
Chapter 119 - Gasoline and Oil Inspection and Regulation	64
Chapter 120 - General Assembly	65
Chapter 120 - General Assembly (Continuation)	66
Chapter 120 - General Assembly (Continuation)	67
Chapter 120C - Lobbying	67
Chapter 121 - Archives and History	67
Chapter 122 - Hospitals for the Mentally Disordered [Repealed.]	67
Chapter 122A - North Carolina Housing Finance Agency	67
Chapter 122B - North Carolina Agricultural Facilities Finance Act [Repealed.]	67
Chapter 122C - Mental Health, Developmental Disabilities, and Substance Abuse Act of 1985	67
Chapter 122C - Mental Health, Developmental Disabilities, and Substance Abuse Act of 1985 (Continuation)	68
Chapter 122D - North Carolina Agricultural Finance Act	68

Chapter 122E - North Carolina Housing Trust and Oil Overcharge Act	68
Chapter 123 - Impeachment	69
Chapter 123A - Industrial Development [Repealed.]	69
Chapter 124 - Internal Improvements	69
Chapter 125 - Libraries	69
Chapter 126 - State Personnel System	69
Chapter 127 - Militia [Repealed.]	69
Chapter 127A - Militia	69
Chapter 127B - Military Affairs	69
Chapter 127C - Advisory Commission on Military Affairs	69
Chapter 128 - Offices and Public Officers	69
Chapter 128 - Offices and Public Officers (Continuation)	70
Chapter 129 - Public Buildings and Grounds	70
Chapter 130 - Public Health [Repealed.]	70
Chapter 130A - Public Health	70
Chapter 130A - Public Health (Continuation)	71
Chapter 130A - Public Health (Continuation)	72
Chapter 130B - Hazardous Waste Management Commission [Repealed.]	72
Chapter 131 - Public Hospitals [Repealed.]	72
Chapter 131A - Health Care Facilities Finance Act	72
Chapter 131B - Licensing of Ambulatory Surgical Facilities [Repealed.]	72
Chapter 131C - Charitable Solicitation Licensure Act [Repealed.]	72
Chapter 131D - Inspection and Licensing of Facilities	72
Chapter 131E - Health Care Facilities and Services	72
Chapter 131E - Health Care Facilities and Services (Continuation)	73
Chapter 131F - Solicitation of Contributions	73
Chapter 132 - Public Records	73
Chapter 133 - Public Works	74
Chapter 134 - Youth Development [Recodified.]	74
Chapter 134A - Youth Services [Repealed.]	74
Chapter 135 - Retirement System for Teachers and State Employees; Social Security; Health Insurance Program for Children	74
Chapter 135 - Retirement System for Teachers and State Employees; Social Security; Health Insurance Program for Children	75
Chapter 136 - Transportation	75
Chapter 136 - Transportation (Continuation)	76
Chapter 137 - Rural Rehabilitation [Repealed.]	76
Chapter 138 - Salaries, Fees and Allowances	76
Chapter 138A - State Government Ethics Act	76
Chapter 139 - Soil and Water Conservation Districts	76

Chapter 140 - State Art Museum; Symphony and Art Societies	76
Chapter 140A - State Awards System	76
Chapter 141 - State Boundaries	76
Chapter 142 - State Debt	76
Chapter 143 - State Departments, Institutions, and Commissions	77
Chapter 143 - State Departments, Institutions, and Commissions (Continuation)	78
Chapter 143 - State Departments, Institutions, and Commissions (Continuation)	79
Chapter 143 - State Departments, Institutions, and Commissions (Continuation)	80
Chapter 143A - State Government Reorganization	80
Chapter 143B - Executive Organization Act of 1973	80
Chapter 143B - Executive Organization Act of 1973 (Continuation)	81
Chapter 143B - Executive Organization Act of 1973 (Continuation)	82
Chapter 143C - State Budget Act	83
Chapter 143D - The State Governmental Accountability and Internal Control Act	83
Chapter 144 - State Flag, Official Governmental Flags, Motto, and Colors	83
Chapter 145 - State Symbols and Other Official Adoptions.	83
Chapter 146 - State Lands	83
Chapter 147 - State Officers	83
Chapter 148 - State Prison System	84
Chapter 149 - State Song and Toast	84
Chapter 150 - Uniform Revocation of Licenses [Repealed.]	84
Chapter 150A - Administrative Procedure Act [Recodified.]	84
Chapter 150B - Administrative Procedure Act	84
Chapter 151 - Constables [Repealed.]	84
Chapter 152 - Coroners	84
Chapter 152A - County Medical Examiner [Repealed.]	84
Chapter 152A - County Medical Examiner [Repealed.] (Continuation)	85
Chapter 153 - Counties and County Commissioners [Repealed.]	85
Chapter 153A - Counties	85
Chapter 153B - Mountain Resources Planning Act	85
Chapter 153C - Uwharrie Regional Resources Act	85
Chapter 154 - County Surveyor [Repealed.]	85
Chapter 155 - County Treasurer [Repealed.]	85
Chapter 156 - Drainage	85
Chapter 156 – Drainage (Continuation)	86

Chapter 157 - Housing Authorities and Projects	86
Chapter 157A - Historic Properties Commissions [Transferred.]	86
Chapter 158 - Local Development	86
Chapter 159 - Local Government Finance	86
Chapter 159 - Local Government Finance (Continuation)	87
Chapter 159A - Pollution Abatement and Industrial Facilities Financing Act [Unconstitutional.]	87
Chapter 159B - Joint Municipal Electric Power and Energy Act	87
Chapter 159C - Industrial and Pollution Control Facilities Financing Act	87
Chapter 159D - The North Carolina Capital Facilities Financing Act	87
Chapter 159E - Registered Public Obligations Act	87
Chapter 159F - North Carolina Energy Development Authority [Repealed.]	87
Chapter 159G - Water Infrastructure	87
Chapter 159H - [Reserved.]	87
Chapter 159I - Solid Waste Management Loan Program and Local Government Special Obligation Bonds	87
Chapter 160 - Municipal Corporations [Repealed And Transferred.]	87
Chapter 160A - Cities and Towns	88
Chapter 160A - Cities and Towns (Continuation)	89
Chapter 160B - Consolidated City-County Act	89
Chapter 160C - Baseball Park Districts [Repealed.]	90
Chapter 161 - Register of Deeds	90
Chapter 162 - Sheriff	90
Chapter 162A - Water and Sewer Systems	90
Chapter 162B Continuity of Local Government in Emergency.	90
Chapter 163 Elections and Election Laws.	90
Chapter 163 Elections and Election Laws. (Continuation)	91
Chapter 164 Concerning the General Statutes of North Carolina.	92
Chapter 165 Veterans.	92
Chapter 166 Civil Preparedness Agencies [Repealed.]	92
Chapter 166A North Carolina Emergency Management Act.	92
Chapter 167 State Civil Air Patrol [Repealed.]	92
Chapter 168 Persons with Disabilities.	92
Chapter 168A Persons With Disabilities Protection Act.	92

§ 105-278.4. Real and personal property used for educational purposes.

(a) Buildings. - Buildings, the land they actually occupy, and additional land reasonably necessary for the convenient use of any such building shall be exempted from taxation if all of the following requirements are met:

(1) Owned by either of the following:

a. An educational institution; or

b. (Effective until July 1, 2012) A nonprofit entity for the sole benefit of a constituent or affiliated institution of The University of North Carolina, an institution as defined in G.S. 116-22, a North Carolina community college, or a combination of these;

b. (Effective July 1, 2012) A nonprofit entity for the sole benefit of a constituent or affiliated institution of The University of North Carolina, a nonprofit postsecondary educational institution as described in G.S. 116-280, a North Carolina community college, or a combination of these;

(2) The owner is not organized or operated for profit and no officer, shareholder, member, or employee of the owner or any other person is entitled to receive pecuniary profit from the owner's operations except reasonable compensation for services;

(3) Of a kind commonly employed in the performance of those activities naturally and properly incident to the operation of an educational institution such as the owner; and

(4) Wholly and exclusively used for educational purposes by the owner or occupied gratuitously by another nonprofit educational institution and wholly and exclusively used by the occupant for nonprofit educational purposes.

(b) Land. - Land (exclusive of improvements); and improvements other than buildings, the land actually occupied by such improvements, and additional land reasonably necessary for the convenient use of any such improvement shall be exempted from taxation if:

(1) Owned by an educational institution that owns real property entitled to exemption under the provisions of subsection (a), above;

(2) Of a kind commonly employed in the performance of those activities naturally and properly incident to the operation of an educational institution such as the owner; and

(3) Wholly and exclusively used for educational purposes by the owner or occupied gratuitously by another nonprofit educational institution (as defined herein) and wholly and exclusively used by the occupant for nonprofit educational purposes.

(c) Partial Exemption. - Notwithstanding the exclusive-use requirements of subsections (a) and (b), above, if part of a property that otherwise meets the requirements of one of those subsections is used for a purpose that would require exemption if the entire property were so used, the valuation of the part so used shall be exempted from taxation.

(d) Public Use. - The fact that a building or facility is incidentally available to and patronized by the general public, so long as there is no material amount of business or patronage with the general public, does not defeat the exemption granted by this section.

(e) Personal Property. - Personal property owned by a church, a religious body, or an educational institution shall be exempted from taxation if:

(1) The owner is not organized or operated for profit, and no officer, shareholder, member, or employee of the owner, or any other person is entitled to receive pecuniary profit from the owner's operations except reasonable compensation for services; and

(2) Used wholly and exclusively for educational purposes by the owner or held gratuitously by a church, religious body, or nonprofit educational institution other than the owner, and wholly and exclusively used for nonprofit educational purposes by the possessor.

(f) Definitions. - The following definitions apply in this section:

(1) Educational institution. - The term includes a university, a college, a school, a seminary, an academy, an industrial school, a public library, a museum, and similar institutions.

(2) Educational purpose. - A purpose that has as its objective the education or instruction of human beings; it comprehends the transmission of information

and the training or development of the knowledge or skills of individual persons. The operation of a student housing facility, a student dining facility, a golf course, a tennis court, a sports arena, a similar sport property, or a similar recreational sport property for the use of students or faculty is also an educational purpose, regardless of the extent to which the property is also available to and patronized by the general public. (1973, c. 695, s. 4; 1991 (Reg. Sess., 1992), c. 926, s. 1; 2004-173, s. 1; 2011-145, s. 9.18(f).)

§ 105-278.5. Real and personal property of religious educational assemblies used for religious and educational purposes.

(a) Buildings, the land they actually occupy, and additional adjacent land reasonably necessary for the convenient use of any such building or for the religious educational programs of the owner, shall be exempted from taxation if:

(1) Owned by a religious educational assembly, retreat, or similar organization;

(2) No officer, shareholder, member, or employee of the owner, or any other person is entitled to receive pecuniary profit from the owner's operations except reasonable compensation for services; and

(3) Of a kind commonly employed in those activities naturally and properly incident to the operation of a religious educational assembly such as the owner; and

(4) Wholly and exclusively used for

a. Religious worship or

b. Purposes of instruction in religious education.

(b) Notwithstanding the exclusive-use requirement of subsection (a), above, if part of a property that otherwise meets the subsection's requirements is used for a purpose that would require exemption if the entire property were so used, the valuation of the part so used shall be exempted from taxation.

(c) The fact that a building or facility is incidentally available to and patronized by the general public, so long as there is no material amount of business or patronage with the general public, shall not defeat the exemption granted by this section.

(d) Personal property owned by a religious educational assembly, retreat, or similar organization shall be exempted from taxation if it is exclusively maintained and used in connection with real property granted exemption under the provisions of subsection (a) or (b), above. (1973, c. 695, s. 4.)

§ 105-278.6. Real and personal property used for charitable purposes.

(a) Real and personal property owned by:

(1) A Young Men's Christian Association or similar organization;

(2) A home for the aged, sick, or infirm;

(3) An orphanage or similar home;

(4) A Society for the Prevention of Cruelty to Animals;

(5) A reformatory or correctional institution;

(6) A monastery, convent, or nunnery;

(7) A nonprofit, life-saving, first aid, or rescue squad organization;

(8) A nonprofit organization providing housing for individuals or families with low or moderate incomes

shall be exempted from taxation if: (i) As to real property, it is actually and exclusively occupied and used, and as to personal property, it is entirely and completely used, by the owner for charitable purposes; and (ii) the owner is not organized or operated for profit.

(b) A charitable purpose within the meaning of this section is one that has humane and philanthropic objectives; it is an activity that benefits humanity or a significant rather than limited segment of the community without expectation of pecuniary profit or reward. The humane treatment of animals is also a charitable purpose.

(c) The fact that a building or facility is incidentally available to and patronized by the general public, so long as there is no material amount of business or patronage with the general public, shall not defeat the exemption granted by this section.

(d) Notwithstanding the exclusive-use requirements of this section, if part of a property that otherwise meets the section's requirements is used for a purpose that would require exemption under subsection (a), above, if the entire property were so used, the valuation of the part so used shall be exempted from taxation.

(e) Real property held by an organization described in subdivision (a)(8) for a charitable purpose under this section as a future site for housing for individuals or families with low or moderate incomes may be classified under this section for no more than 10 years. The taxes that would otherwise be due on real property exempt under this subsection shall be a lien on the property as provided in G.S. 105-355(a). The taxes shall be carried forward in the records of the taxing unit as deferred taxes. The deferred taxes are due and payable in accordance with G.S. 105-277.1F when the property loses its eligibility for deferral as a result of a disqualifying event. A disqualifying event occurs when the property was not used for low- or moderate-income housing within 10 years from the first day of the fiscal year the property was classified under this subsection. In addition to the provisions in G.S. 105-277.1F, all liens arising under this subdivision are extinguished when the property is used for low- or moderate-income housing within the time period allowed under this subsection. (1973, c. 695, s. 4; 1975, c. 808; 1993, c. 230, s. 1; 2008-35, s. 2.6; 2009-481, s. 2; 2010-95, s. 18; 2011-368, s. 1.)

§ 105-278.6A. Qualified retirement facility.

(a) Classification. - Buildings, the land they actually occupy, additional adjacent land reasonably necessary for the convenient use of the buildings, and personal property owned by a qualified retirement facility and used in the operation of that facility are designated a special class of property under Section 2(2) of Article V of the North Carolina Constitution and are excluded from taxation to the extent provided in this section.

(b) Definitions. - The following definitions apply in section:

(1) Charity care. - The unreimbursed costs to the facility of providing health care, housing, or other services to a resident who is uninsured, underinsured, or otherwise unable to pay for all or part of the services rendered.

(2) Community benefits. - The unreimbursed costs to the facility of providing the following:

a. Services, including health, recreation, community research, and education activities provided to the community at large, including the elderly.

b. Charitable donations.

c. Donated volunteer services.

d. Donations and voluntary payments to government agencies.

(3) Financial reporting period. - The calendar year or tax year ending prior to the date the retirement facility applies for an exclusion under this section.

(4) Resident revenue. - Annual revenue paid by a resident for goods and services and one year's share of the initial resident fee amortized in accordance with generally accepted accounting principles.

(5) Retirement facility. - A community that meets all of the following conditions:

a. It is licensed under Article 64 of Chapter 58 of the General Statutes.

b. It is designed for elderly residents.

c. It includes independent living units for elderly residents.

d. It includes a skilled nursing facility or an adult care facility.

(6) Unreimbursed costs. - The costs a facility incurs for providing charity care or community benefits after subtracting payment or reimbursement received from any source for the care or benefits. Unreimbursed costs include costs paid from funds generated by a program described in subdivision (c)(5) of this section.

(c) Total Exclusion. - A retirement facility qualifies for total exclusion under this section if it meets all of the following conditions:

(1) It is exempt from tax under Article 4 of this Chapter and private shareholders do not benefit from its operations.

(2) All of its revenues, less operating and capital expenses, are applied to providing uncompensated goods and services to the elderly and to the local community, or are applied to an endowment or a reserve for these purposes.

(3) Its charter provides that in the event of dissolution, its assets will revert or be conveyed to an entity that is organized exclusively for charitable, educational, scientific, or religious purposes, and is an exempt organization under section 501(c)(3) of the Code.

(4) Repealed by Session Laws 2001-17, s. 1, effective July 1, 2001.

(5) It has an active program to generate funds through one or more sources, such as gifts, grants, trusts, devises, endowment, or an annual giving program, to assist the retirement facility in serving persons who might not be able to reside there without financial assistance or subsidy.

(6) It meets at least one of the following conditions:

a. The facility serves all residents without regard to the residents' ability to pay.

b. At least five percent (5%) of the facility's resident revenue for the financial reporting period is provided in charity care to its residents, in community benefits, or in both.

(d) Partial Exclusion. - A retirement facility qualifies for a partial exclusion under this subsection if it meets conditions under subdivisions (c) (1) through (c)(5) of this section and at least one percent (1%) of the facility's resident revenue for the financial reporting period is provided in charity care to its residents, in community benefits, or in both. The percentage of the retirement facility's assessed value that is excluded from taxation is the applicable percentage provided in the following table, based on the minimum percentage of the facility's resident revenue that it provides in charity care to its residents, in community benefits, or in both:

Percentage of Partial Exclusion Revenue	Minimum Resident
80%	4%
60%	3%
40%	2%
20%	1%

(e) Application for Exclusion. - The application requirements of G.S. 105-282.1 apply to this section. (1939, c. 310, s. 303; 1961, c. 1169, s. 8; 1967, c. 1185; 1971, c. 806, s. 1; c. 1121, s. 3; 1973, cc. 290, 451; c. 476, s. 128; c. 484; c. 695, s. 1; c. 790, s. 1; cc. 904, 962, 1028, 1034, 1077; c. 1262, s. 23; c. 1264, s. 1; 1975, cc. 566, 755; c. 764, s. 6; 1977, c. 771, s. 4; c. 782, s. 2; c. 1001, ss. 1, 2; 1977, 2nd Sess., c. 1200, s. 4; 1979, c. 200, s. 1; 1979, 2nd Sess., c. 1092; 1981, c. 86, s. 1; 1981 (Reg. Sess., 1982), c. 1244, ss. 1, 2; 1983, c. 643, ss. 1, 2; c. 693; 1983 (Reg. Sess., 1984), c. 1060; 1985, c. 510, s. 1; c. 656, s. 37; 1985 (Reg. Sess., 1986), c. 982, s. 18; 1987, c. 356; c. 622, s. 2; c. 747, s. 8; c. 777, s. 6; c. 813, ss. 5, 6, 22; c. 850, s. 17; 1987 (Reg. Sess., 1988), c. 1041, s. 1.1; 1989, c. 148, s. 4; c. 168, s. 6; c. 705; c. 723, s. 1; c. 727, ss. 28, 29; 1991, c. 717, s. 1; 1991 (Reg. Sess., 1992), c. 975, s. 2; 1993, c. 459, s. 2; 1993 (Reg. Sess., 1994), c. 745, s. 39; 1995, c. 41, s. 2; c. 509, s. 51; 1995 (Reg. Sess., 1996), c. 646, s. 12; 1997-23, ss. 1, 3, 9; 1997-443, s. 11A.119(a); 1997-456, s. 27; 1998-55, ss. 10, 18; 1998-212, s. 29A.18(a); 1999-191, s. 1; 2000-20, s. 2; 2001-17, s. 1; 2011-284, s. 70.)

§ 105-278.7. Real and personal property used for educational, scientific, literary, or charitable purposes.

(a) Buildings, the land they actually occupy, and additional adjacent land necessary for the convenient use of any such building shall be exempted from taxation if wholly owned by an agency listed in subsection (c), below, and if:

(1) Wholly and exclusively used by its owner for nonprofit educational, scientific, literary, or charitable purposes as defined in subsection (f), below; or

(2) Occupied gratuitously by an agency listed in subsection (c), below, other than the owner, and wholly and exclusively used by the occupant for nonprofit educational, scientific, literary, charitable, or cultural purposes.

(b) Personal property shall be exempted from taxation if wholly owned by an agency listed in subsection (c), below, and if:

(1) Wholly and exclusively used by its owner for nonprofit educational, scientific, literary, or charitable purposes; or

(2) Gratuitously made available to an agency listed in subsection (c), below, other than the owner, and wholly and exclusively used by the possessor for nonprofit educational, scientific, literary, or charitable purposes.

(c) The following agencies, when the other requirements of this section are met, may obtain property tax exemption under this section:

(1) A charitable association or institution,

(2) An historical association or institution,

(3) A veterans' organization or association,

(4) A scientific association or institution,

(5) A literary association or institution,

(6) A benevolent association or institution, or

(7) A nonprofit community or neighborhood organization.

(d) Notwithstanding the exclusive-use requirements of subsection (a), above, if part of a property that otherwise meets the subsection's requirements is used for a purpose that would require exemption if the entire property were so used, the valuation of the part so used shall be exempted from taxation.

(e) The fact that a building or facility is incidentally available to and patronized by the general public, so long as there is no material amount of business or patronage with the general public, shall not defeat the exemption granted by this section.

(f)   Within the meaning of this section:

(1)   An educational purpose is one that has as its objective the education or instruction of human beings; it comprehends the transmission of information and the training or development of the knowledge or skills of individual persons.

(2)   A scientific purpose is one that yields knowledge systematically through research, experimentation, or other work done in one or more of the natural sciences.

(3)   A literary purpose is one that pertains to letters or literature, especially writing, publishing, and the study of literature. It includes the literature of the stage and screen as well as the performance or exhibition of works based on literature.

(4)   A charitable purpose is one that has humane and philanthropic objectives; it is an activity that benefits humanity or a significant rather than limited segment of the community without expectation of pecuniary profit or reward. The humane treatment of animals is also a charitable purpose.

(5)   A cultural purpose is one that is conducive to the enlightenment and refinement of taste acquired through intellectual and aesthetic training, education, and discipline. (1973, c. 695, s. 4; 1995 (Reg. Sess., 1996), c. 646, s. 15; 2005-435, ss. 59(b), 59(c).)

§ 105-278.8. Real and personal property used for charitable hospital purposes.

(a)   Real and personal property held for or owned by a hospital organized and operated as a nonstock, nonprofit, charitable institution (without profit to members or their successors) shall be exempted from taxation if actually and exclusively used for charitable hospital purposes.

(b)   Notwithstanding the exclusive-use requirements of subsection (a), above, if part of a property that otherwise meets that subsection's requirements is used for a purpose that would require exemption under that subsection if the entire property were so used, the valuation of the part so used shall be exempted from taxation.

(c)   Within the meaning of this section, a charitable hospital purpose is a hospital purpose that has humane and philanthropic objectives; it is a hospital activity that benefits humanity or a significant rather than limited segment of the community without expectation of pecuniary profit or reward. However, the fact that a qualifying hospital charges patients who are able to pay for services rendered does not defeat the exemption granted by this section. (1973, c. 695, s. 4.)

§ 105-278.9. Repealed by Session Laws 1985 (Reg. Sess., 1986), c. 982, s. 21.

§ 105-279. Repealed by Session Laws 1981, c. 819, s. 2.

§ 105-280. Repealed by Session Laws 1973, c. 695, s. 4.

§ 105-281. Repealed by Session Laws 1973, c. 695, s. 10.

§ 105-282. Repealed by Session Laws 1973, c. 695, s. 8.

§ 105-282.1. Applications for property tax exemption or exclusion; annual review of property exempted or excluded from property tax.

(a)   Application. - Every owner of property claiming exemption or exclusion from property taxes under the provisions of this Subchapter has the burden of establishing that the property is entitled to it. If the property for which the exemption or exclusion is claimed is appraised by the Department of Revenue, the application shall be filed with the Department. Otherwise, the application shall be filed with the assessor of the county in which the property is situated. An application must contain a complete and accurate statement of the facts that entitle the property to the exemption or exclusion and must indicate the municipality, if any, in which the property is located. Each application filed with the Department of Revenue or an assessor shall be submitted on a form approved by the Department. Application forms shall be made available by the assessor and the Department, as appropriate.

Except as provided below, an owner claiming an exemption or exclusion from property taxes must file an application for the exemption or exclusion annually during the listing period.

(1) No application required. - Owners of the following exempt or excluded property do not need to file an application for the exemption or exclusion to be entitled to receive it:

a. Property exempt from taxation under G.S. 105-278.1 or G.S. 105-278.2.

b. Special classes of property excluded from taxation under G.S. 105-275(15), (16), (26), (31), (32a), (33), (34), (37), (40), (42), or (44).

c. Property classified for taxation at a reduced valuation under G.S. 105-277(g) or G.S. 105-277.9.

(2) Single application required. - An owner of one or more of the following properties eligible for a property tax benefit must file an application for the benefit to receive it. Once the application has been approved, the owner does not need to file an application in subsequent years unless new or additional property is acquired or improvements are added or removed, necessitating a change in the valuation of the property, or there is a change in the use of the property or the qualifications or eligibility of the taxpayer necessitating a review of the benefit.

a. Property exempted from taxation under G.S. 105-278.3, 105-278.4, 105-278.5, 105-278.6, 105-278.7, or 105-278.8.

b. Special classes of property excluded from taxation under G.S. 105-275(3), (7), (8), (12), (17), (18), (19), (20), (21), (31e), (35), (36), (38), (39), (41), or (45) or under G.S. 131A-21.

c. Special classes of property classified for taxation at a reduced valuation under G.S. 105-277(h), 105-277.1, 105-277.1C, 105-277.10, 105-277.13, 105-277.14, 105-277.15, 105-277.17, or 105-278.

d. Property owned by a nonprofit homeowners' association but where the value of the property is included in the appraisals of property owned by members of the association under G.S. 105-277.8.

e.   Repealed by Session Laws 2008-35, s. 1.2, effective for taxes imposed for taxable years beginning on or after July 1, 2008.

(a1)   Late Application. - Upon a showing of good cause by the applicant for failure to make a timely application, an application for exemption or exclusion filed after the close of the listing period may be approved by the Department of Revenue, the board of equalization and review, the board of county commissioners, or the governing body of a municipality, as appropriate. An untimely application for exemption or exclusion approved under this subsection applies only to property taxes levied by the county or municipality in the calendar year in which the untimely application is filed.

(b)   Approval and Appeal Process. - The Department of Revenue or the assessor to whom an application for exemption or exclusion is submitted must review the application and either approve or deny the application. Approved applications shall be filed and made available to all taxing units in which the exempted or excluded property is situated. If the Department denies an application for exemption or exclusion, it shall notify the taxpayer, who may appeal the denial to the Property Tax Commission.

If an assessor denies an application for exemption or exclusion, the assessor must notify the owner of the decision and the owner may appeal the decision to the board of equalization and review or the board of county commissioners, as appropriate, and from the county board to the Property Tax Commission. If the notice of denial covers property located within a municipality, the assessor shall send a copy of the notice and a copy of the application to the governing body of the municipality. The municipal governing body shall then advise the owner whether it will adopt the decision of the county board or require the owner to file a separate appeal with the municipal governing body. In the event the owner is required to appeal to the municipal governing body and that body renders an adverse decision, the owner may appeal to the Property Tax Commission. Nothing in this subsection shall prevent the governing body of a municipality from denying an application which has been approved by the assessor or by the county board provided the owner's rights to notice and hearing are not abridged. Applications handled separately by a municipality shall be filed in the office of the person designated by the governing body, or in the absence of such designation, in the office of the chief fiscal officer of the municipality.

(c)   Discovery of Property. - When an owner of property that may be eligible for exemption or exclusion neither lists the property nor files an application for exemption or exclusion, the assessor or the Department of Revenue, as appropriate, shall proceed to discover the property. If, upon appeal, the owner demonstrates that the property meets the conditions for exemption or exclusion, the body hearing the appeal may approve the exemption or exclusion. Discovery of the property by the Department or the county shall automatically constitute a discovery by any taxing unit in which the property has a taxable situs.

(d) Roster of Exempted and Excluded Property. - The assessor shall prepare and maintain a roster of all property in the county that is granted tax relief through classification or exemption. On or before November 1 of each year, the assessor must send a report to the Department of Revenue summarizing the information contained in the roster. The report must be in the format required by the Department. The assessor must also send the Department a copy of the roster upon the request of the Department. As to affected real and personal property, the roster shall set forth:

(1) The name of the owner of the property.

(2) A brief description of the property.

(3) A statement of the use to which the property is put.

(4) A statement of the value of the property.

(5) The total value of exempt property in the county and in each municipality therein.

(e) Annual Review of Exempted or Excluded Property. - Pursuant to G.S. 105-296(l), the assessor must annually review at least one-eighth of the parcels in the county exempted or excluded from taxation to verify that the parcels qualify for the exemption or exclusion. (1973, c. 695, s. 8; c. 1252; 1981, c. 54, ss. 2, 3; c. 86, s. 2; c. 915; 1985 (Reg. Sess., 1986), c. 982, s. 22; 1987, c. 45, s. 1; c. 295, ss. 5, 6; c. 680, ss. 1-3; c. 813, s. 13; 1989, c. 674, s. 2; c. 723, s. 2; 1991, c. 34, s. 1; 1991 (Reg. Sess., 1992), c. 975, s. 3; 1993, c. 459, s. 3; 1995, c. 41, s. 7; 1995 (Reg. Sess., 1996), c. 646, s. 16; 1997-23, s. 4; 2000-140, s. 72(b); 2001-139, s. 1; 2007-484, s. 43.7T(b); 2007-497, s. 2.4; 2008-35, s. 1.3; 2008-107, s. 28.11(g); 2008-171, ss. 3, 7(c); 2009-445, s. 23(a), (c)-(e); 2009-481, s. 3.)

§§ 105-282.2 through 105-282.6. Reserved for future codification purposes.

Article 12A.

Taxation of Lessees and Users of Tax-Exempt Cropland or Forestland.

§ 105-282.7. Taxation of lessees and users of tax-exempt cropland or forestland.

(a)   When any cropland or forestland owned by the United States, the State, a county or a municipal corporation is leased, loaned or otherwise made available to and used by a person, as defined in G.S. 105-273(12), in connection with a business conducted for profit, the lessee or user of the property is subject to taxation to the same extent as if the lessee or user owned the property. As used in this section, "forestland" has the same meaning as in G.S. 105-277.2(2), and "cropland" means agricultural land and horticultural land as defined in G.S. 105-277.2(1) and (3) respectively.

(b)   This section does not apply to cropland or forestland for which payments in lieu of taxes are made in amounts equivalent to the amount of tax that could otherwise be lawfully assessed.

(c)   Taxes levied pursuant to this Article are levied on the privilege of leasing or otherwise using tax-exempt cropland or forestland in connection with a business conducted for profit. The purpose of these taxes is to eliminate the competitive advantage accruing to profit-making enterprises from the use of tax-exempt property. (1981, c. 819, s. 1.)

§ 105-282.8. Assessment and collection.

The taxes levied under this Article shall be assessed to the lessee or user of the exempt property and shall be collected in the same manner and to the extent as if the lessee or user owned the property. The taxes are a debt due from the lessee or user to the taxing unit in which the property is located and are recoverable as other actions to collect a debt. (1981, c. 819, s. 1.)

Article 13.

Standards for Appraisal and Assessment.

§ 105-283. Uniform appraisal standards.

All property, real and personal, shall as far as practicable be appraised or valued at its true value in money. When used in this Subchapter, the words "true value" shall be interpreted as meaning market value, that is, the price estimated in terms of money at which the property would change hands between a willing and financially able buyer and a willing seller, neither being under any compulsion to buy or to sell and both having reasonable knowledge of all the uses to which the property is adapted and for which it is capable of being used. For the purposes of this section, the acquisition of an interest in land by an entity having the power of eminent domain with respect to the interest acquired shall not be considered competent evidence of the true value in money of comparable land. (1939, c. 310, s. 500; 1953, c. 970, s. 5; 1955, c. 1100, s. 2; 1959, c. 682; 1967, c. 892, s. 7; 1969, c. 945, s. 1; 1971, c. 806, s. 1; 1973, c. 695, s. 11; 1977, 2nd Sess., c. 1297.)

§ 105-284. Uniform assessment standard.

(a)   Except as otherwise provided in this section, all property, real and personal, shall be assessed for taxation at its true value or use value as determined under G.S. 105-283 or G.S. 105-277.6, and taxes levied by all counties and municipalities shall be levied uniformly on assessments determined in accordance with this section.

(b)   The assessed value of public service company system property subject to appraisal by the Department of Revenue under G.S. 105-335(b)(1) shall be determined by applying to the allocation of such value to each county a percentage to be established by the Department of Revenue. The percentage to be applied shall be either:

(1)   The median ratio established in sales assessment ratio studies of real property conducted by the Department of Revenue in the county in the year the county conducts a reappraisal of real property and in the fourth and seventh years thereafter; or

(2)   A weighted average percentage based on the median ratio for real property established by the Department of Revenue as provided in subdivision (1) and a one hundred percent (100%) ratio for personal property. No percentage shall be applied in a year in which the median ratio for real property is ninety percent (90%) or greater.

If the median ratio for real property in any county is below ninety percent (90%) and if the county assessor has provided information satisfactory to the Department of Revenue that the county follows accepted guidelines and practices in the assessment of business personal property, the weighted average percentage shall be applied to public service company property. In calculating the weighted average percentage, the Department shall use the assessed value figures for real and personal property reported by the county to the Local Government Commission for the preceding year. In any county which fails to demonstrate that it follows accepted guidelines and practices, the percentage to be applied shall be the median ratio for real property. The percentage established in a year in which a sales assessment ratio study is conducted shall continue to be applied until another study is conducted by the Department of Revenue.

(c)   Notice of the median ratio and the percentage to be applied for each county shall be given by the Department of Revenue to the chairman of the board of commissioners not later than April 15 of the year for which it is to be effective. Notice shall also be given at the same time to the public service companies whose property values are subject to adjustment under this section. Either the county or an affected public service company may challenge the real property ratio or the percentage established by the Department of Revenue by giving notice of exception within 30 days after the mailing of the Department's notice. Upon receipt of such notice of exception, the Department shall arrange a conference with the challenging party or parties to review the matter. Following the conference, the Department shall notify the challenging party or parties of its final determination in the matter. Either party may appeal the Department's determination to the Property Tax Commission by giving notice of appeal within 30 days after the mailing of the Department's decision.

(d)   Property that is in a development financing district and that is subject to an agreement entered into pursuant to G.S. 159-108 shall be assessed at its true value or at the minimum value set out in the agreement, whichever is greater.(1939, c. 310, s. 500; 1953, c. 970, s. 5; 1955, c. 1100, s. 2; 1959, c. 682; 1967, c. 892, s. 7; 1969, c. 945, s. 1; 1971, c. 806, s. 1; 1973, c. 695, s. 12; 1985, c. 601, s. 1; 1987 (Reg. Sess., 1988), c. 1052, s. 1; 2003-403, s. 20.)

Article 14.

Time for Listing and Appraising Property for Taxation.

§ 105-285. Date as of which property is to be listed and appraised.

(a) Annual Listing Required. - All property subject to ad valorem taxation shall be listed annually.

(b) Personal Property; General Rule. - Except as otherwise provided in this Chapter, the value, ownership, and place of taxation of personal property, both tangible and intangible, shall be determined annually as of January 1.

(c) Repealed by Session Laws 1987, c. 813, s. 12.

(d) Real Property. - The value of real property shall be determined as of January 1 of the years prescribed by G.S. 105-286 and G.S. 105-287. The ownership of real property shall be determined annually as of January 1, except in the following situation: When any real property is acquired after January 1, but prior to July 1, and the property was not subject to taxation on January 1 on account of its exempt status, it shall be listed for taxation by the transferee as of the date of acquisition and shall be appraised in accordance with its true value as of January 1 preceding the date of acquisition; and the property shall be taxed for the fiscal year of the taxing unit beginning on July 1 of the year in which it is acquired. The person in whose name such property is listed shall have the right to appeal the listing, appraisal, and assessment of the property in the same manner as that provided for listings made as of January 1.

In the event real property exempt as of January 1 is, prior to July 1, acquired from a governmental unit that by contract is making payments in lieu of taxes to the taxing unit for the fiscal period beginning July 1 of the year in which the property is acquired, the tax on such property for the fiscal period beginning on July 1 immediately following acquisition shall be one half of the amount of the tax that would have been imposed if the property had been listed for taxation as of January 1. (1939, c. 310, s. 302; 1945, c. 973; 1971, c. 806, s. 1; 1973, c. 735; 1985, c. 656, s. 21; 1987, c. 813, s. 12; 1993, c. 485, s. 17.)

§ 105-286. Time for general reappraisal of real property.

(a) Octennial Cycle. - Each county must reappraise all real property in accordance with the provisions of G.S. 105-283 and G.S. 105-317 as of January 1 of the year set out in the following schedule and every eighth year thereafter, unless the county is required to advance the date under subdivision (2) of this section or chooses to advance the date under subdivision (3) of this section.

(1) Schedule of Initial Reappraisals.

Division One - 1972: Avery, Camden, Cherokee, Cleveland, Cumberland, Guilford, Harnett, Haywood, Lee, Montgomery, Northampton, and Robeson.

Division Two - 1973: Caldwell, Carteret, Columbus, Currituck, Davidson, Gaston, Greene, Hyde, Lenoir, Madison, Orange, Pamlico, Pitt, Richmond, Swain, Transylvania, and Washington.

Division Three - 1974: Ashe, Buncombe, Chowan, Franklin, Henderson, Hoke, Jones, Pasquotank, Rowan, and Stokes.

Division Four - 1975: Alleghany, Bladen, Brunswick, Cabarrus, Catawba, Dare, Halifax, Macon, New Hanover, Surry, Tyrrell, and Yadkin.

Division Five - 1976: Bertie, Caswell, Forsyth, Iredell, Jackson, Lincoln, Onslow, Person, Perquimans, Rutherford, Union, Vance, Wake, Wilson, and Yancey.

Division Six - 1977: Alamance, Durham, Edgecombe, Gates, Martin, Mitchell, Nash, Polk, Randolph, Stanly, Warren, and Wilkes.

Division Seven - 1978: Alexander, Anson, Beaufort, Clay, Craven, Davie, Duplin, and Granville.

Division Eight - 1979: Burke, Chatham, Graham, Hertford, Johnston, McDowell, Mecklenburg, Moore, Pender, Rockingham, Sampson, Scotland, Watauga, and Wayne.

(2) Mandatory Advancement. - A county whose population is 75,000 or greater according to the most recent annual population estimates certified to the Secretary by the State Budget Officer must conduct a reappraisal of real property when the county's sales assessment ratio determined under G.S. 105-289(h) is less than .85 or greater than 1.15, as indicated on the notice the county receives under G.S. 105-284. A reappraisal required under this

subdivision must become effective no later than January 1 of the earlier of the following years:

a. The third year following the year the county received the notice.

b. The eighth year following the year of the county's last reappraisal.

(3) Optional Advancement. - A county may conduct a reappraisal of real property earlier than required by subdivision (1) or (2) of this subsection if the board of county commissioners adopts a resolution providing for advancement of the reappraisal. The resolution must designate the effective date of the advanced reappraisal and may designate a new reappraisal cycle that is more frequent than the octennial cycle set in subdivision (1) of this subsection. The board of county commissioners must promptly forward a copy of the resolution adopted under this subdivision to the Department of Revenue. A more frequent reappraisal cycle designated in a resolution adopted under this subdivision continues in effect after a mandatory reappraisal required under subdivision (2) of this subsection unless the board of county commissioners adopts another resolution that designates a different date for the county's next reappraisal.

(b), (c) Repealed by Session Laws 2008-146, s. 1.1, effective July 1, 2009. (1939, c. 310, s. 300; 1941, c. 282, ss. 1, 11/2; 1943, c. 634, s. 1; 1945, c. 5; 1947, c. 50; 1949, c. 109; 1951, c. 847; 1953, c. 395; 1955, c. 1273; 1957, c. 1453, s. 1; 1959, c. 704, s. 1; 1971, c. 806, s. 1; 1973, c. 476, s. 193; 1987, c. 45, s. 1; 2008-146, s. 1.1.)

§ 105-287. Changing appraised value of real property in years in which general reappraisal is not made.

(a) In a year in which a general reappraisal of real property in the county is not made under G.S. 105-286, the property shall be listed at the value assigned when last appraised unless the value is changed in accordance with this section. The assessor shall increase or decrease the appraised value of real property, as determined under G.S. 105-286, to recognize a change in the property's value resulting from one or more of the following reasons:

(1) Correct a clerical or mathematical error.

(2) Correct an appraisal error resulting from a misapplication of the schedules, standards, and rules used in the county's most recent general reappraisal.

(2a) Recognize an increase or decrease in the value of the property resulting from a conservation or preservation agreement subject to Article 4 of Chapter 121 of the General Statutes, the Conservation and Historic Preservation Agreements Act.

(2b) Recognize an increase or decrease in the value of the property resulting from a physical change to the land or to the improvements on the land, other than a change listed in subsection (b) of this section.

(2c) Recognize an increase or decrease in the value of the property resulting from a change in the legally permitted use of the property.

(3) Recognize an increase or decrease in the value of the property resulting from a factor other than one listed in subsection (b).

(b) In a year in which a general reappraisal of real property in the county is not made, the assessor may not increase or decrease the appraised value of real property, as determined under G.S. 105-286, to recognize a change in value caused by:

(1) Normal, physical depreciation of improvements;

(2) Inflation, deflation, or other economic changes affecting the county in general; or

(3) Betterments to the property made by:

a. Repainting buildings or other structures;

b. Terracing or other methods of soil conservation;

c. Landscape gardening;

d. Protecting forests against fire; or

e. Impounding water on marshland for non-commercial purposes to preserve or enhance the natural habitat of wildlife.

(c) An increase or decrease in the appraised value of real property authorized by this section shall be made in accordance with the schedules, standards, and rules used in the county's most recent general reappraisal. An increase or decrease in appraised value made under this section is effective as of January 1 of the year in which it is made and is not retroactive. The reason for an increase or decrease in appraised value made under this section need not be under the control of or at the request of the owner of the affected property. This section does not modify or restrict the provisions of G.S. 105-312 concerning the appraisal of discovered property.

(d) Notwithstanding subsection (a), if a tract of land has been subdivided into lots and more than five acres of the tract remain unsold by the owner of the tract, the assessor may appraise the unsold portion as land acreage rather than as lots. A tract is considered subdivided into lots when the lots are located on streets laid out and open for travel and the lots have been sold or offered for sale as lots since the last appraisal of the property. (1939, c. 310, ss. 301, 500; 1953, c. 970, s. 5; 1955, c. 901; c. 1100, s. 2; 1959, c. 682; c. 704, s. 2; 1963, c. 414; 1967, c. 892, s. 7; 1969, c. 945, s. 1; 1971, c. 806, s. 1; 1973, c. 695, s. 10; c. 790, s. 2; 1987, c. 655; 1997-226, s. 4; 2001-139, s. 2; 2008-146, s. 1.2.)

Article 15.

Duties of Department and Property Tax Commission as to Assessments.

§ 105-288. Property Tax Commission.

(a) Creation and Membership. - The Property Tax Commission is created. It consists of five members, three of whom are appointed by the Governor and two of whom are appointed by the General Assembly. Of the two appointments by the General Assembly, one shall be made upon the recommendation of the Speaker of the House of Representatives and the other shall be made upon the recommendation of the President Pro Tempore of the Senate. The terms of the members are for four years and expire on June 30. The General Assembly shall make its appointments in accordance with G.S. 120-121 and shall fill a vacancy in accordance with G.S. 120-122. A vacancy occurs on the Commission when a member resigns, is removed, or dies. The person appointed to fill a vacancy shall serve for the balance of the unexpired term. The Governor may remove any member for misfeasance, malfeasance, or nonfeasance.

The Commission shall have a chair and a vice-chair. The Governor shall designate one of the Commission members as the chair, to serve at the pleasure of the Governor. The members of the Commission shall elect a vice-chair from among its membership. The vice-chair serves until the member's regularly appointed term expires.

(b) Duties. - The Property Tax Commission constitutes the State Board of Equalization and Review for the valuation and taxation of property in the State. It shall hear appeals from the appraisal and assessment of the property of public service companies as defined in G.S. 105-333. The Commission may adopt rules needed to fulfill its duties.

(c) Oath. - Each member of the Property Tax Commission, as the appointed holder of an office, shall take the oath required by Article VI, § 7 of the North Carolina Constitution with the following phrase added to it: "that I will not allow my actions as a member of the Property Tax Commission to be influenced by personal or political friendships or obligations,".

(d) Expenses. - The members of the Property Tax Commission shall receive travel and subsistence expenses in accordance with G.S. 138-5 and a salary as provided for by the Commission when hearing cases, meeting to decide cases, and attending training or continuing education classes on property taxes or judicial procedure. The Secretary of Revenue shall supply all the clerical and other services required by the Commission. All expenses of the Commission and the Department of Revenue in performing the duties enumerated in this Article shall be paid as provided in G.S. 105-501.

(e) Meetings. - The Property Tax Commission shall meet at least once in each quarter and may hold special meetings at any time and place within the State at the call of the Chair or upon the written request of at least three members. At least 15 days' notice shall be given to each member with respect to each special meeting. A majority of the Commission members constitutes a quorum for the transaction of business. (1939, c. 310, ss. 200, 201; 1941, c. 327, s. 6; 1947, c. 184; 1961, c. 547, s. 1; 1967, c. 1196, ss. 1, 2; 1971, c. 806, s. 1; 1973, c. 476, s. 193; 1991, c. 110, s. 1; 1991 (Reg. Sess., 1992), c. 1007, s. 20; c. 1016, s. 2; 1995, c. 41, s. 5; 2000-67, s. 7.11; 2005-276, s. 22.5(a); 2007-308, s. 1.)

§ 105-289. Duties of Department of Revenue.

(a) It is the duty of the Department of Revenue:

(1) To discharge the duties prescribed by law and to enforce the provisions of this Subchapter.

(2) To exercise general and specific supervision over the valuation and taxation of property by taxing units throughout the State.

(3) To appraise the property of public service companies.

(4) To keep full and accurate records of the Commission's official proceedings.

(5) To prepare and distribute annually to each assessor the manual developed by the Use-Value Advisory Board under G.S. 105-277.7 that establishes the cash rental rates for agricultural lands and horticultural lands and the net income ranges for forestland.

(6) To establish requirements for horticultural land, used to produce evergreens intended for use as Christmas trees, in lieu of a gross income requirement until evergreens are harvested from the land, and to establish a gross income requirement for this type horticultural land, that differs from the income requirement for other horticultural land, when evergreens are harvested from the land.

(7) To conduct studies of the cash rents for agricultural and horticultural lands on a county or a regional basis, such as the Major Land Resource Area map designated and developed by the U.S. Department of Agriculture. The results of the studies must be furnished to the North Carolina Use-Value Advisory Board. The studies may be conducted on any reasonable basis and timetable that will be reflective of rents and values for each local area based on the productivity of the land.

(b), (c) Repealed by Session Laws 1973, c. 476, s. 193.

(d) In exercising general and specific supervision over the valuation and taxation of property, the Department shall provide the following:

(1) A continuing program of education and training for local tax officials in the conduct of their duties;

(2) A program for testing the qualifications of an assessor and other persons engaged in the appraisal of property for a county or municipality;

(3) A certification program for an assessor and other persons engaged in the appraisal of property for a county or municipality; and

(4) Assistance to the county and/or the county attorney in developing the specifications for the proposed contract sent to the Department for review pursuant to G.S. 105-299.

The Department shall promulgate regulations to carry out its duties under this subsection.

(e) The Department of Revenue may furnish the following information to a local tax official:

(1) Information contained in a report to it or to any other State department; and

(2) Information the Department has in its possession that may assist a local tax official in securing complete tax listings, appraising or assessing taxable property, collecting taxes, or presenting information in administrative or judicial proceedings involving the listing, appraisal, or assessment of property.

A local tax official may use information obtained from the Department under this subsection only for the purposes stated in subdivision (2). A local tax official may not divulge or make public this information except as required in administrative or judicial proceedings under this Subchapter. A local tax official who makes improper use of or discloses information obtained from the Department under this subsection is punishable as provided in G.S. 153A-148.1 or G.S. 160A-208.1, as appropriate.

The Department may not furnish information to a local tax official pursuant to this subsection unless it has obtained a written certification from the official stating that the official is familiar with the provisions of this subsection and G.S. 153A-148.1 or G.S. 160A-208.1, as appropriate, and that information obtained from the Department under this subsection will be used only for the purposes stated in subdivision (2).

(f)   To advise local tax officials of their duties concerning the listing, appraisal, and assessment of property and the levy and collection of property taxes.

(g)   To see that proper proceedings are brought to enforce the statutes pertaining to taxation and the collection of penalties and liabilities imposed by law upon public officers, officers of corporations, and individuals who fail, refuse, or neglect to comply with the provisions of this Subchapter and other laws with respect to the taxation of property, and to call upon the Attorney General of this State or any prosecuting attorney of this State to assist in the execution of the powers conferred by the laws of this State with respect to the taxation of property.

(h)   To make annual studies of the ratio of the appraised value of real property to its true value and to establish for each county the median ratio as determined by the studies for each calendar year. The studies for each calendar year shall be completed by April 15 of the following calendar year. The studies shall be conducted in accordance with generally accepted principles and procedures for sales assessment ratio studies.

(i)   To maintain a register of appraisal firms, mapping firms and other persons or firms having expertise in one or more of the duties of the assessor; to review the qualifications and work of such persons or firms; and to advise county officials as to the professional and financial capabilities of such persons or firms to assist the assessor in carrying out his duties under this Subchapter. The register shall include a copy of the report filed by the counties pursuant to G.S. 105-322(g)(4). It shall also include the average median sales assessment ratio and the coefficient of dispersion achieved in each county for the first two years following the county's effective date of revaluation. To be registered with the Department of Revenue, such persons or firms shall annually file a report with the Department setting forth the following information:

(1)   A statement of the firm's ownership,

(2)   A statement of the firm's financial condition,

(3)   A list of the firm's principal officers with a statement of their qualifications and experience,

(4)   A list of the firm's employees with a statement of their education, training and experience, and

(5) A full and complete resume of each employee which the firm proposes to place in a supervisory position in any mapping or revaluation project for a county in this State. (1939, c. 310, s. 202; 1955, c. 1350, s. 10; 1967, c. 1196, s. 3; 1969, c. 7, s. 1; 1971, c. 806, s. 1; 1973, c. 47, s. 2; c. 476, s. 193; 1975, c. 275, s. 9; c. 508, s. 1; 1981, c. 387, ss. 1, 2; 1983, c. 813, s. 1; 1985, c. 601, s. 3; c. 628, s. 3; 1987, c. 45, s. 1; c. 46, s. 1; c. 440, s. 1; c. 830, s. 84(a); 1987 (Reg. Sess., 1988), c. 1052, s. 1; 1989, c. 79, ss. 2, 4; c. 736, s. 3; 1991, c. 110, s. 2; 1993, c. 485, s. 35; 2002-184, s. 5; 2005-313, s. 6.)

§ 105-289.1. Repealed by Session Laws 1987, c. 813, s. 12.

§ 105-290. Appeals to Property Tax Commission.

(a) Duty to Hear Appeals. - In its capacity as the State board of equalization and review, the Property Tax Commission shall hear and adjudicate appeals from boards of county commissioners and from county boards of equalization and review as provided in this section.

(b) Appeals from Appraisal and Listing Decisions. - The Property Tax Commission shall hear and decide appeals from decisions concerning the listing, appraisal, or assessment of property made by county boards of equalization and review and boards of county commissioners. Any property owner of the county may except to an order of the county board of equalization and review or the board of county commissioners concerning the listing, appraisal, or assessment of property and appeal the order to the Property Tax Commission.

(1) In these cases, taxpayers and persons having ownership interests in the property subject to taxation may file separate appeals or joint appeals at the election of one or more of the taxpayers. It is the intent of this provision that all owners of a single item of personal property or tract or parcel of real property be allowed to join in one appeal and also that any taxpayer be allowed to include in one appeal all objections timely presented regardless of the fact that the listing or valuation of more than one item of personal property or tract or parcel of real property is the subject of the appeal.

(2) When an appeal is filed, the Property Tax Commission shall provide a hearing before representatives of the Commission or the full Commission as specified in this subdivision.

a. Hearing by Commission Representatives. - The Commission may authorize one or more members of the Commission or employees of the Department of Revenue to hear an appeal, to make examinations and investigations, to have made from stenographic notes a full and complete record of the evidence offered at the hearing, and to make recommended findings of fact and conclusions of law. Should the Commission elect to follow this procedure, it shall fix the time and place at which its representatives will hear the appeal and, at least 10 days before the hearing, give written notice of the hearing to the appellant and to the clerk of the board of commissioners of the county from which the appeal is taken. At the hearing the Commission's representatives shall hear all evidence and affidavits offered by the appellant and appellee county and may exercise the authority granted by subsection (d), below, to obtain information pertinent to decision of the appeal. The representatives conducting the hearing shall submit to the Commission and to the appellant and appellee their recommended findings of fact and conclusions of law. Upon the request of any party, the representatives conducting the hearing shall also submit to the Commission and to the appellant and appellee a full record of the proceeding. The cost of providing the full record of the proceeding shall be borne by the party requesting it, unless the Commission determines for good cause that the cost should be borne by the Commission. The Commission shall review the record, the recommended findings of fact and conclusions of law, and any written arguments that may be submitted to the Commission by the appellant or appellee within 15 days following the date on which the findings and conclusions were submitted to the parties and shall take one of the following actions:

1. Accept the recommended findings of fact and conclusions of law and issue an appropriate order as provided in subdivision (b)(3), below.

2. Make new findings of fact or conclusions of law based upon the materials submitted by the Commission's representatives and issue an appropriate order as provided in subdivision (b)(3), below.

3. Rehear the appeal under the procedure provided in subdivision (b)(2)b, below, with respect to any portion of the record or recommended findings of fact or conclusions of law.

b. Hearing by Full Commission. - Should the Commission elect not to employ the procedure provided in subdivision (b)(2)a, above, it shall fix a time and place at which the Commission shall hear the appeal and, at least 10 days before the hearing, give written notice of the hearing to the appellant and to the clerk of the board of commissioners of the county from which the appeal is taken. At the hearing the Commission shall hear all evidence and affidavits offered by the appellant and appellee county and may exercise the authority granted by subsection (d), below, to obtain information pertinent to decision of the appeal. The Commission shall make findings of fact and conclusions of law and issue an appropriate order as provided in subdivision (b)(3), below.

(3) On the basis of the findings of fact and conclusions of law made after any hearing provided for by this subsection (b), the Property Tax Commission shall enter an order (incorporating the findings and conclusions) reducing, increasing, or confirming the valuation or valuations appealed or listing or removing from the tax lists the property whose listing has been appealed. A certified copy of the order shall be delivered to the appellant and to the clerk of the board of commissioners of the county from which the appeal was taken, and the abstracts and tax records of the county shall be corrected to reflect the Commission's order.

(4) Interest on Overpayments. - When an order of the Property Tax Commission reduces the valuation of property or removes the property from the tax lists and, based on the order, the taxpayer has paid more tax than is due on the property, the taxpayer is entitled to receive interest on the overpayment in accordance with this subdivision. An overpayment of tax bears interest at the rate set under G.S. 105-241.21 from the date the interest begins to accrue until a refund is paid. Interest accrues from the later of the date the tax was paid and the date the tax would have been considered delinquent under G.S. 105-360. A refund is considered paid on a date determined by the governing body of the taxing unit that is no sooner than five days after a refund check is mailed.

(c) Appeals from Adoption of Schedules, Standards, and Rules. - It shall be the duty of the Property Tax Commission to hear and to adjudicate appeals from orders of boards of county commissioners adopting schedules of values, standards, and rules under the provisions of G.S. 105-317 as prescribed in this subsection (c), and the adoption of such schedules, standards, and rules shall not be subject to appeal under any other provision of this Subchapter.

(1) A property owner of the county who, either separately or in conjunction with other property owners of the county, asserts that the schedules of values, standards, and rules adopted by order of the board of county commissioners do not meet the true value or present-use value appraisal standards established by G.S. 105-283 and G.S. 105-277.2(5), respectively, may appeal the order to the Property Tax Commission within 30 days of the date when the order adopting

the schedules, standards, and rules was first published, as required by G.S. 105-317(c).

(2) Upon such an appeal the Property Tax Commission shall proceed to hear the appeal in accordance with the procedures provided in subdivisions (b)(1) and (b)(2), above, and in scheduling the hearing upon such an appeal, the Commission shall give it priority over appeals that may be pending before the Commission under the provisions of subsection (b), above. The decision of the Commission upon such an appeal shall be embodied in an order as provided in subdivision (c)(3), below.

(3) On the basis of the findings of fact and conclusions of law made after any hearing provided for by this subsection (c), the Property Tax Commission shall enter an order (incorporating the findings and conclusions):

a. Modifying or confirming the order adopting the schedules, standards, and rules challenged, or

b. Requiring the board of county commissioners to revise or modify its order of adoption in accordance with the instructions of the Commission and to present the order as thus revised or modified for approval by the Commission under rules and regulations prescribed by the Commission.

(d) Witnesses and Documents. - Upon its own motion or upon the request of any party to an appeal, the Property Tax Commission, or any member of the Commission, or any employee of the Department of Revenue so authorized by the Commission shall examine witnesses under oath administered by any member of the Commission or any employee of the Department so authorized by the Commission, and examine the documents of any person if there is ground for believing that information contained in such documents is pertinent to the decision of any appeal pending before the Commission, regardless of whether such person is a party to the proceeding before the Commission. Witnesses and documents examined under the authority of this subsection (d) shall be examined only after service of a subpoena as provided in subdivision (d)(1), below. The travel expenses of any witness subpoenaed and the cost of serving any subpoena shall be borne by the party that requested the subpoena.

(1) The Property Tax Commission, a member of the Commission, or any employee of the Department of Revenue authorized by the Commission, is authorized and empowered to subpoena witnesses and to subpoena documents upon a subpoena to be signed by the chairman of the Commission directed to

the witness or witnesses or to the person or persons having custody of the documents sought. Subpoenas issued under this subdivision may be served by any officer authorized to serve subpoenas.

(2)   Any person who shall willfully fail or refuse to appear, to produce subpoenaed documents in response to a subpoena, or to testify as provided in this subsection (d) shall be guilty of a Class 1 misdemeanor.

(3)   Upon a motion, the Property Tax Commission, or a member of the Commission may quash a subpoena if, after a hearing, the Commission finds any of the following:

a.   The subpoena requires the production of evidence that does not relate to a matter in issue.

b.   The subpoena fails to describe with sufficient particularity the evidence required to be produced.

c.   The subpoena is subject to being quashed for any other reason sufficient in law.

(d1)   Hearing on Motion to Quash Subpoena; Appeal. - A hearing on a motion to quash a subpoena pursuant to subdivision (d)(3) of this section shall be heard at least 10 days prior to the hearing for which the subpoena was issued. The denial of a motion to quash a subpoena is subject to immediate judicial review in the Superior Court of Wake County or in the superior court of the county where the person subject to the subpoena resides.

(e)   Time Limits for Appeals. - A notice of appeal from an order of a board of county commissioners, other than an order adopting a uniform schedule of values, or from a board of equalization and review shall be filed with the Property Tax Commission within 30 days after the date the board mailed a notice of its decision to the property owner. A notice of appeal from an order adopting a schedule of values shall be filed within the time set in subsection (c).

(f)   Notice of Appeal. - A notice of appeal filed with the Property Tax Commission shall be in writing and shall state the grounds for the appeal. A property owner who files a notice of appeal shall send a copy of the notice to the appropriate county assessor.

(g) What Constitutes Filing. - A notice of appeal submitted to the Property Tax Commission by a means other than United States mail is considered to be filed on the date it is received in the office of the Commission. A notice of appeal submitted to the Property Tax Commission by United States mail is considered to be filed on the date shown on the postmark stamped by the United States Postal Service. If an appeal submitted by United States mail is not postmarked or the postmark does not show the date of mailing, the appeal is considered to be filed on the date it is received in the office of the Commission. A property owner who files an appeal with the Commission has the burden of proving that the appeal is timely. (1939, c. 310, ss. 202, 1107, 1109; 1955, c. 1350, s. 10; 1967, c. 1196, s. 3; 1969, c. 7, ss. 1, 2; 1971, c. 806, s. 1; 1973, c. 476, s. 193; 1987, c. 295, ss. 3, 9; c. 680, ss. 4, 5; 1989 (Reg. Sess., 1990), c. 1005, ss. 1, 2; 1991 (Reg. Sess., 1992), c. 1016, s. 1; 1993, c. 539, s. 713; 1994, Ex. Sess., c. 24, s. 14(c); 1997-205, s. 1; 2007-251, ss. 3, 4; 2007-491, s. 44(1)a.)

§ 105-291. Powers of Department and Commission.

(a) General Powers. - The Department of Revenue is authorized to exercise all powers reasonably necessary to perform the duties imposed upon it by this Subchapter and other laws of this State.

(b) Rule-Making Power. - The Department may adopt such rules and regulations, not inconsistent with law, as the Department may deem necessary to perform the duties or responsibilities of this Chapter.

(c) General Investigatory Authority. - In exercising general and specific supervision over the valuation and taxation of property, the Department or any authorized deputy shall have power to examine witnesses under oath administered by any member or authorized deputy and to examine the documents of any State department, county, city, town, or taxpayer if there is ground for believing that the witnesses have or that the documents contain information pertinent to the subject of the Department's inquiry. Witnesses and documents examined under the authority of this subsection (c) may be obtained through service of subpoenas as provided in subdivision (c)(1), below.

(1) To obtain the testimony of witnesses or to obtain access to the documents enumerated in this subsection (c), the Department or any authorized deputy is authorized and empowered to subpoena witnesses and to subpoena documents upon a subpoena to be signed by the Secretary of Revenue directed

to the witness or to the person having custody of the documents sought, and to be served by any officer authorized to serve subpoenas.

(2) Any person who shall willfully fail or refuse to appear; to produce subpoenaed documents before the Department or authorized deputy in response to a subpoena; or to testify as provided in this subsection (c) shall be guilty of a Class 1 misdemeanor.

(d) Certification of Actions. - The Property Tax Commission shall have power to certify copies of its records, orders, and proceedings by attesting the copies with its official seal, and copies of records, orders, or proceedings so certified shall be received in evidence in all courts of this State with like effect as certified copies of other public records.

(e) Power to Require Reports. - In its discretion, the Department may require tax supervisors, clerks of boards of county commissioners, and county accountants to file with it, when called for, complete reports of the appraised and assessed value of all real and personal property in the counties, itemized as the Department may prescribe.

(f) Power to Prescribe Record Forms. - The Department may prescribe the forms, books, and records to be used in the listing, appraisal, and assessment of property and in the levying and collection of property taxes, and how the same shall be kept.

(g) Power to Recommend Appraisal Standards. - The Department may develop and recommend standards and rules to be used by tax supervisors and other responsible officials in the appraisal of specific kinds and categories of property for taxation. (1939, c. 310, s. 203; 1945, c. 955; 1951, c. 798; 1971, c. 806, s. 1; 1973, c. 476, s. 193; 1993, c. 539, s. 714; 1994, Ex. Sess., c. 24, s. 14(c).)

§§ 105-292 through 105-293: Repealed by Session Laws 1973, c. 476, s. 193.

Article 16.

County Listing, Appraisal, and Assessing Officials.

§ 105-294. County assessor.

(a) Appointment. - Persons occupying the position of county assessor on July 1, 1983, shall continue in office until the first Monday in July, 1983. At its first regular meeting in July, 1983, and every two years or four years thereafter, as appropriate, the board of county commissioners of each county shall appoint a county assessor to serve a term of not less than two nor more than four years; provided, however, that no person shall be eligible for initial appointment to a term of more than two years unless such person is deemed to be qualified as provided in subsection (b) of this section or has been certified by the Department of Revenue as provided in subsection (c) of this section. The board of commissioners may remove the assessor from office during his term for good cause after giving him notice in writing and an opportunity to appear and be heard at a public session of the board. Whenever a vacancy occurs in this office, the board of county commissioners shall appoint a qualified person to serve as county assessor for the period of the unexpired term.

(b) Persons who held the position of assessor on July 1, 1971, and continue to hold the position, and persons who have been certified for appointment as assessor by the Department of Revenue between July 1, 1971, and July 1, 1983, are deemed to be qualified to serve as county assessor. Any other person selected to serve as county assessor must meet the following requirements:

(1) Be at least 21 years of age as of the date of appointment;

(2) Hold a high school diploma or certificate of equivalency, or in the alternative, have five years employment experience in a vocation which is reasonably related to the duties of a county assessor;

(3) Within two years of the date of appointment, achieve a passing score in courses of instruction approved by the Department of Revenue covering the following topics:

a. The laws of North Carolina governing the listing, appraisal, and assessment of property for taxation;

b. The theory and practice of estimating the fair market value of real property for ad valorem tax purposes;

c. The theory and practice of estimating the fair market value of personal property for ad valorem tax purposes; and

d. Property assessment administration.

(4) Upon completion of the required four courses, achieve a passing grade in a comprehensive examination in property tax administration conducted by the Department of Revenue.

(c) Certification. - Persons meeting all of the requirements of this section shall be certified by the Department of Revenue. From the date of appointment until the date of certification, persons appointed to serve as county assessor are deemed to be serving in an acting capacity. Any person who fails to qualify within two years after the date of initial appointment shall not be eligible for reappointment until all of the requirements have been met.

(d) In order to retain the position of county assessor, every person serving as county assessor, including those persons deemed to be qualified under the provisions of this act, shall, in each period of 24 months, attend at least 30 hours of instruction in the appraisal or assessment of property as provided in regulations of the Department of Revenue.

(e) The compensation and expenses of the county assessor shall be determined by the board of county commissioners.

(f) Alternative to separate office of county assessor. - Pursuant to Act [Article] VI, Section 9 of the North Carolina Constitution, the office of county assessor is hereby declared to be an office that may be held concurrently with any other appointive or elective office except that of member of the board of county commissioners. (1939, c. 310, ss. 400, 401; 1953, c. 970, ss. 1, 2; 1971, c. 806, s. 1; 1973, c. 476, s. 193; 1983, c. 813, s. 2; 1987, c. 45, ss. 1, 2; 1997-23, s. 5.)

§ 105-295. Oath of office for assessor.

The assessor, as the holder of an appointed office, shall take the oath required by Article VI, § 7 of the North Carolina Constitution with the following phrase added to it: "that I will not allow my actions as assessor to be influenced by personal or political friendships or obligations,". The oath must be filed with the clerk of the board of county commissioners. (1939, c. 310, s. 402; 1971, c. 806, s. 1; 1987, c. 45, s. 1; 1991, c. 110, s. 4; 1991 (Reg. Sess., 1992), c. 1007, s. 21.)

§ 105-296. Powers and duties of assessor.

(a) The county assessor shall have general charge of the listing, appraisal, and assessment of all property in the county in accordance with the provisions of law. He shall perform the duties imposed upon him by law, and he shall have and exercise all powers reasonably necessary in the performance of his duties not inconsistent with the Constitution or the laws of this State.

(b) Within budgeted appropriations, he shall employ listers, appraisers, and clerical assistants necessary to carry out the listing, appraisal, assessing, and billing functions required by law. The assessor may allocate responsibility among such employees by territory, by subject matter, or on any other reasonable basis. Each person employed by the assessor as a real property appraiser or personal property appraiser shall during the first year of employment and at least every other year thereafter attend a course of instruction in his area of work. At the end of the first year of their employment, such persons shall also achieve a passing score on a comprehensive examination in property tax administration conducted by the Department of Revenue.

(c) At least 10 days before the date as of which property is to be listed, the assessor shall advertise in a newspaper having general circulation in the county and post in at least five public places in each township in the county a notice containing all of the items listed in this subsection. If the listing period is extended in any county by the board of county commissioners, the assessor shall advertise in the newspaper in which the original notice was published and post in the same places a notice of the extension and of the times during which and the place or places at which lists will be accepted during the extended period. The items that must be included in the notice are:

(1) The date as of which property is to be listed.

(2) The date on which listing will begin.

(3) The date on which listing will end.

(4) The times between the date mentioned in subdivision (c)(2), above, and the date mentioned in subdivision (c)(3), above, during which lists will be accepted.

(5)   The place or places at which lists will be accepted at the times established under subdivision (c)(4), above.

(6)   A statement that all persons who, on the date as of which property is to be listed, own property subject to taxation must list such property within the period set forth in the notice and that any person who fails to do so will be subject to the penalties prescribed by law.

(7)   If the county has provided for electronic listing of personal property under G.S. 105-310.1, a statement that the county allows electronic listing of personal property and the timetable and procedures for electronic listing.

(d)   through (f) Repealed by Session Laws 1987, c. 43, s. 2.

(g)   He shall have power to subpoena any person for examination under oath and to subpoena documents whenever he has reasonable grounds for the belief that such person has knowledge or that such documents contain information that is pertinent to the discovery or valuation of any property subject to taxation in the county or that is necessary for compliance with the requirements as to what the tax list shall contain. The subpoena shall be signed by the chairman of the board of equalization and review if that board is in session; otherwise, it shall be signed by the chairman of the board of county commissioners. It shall be served by an officer qualified to serve subpoenas. Any person who shall wilfully fail or refuse to appear, produce subpoenaed documents, or testify concerning the subject of the inquiry shall be guilty of a Class 1 misdemeanor.

(h)   Only after the abstract has been carefully reviewed can the assessor require any person operating a business enterprise in the county to submit a detailed inventory, statement of assets and liabilities, or other similar information pertinent to the discovery or appraisal of property taxable in the county. Inventories, statements of assets and liabilities, or other information secured by the assessor under the terms of this subsection, but not expressly required by this Subchapter to be shown on the abstract itself, shall not be open to public inspection but shall be made available, upon request, to representatives of the Department of Revenue or of the Division of Employment Security (DES) of the Department of Commerce. Any assessor or other official or employee disclosing information so obtained, except as may be necessary in listing or appraising property in the performance of official duties, or in the administrative or judicial proceedings relating to listing, appraising, or other official duties, shall be guilty of a Class 3 misdemeanor and punishable only by a fine not exceeding fifty dollars ($50.00).

(i)   Prior to the first meeting of the board of equalization and review, the assessor may, for good cause, change the appraisal of any property subject to assessment for the current year. Written notice of a change in assessment shall be given to the taxpayer at his last known address prior to the first meeting of the board of equalization and review.

(j)   The assessor must annually review at least one eighth of the parcels in the county classified for taxation at present-use value to verify that these parcels qualify for the classification. By this method, the assessor must review the eligibility of all parcels classified for taxation at present-use value in an eight-year period. The period of the review process is based on the average of the preceding three years' data. The assessor may request assistance from the Farm Service Agency, the Cooperative Extension Service, the North Carolina Forest Service of the Department of Agriculture and Consumer Services, or other similar organizations.

The assessor may require the owner of classified property to submit any information, including sound management plans for forestland, needed by the assessor to verify that the property continues to qualify for present-use value taxation. The owner has 60 days from the date a written request for the information is made to submit the information to the assessor. If the assessor determines the owner failed to make the information requested available in the time required without good cause, the property loses its present-use value classification and the property's deferred taxes become due and payable as provided in G.S. 105-277.4(c). If the property loses its present-use value classification for failure to provide the requested information, the assessor must reinstate the property's present-use value classification when the owner submits the requested information within 60 days after the disqualification unless the information discloses that the property no longer qualifies for present-use value classification. When a property's present-use value classification is reinstated, it is reinstated retroactive to the date the classification was revoked and any deferred taxes that were paid as a result of the revocation must be refunded to the property owner. The owner may appeal the final decision of the assessor to the county board of equalization and review as provided in G.S. 105-277.4(b1).

In determining whether property is operating under a sound management program, the assessor must consider any weather conditions or other acts of nature that prevent the growing or harvesting of crops or the realization of income from cattle, swine, or poultry operations. The assessor must also allow the property owner to submit additional information before making this determination.

(k) He shall furnish information to the Department of Revenue as required by the Department to conduct studies in accordance with G.S. 105-289(h).

(l) The assessor shall annually review at least one-eighth of the parcels in the county exempted or excluded from taxation to verify that these parcels qualify for the exemption or exclusion. By this method, the assessor shall review the eligibility of all parcels exempted or excluded from taxation in an eight-year period. The assessor may require the owner of exempt or excluded property to make available for inspection any information reasonably needed by the assessor to verify that the property continues to qualify for the exemption or exclusion. The owner has 60 days from the date a written request for the information is made to submit the information to the assessor. If the assessor determines that the owner failed to make the information requested available in the time required without good cause, then the property loses its exemption or exclusion. If the property loses its exemption or exclusion for failure to provide the requested information, the assessor must reinstate the property's exemption or exclusion when the owner makes the requested information available within 60 days after the disqualification unless the information discloses that the property is no longer eligible for the exemption or exclusion.

(m) The assessor shall annually review the transportation corridor official maps and amendments to them filed with the register of deeds pursuant to Article 2E of Chapter 136 of the General Statutes. The assessor must indicate on all tax maps maintained by the county or city that portion of the properties embraced within a transportation corridor and must note any variance granted for the property for such period as the designation remains in effect. The assessor must tax the property within a transportation corridor as required under G.S. 105-277.9. (1939, c. 310, ss. 403, 404; 1953, c. 970, s. 3; 1955, c. 1012, s. 1; 1957, c. 202; 1959, c. 740, s. 3; 1963, c. 302; 1971, c. 806, s. 1; 1973, c. 560; 1983, c. 813, s. 3; 1985, c. 518, s. 2; 1987, c. 43, s. 2; c. 45, ss. 1, 2; c. 830, s. 84(b); 1987 (Reg. Sess., 1988), c. 1044, s. 13; 1991, c. 34, s. 2; c. 77, s. 1; 1993, c. 539, ss. 715, 716; 1994, Ex. Sess., c. 24, s. 14(c); 2001-139, ss. 3-5; 2002-184, s. 6; 2005-313, s. 7; 2005-386, s. 1.4; 2011-145, s. 13.25(pp); 2011-238, s. 2; 2011-401, s. 5.1; 2013-155, s. 8.)

§ 105-297. Assistant assessor.

The board of county commissioners may, upon the recommendation of the assessor, appoint one or more assistant assessors. The board may delegate to assistant assessors appointed under this section responsibility for the appraisal of real property, the listing and appraisal of business property, or such other duties as the board deems advisable. Pursuant to Article VI, Sec. 9, of the North Carolina Constitution, the office of assistant assessor is hereby declared to be an office that may be held concurrently with any other appointive office. (1939, c. 310, s. 409; 1955, c. 866; 1963, c. 625; 1967, cc. 59, 293; 1971, c. 802, s. 11; c. 806, s. 1; 1987, c. 45, s. 1.)

§ 105-298: Repealed by Session Laws 1987, c. 43, s. 3.

§ 105-299. (Effective until July 1, 2013 - see notes) Employment of experts.

The board of county commissioners may employ appraisal firms, mapping firms or other persons or firms having expertise in one or more of the duties of the assessor to assist the assessor in the performance of these duties. The county may also assign to county agencies, or contract with State or federal agencies for, any duties involved with the approval or auditing of use-value accounts. The county may make available to these persons any information it has that will facilitate the performance of a contract entered into pursuant to this section. Persons receiving this information are subject to the provisions of G.S. 105-289(e) and G.S. 105-259 regarding the use and disclosure of information provided to them by the county. Any person employed by an appraisal firm whose duties include the appraisal of property for the county must be required to demonstrate that he or she is qualified to carry out these duties by achieving a passing grade on a comprehensive examination in the appraisal of property administered by the Department of Revenue. In the employment of these firms, primary consideration must be given to the firms registered with the Department of Revenue pursuant to G.S. 105-289(i). A copy of the specifications to be submitted to potential bidders and a copy of the proposed contract may be sent by the board to the Department of Revenue for review before the invitation or acceptance of any bids. Contracts for the employment of these firms or persons are contracts for personal services and are not subject to the provisions of Article 8, Chapter 143, of the General Statutes. (1939, c. 310, s. 408; 1971, c.

806, s. 1; 1973, c. 476, s. 193; 1975, c. 508, s. 2; 1983, c. 813, s. 4; 1985, c. 601, s. 2; 1989, c. 79; 2002-184, s. 7; 2003-416, s. 9.)

§ 105-299. (Effective July 1, 2013 until July 1, 2015 - see notes) Employment of experts.

The board of county commissioners may employ appraisal firms, mapping firms or other persons or firms having expertise in one or more of the duties of the assessor to assist the assessor in the performance of these duties. The county may also assign to county agencies, or contract with State or federal agencies for, any duties involved with the approval or auditing of use-value accounts. The county may make available to these persons any information it has that will facilitate the performance of a contract entered into pursuant to this section. Persons receiving this information are subject to the provisions of G.S. 105-289(e) and G.S. 105-259 regarding the use and disclosure of information provided to them by the county. Any person employed by an appraisal firm whose duties include the appraisal of property for the county must be required to demonstrate that he or she is qualified to carry out these duties by achieving a passing grade on a comprehensive examination in the appraisal of property administered by the Department of Revenue. In the employment of these firms, primary consideration must be given to the firms registered with the Department of Revenue pursuant to G.S. 105-289(i). A copy of the specifications to be submitted to potential bidders and a copy of the proposed contract may be sent by the board to the Department of Revenue for review before the invitation or acceptance of any bids. Contracts for the employment of these firms or persons are contracts for personal services and are not subject to the provisions of Article 8, Chapter 143, of the General Statutes. If the board of county commissioners employs any person or firm to assist the assessor in the performance of the assessor's duties, the person or firm may not be compensated, in whole or in part, on a contingent fee basis or any other similar method that may impair the assessor's independence or the perception of the assessor's independence by the public. (1939, c. 310, s. 408; 1971, c. 806, s. 1; 1973, c. 476, s. 193; 1975, c. 508, s. 2; 1983, c. 813, s. 4; 1985, c. 601, s. 2; 1989, c. 79; 2002-184, s. 7; 2003-416, s. 9; 2012-152, s. 2; 2012-194, s. 61.5(b).)

§ 105-299. (Effective July 1, 2015 - see notes) Employment of experts.

The board of county commissioners may employ appraisal firms, mapping firms or other persons or firms having expertise in one or more of the duties of the assessor to assist the assessor in the performance of these duties. The county may also assign to county agencies, or contract with State or federal agencies for, any duties involved with the approval or auditing of use-value accounts. The county may make available to these persons any information it has that will facilitate the performance of a contract entered into pursuant to this section. Persons receiving this information are subject to the provisions of G.S. 105-289(e) and G.S. 105-259 regarding the use and disclosure of information provided to them by the county. Any person employed by an appraisal firm whose duties include the appraisal of property for the county must be required to demonstrate that he or she is qualified to carry out these duties by achieving a passing grade on a comprehensive examination in the appraisal of property administered by the Department of Revenue. In the employment of these firms, primary consideration must be given to the firms registered with the Department of Revenue pursuant to G.S. 105-289(i). A copy of the specifications to be submitted to potential bidders and a copy of the proposed contract may be sent by the board to the Department of Revenue for review before the invitation or acceptance of any bids. Contracts for the employment of these firms or persons are contracts for personal services and are not subject to the provisions of Article 8, Chapter 143, of the General Statutes. (1939, c. 310, s. 408; 1971, c. 806, s. 1; 1973, c. 476, s. 193; 1975, c. 508, s. 2; 1983, c. 813, s. 4; 1985, c. 601, s. 2; 1989, c. 79; 2002-184, s. 7; 2003-416, s. 9; 2012-152, s. 2; 2012-194, s. 61.5(b).)

§ 105-300. Tax commission.

In all counties having a tax commission or comparable agency, the commission or agency shall, except for levying taxes, perform all the duties required by this Subchapter to be performed by the board of equalization and review and the board of county commissioners. All expenses incurred by the tax commission or agency or its appointees in accordance with this Subchapter shall be paid by the county. Pursuant to Article VI, Sec. 9, of the North Carolina Constitution, the office of member of a tax commission or comparable agency is hereby declared to be an office that may not be held concurrently with any other elective or appointive office. (1939, c. 310, s. 410; 1971, c. 806, s. 1.)

Article 17.

Administration of Listing.

§ 105-301. Place for listing real property.

All taxable real property that is not required by this Subchapter to be appraised originally by the Department of Revenue shall be listed in the county in which it is situated. If all or part of the real property is situated within the boundaries of a municipal corporation, this fact shall be specified on the abstract as required by G.S. 105-309. Nothing in this section shall be construed to conflict with the provisions of G.S. 105-326 through 105-328. (1939, c. 310, s. 700; 1971, c. 806, s. 1; 1973, c. 476, s. 193.)

§ 105-302. In whose name real property is to be listed.

(a)   Taxable real property shall be listed in the name of the owner, and it shall be the owner's duty to list it unless the board of county commissioners shall have adopted a permanent listing system as provided in G.S. 105-303(b). For purposes of this section, the board of county commissioners may require that real property be listed in the name of the owner of record as of the day as of which property is to be listed under G.S. 105-285.

(b)   If real property is listed in the name of one other than the person in whose name it should be listed, and the name of the proper person is later ascertained, the abstract and tax records shall be corrected to list the property in the name of the person in whose name it should have been listed. The corrected listing shall have the same force and effect as if the real property had been listed in the name of the proper person in the first instance.

(c)   For purposes of this Subchapter:

(1)   The owner of the equity of redemption in real property subject to a mortgage or deed of trust shall be considered the owner of the property, and such real property shall be listed in the name of the owner of the equity of redemption.

(2)   Real property owned by a corporation shall be listed in the name of the corporation.

(3)   Real property owned by an unincorporated association shall be listed in the name of the association.

(4)   Real property owned by a partnership shall be listed in the name of the partnership.

(5)   Real property held in connection with a sole proprietorship shall be listed in the name of the owner, and the name and address of the proprietorship shall be noted on the abstract.

(6)   Real property of which a decedent died possessed, if not under the control of an executor or administrator, shall be listed in the names of the heirs or devisees if known, but such property may be listed as property of "the heirs" or "the devisees" of the decedent, without naming them, until they have given the assessor notice of their names and of the division of the estate. It shall be the duty of an executor or administrator having control of real property to list it in his fiduciary capacity, as required by subdivision (c)(7), below, until he is divested of control of the property. However, the right of an administrator or executor of a deceased person to petition for the sale of real property to make assets shall not be considered control of the real property for the purposes of this subdivision.

(7)   Real property, the title to which is held by a trustee, guardian, or other fiduciary, shall be listed by the fiduciary in his fiduciary capacity except as otherwise provided in this section.

(8)   A life tenant or tenant for the life of another shall be considered the owner of real property, and it shall be his duty to list the property for taxation, indicating on the abstract that he is a life tenant or tenant for the life of another named individual.

(9)   Upon request to and with the approval of the assessor, undivided interests in real property owned by tenants in common who are not copartners may be listed by the respective owners in accordance with their respective undivided interests. Otherwise, real property held by tenants in common shall be listed in the names of all the owners.

(10)   Real property owned by husband and wife as tenants by the entirety shall be listed on a single abstract in the names of both tenants, and the nature of their ownership shall be indicated thereon.

(11)   When land is owned by one party and improvements thereon or special rights (such as mineral, timber, quarry, waterpower, or similar rights) therein are owned by another party, the parties shall list their interests separately unless, in accordance with contractual relations between them, both the land and the improvements and special rights are listed in the name of the owner of the land.

(12)   If the person in whose name real property should be listed is unknown, or if title to real property is in dispute, the property shall be listed in the name of the occupant or, if there be no occupant, in the name of "unknown owner." Such a listing shall not affect the validity of the lien for taxes created by G.S. 105-355. When the name of the owner is later ascertained, the provisions of subsection (b), above, shall apply.

(13)   Real property, owned under a time-sharing arrangement but managed by a homeowners association or other managing entity, shall be listed in the name of the managing entity. (1939, c. 310, s. 701; 1971, c. 806, s. 1; 1983, c. 785, s. 1; 1987, c. 45, s. 1.)

§ 105-302.1. Reports on properties listed in name of unknown owner.

In order to promote the discovery of "State lands" as defined by G.S. 146-64(6), it shall be the duty of all assessors upon request to furnish the State of North Carolina a report on all properties listed in the name of "unknown owner" pursuant to G.S. 105-302(c)(12) in their respective tax jurisdictions. Such report shall be forwarded to the Secretary of the North Carolina Department of Administration. The report shall contain all information available to the assessor concerning the location and identification of the properties in question. (1979, c. 45, s. 1; 1987, c. 45, s.1)

§ 105-303. Obtaining information on real property transfers; permanent listing.

(a)   To facilitate the accurate listing of real property for taxation, the board of county commissioners may require the register of deeds to comply with the provisions of subdivision (a)(1), below, or it may require him to comply with the provisions of subdivision (a)(2), below:

(1) When any conveyance of real property (other than a deed of trust or mortgage) is recorded, the board of county commissioners may require the register of deeds to certify to the assessor:

a. The name of the person conveying the property.

b. The name and address of the person to whom the property is being conveyed.

c. A description of the property sufficient to locate and identify it.

d. A statement as to whether the parcel is conveyed in whole or in part.

(2) When any conveyance of real property (other than a deed of trust or mortgage) is submitted for recordation, the board of county commissioners may require the register of deeds to refuse to record it unless it has been presented to the assessor and the assessor has noted thereon that he has obtained the information he desires from the conveyance and from the person recording it.

(b) The board of commissioners of each county must install a permanent listing system. Each county must obtain the approval of the Department of Revenue for its permanent listing system. Under such a system the provisions of subdivisions (b)(1) through (b)(4) of this subsection apply.

(1) The assessor is responsible for listing all real property on the abstracts and tax records each year in the name of the owner of record as of the day as of which property is to be listed under G.S. 105-285.

(2) Persons whose duty it is to list real property under the provisions of G.S. 105-302 are relieved of that duty, but annually, during the listing period established by G.S. 105-307, these persons must furnish the assessor with the information concerning improvements on and separate rights in real property required by G.S. 105-309(c)(3) through (c)(5).

(3) The penalties imposed by G.S. 105-308 and 105-312 do not apply to failure to list real property for taxation, but they apply to failure to comply with the provisions of subdivision (b)(2) of this subsection with respect to reporting the construction or acquisition of improvements on and separate rights in real property. In such a case, the penalty prescribed by G.S. 105-312 shall be computed on the basis of the tax imposed on the improvements and separate rights.

(4) The Department of Revenue may authorize the board of county commissioners to make additional modifications of the listing requirements of this Subchapter, as long as the modifications do not conflict with subdivisions (b)(1) through (b)(3) of this subsection. (1939, c. 310, s. 701; 1971, c. 806, s. 1; 1973, c. 476, s. 193; c. 789; 1987, c. 43, s. 4; c. 45, s. 1; 1999-297, s. 3.)

§ 105-304. Place for listing tangible personal property.

(a) Listing Instructions. - This section applies to all taxable tangible personal property that has a tax situs in this State and that is not required by this Subchapter to be appraised originally by the Department of Revenue. The place in this State at which this property is taxable is determined according to the rules provided in this section. The person whose duty it is to list property must list it in the county in which the place of taxation is located, indicating on the abstract the information required by G.S. 105-309(d). If the place of taxation lies within a city or town that requires separate listing under G.S. 105-326(a), the person whose duty it is to list must also list the property for taxation in the city or town.

(a1) Repealed by Session Laws 2011-238, s. 1, effective June 23, 2011.

(b) Definitions. - The following definitions apply in this section:

(1) Situated. - More or less permanently located.

(2) Business premises. - The term includes, for purposes of illustration, the following: Store, mill, dockyard, piling ground, shop, office, mine, farm, factory, warehouse, rental real estate, place for the sale of property (including the premises of a consignee), and place for storage (including a public warehouse).

(3) Repealed by Session Laws 2011-238, s. 1, effective June 23, 2011.

(c) General Rule. - Except as otherwise provided in subsections (d) through (h) of this section, tangible personal property is taxable at the residence of the owner. For purposes of this section:

(1) The residence of an individual person who has two or more places in this State at which the individual occasionally dwells is the place at which the

individual dwelt for the longest period of time during the calendar year immediately preceding the date as of which property is to be listed for taxation.

(2) The residence of a domestic or foreign taxpayer other than an individual person is the place at which its principal North Carolina place of business is located.

(d) Property of Taxpayers With No Fixed Residence in This State. -

(1) Tangible personal property owned by an individual nonresident of this State is taxable at the place in this State at which the property is situated.

(2) Tangible personal property owned by a domestic or foreign taxpayer (other than an individual person) that has no principal office in this State is taxable at the place in this State at which the property is situated.

(e) Farm Products. - Farm products produced in this State, if owned by their producer, are taxable at the place in this State at which they were produced.

(f) Property Situated or Commonly Used at Premises Other Than Owner's Residence. - Subject to the provisions of subsection (e) of this section:

(1) Tangible personal property situated at or commonly used in connection with a temporary or seasonal dwelling owned or leased by the owner of the personal property is taxable at the place at which the temporary or seasonal dwelling is situated.

(2) Tangible personal property situated at or commonly used in connection with a business premises hired, occupied, or used by the owner of the personal property (or by the owner's agent or employee) is taxable at the place at which the business premises is situated. Tangible personal property that may be used by the public generally or that is used to sell or vend merchandise to the public falls within the provisions of this subdivision.

(3) Tangible personal property situated at or commonly used in connection with a premise owned, hired, occupied, or used by a person who is in possession of the personal property under a business agreement with the property's owner is taxable at the place at which the possessor's premise is situated. For purposes of this subdivision, the term "business agreement" means a commercial lease, a bailment for hire, a consignment, or a similar business arrangement.

(4) In applying the provisions of subdivisions (1), (2), and (3) of this subsection, the temporary absence of tangible personal property from the place at which it is taxable under one of those subdivisions on the day as of which property is to be listed does not affect the application of the rules established in those subdivisions. The presence of tangible personal property at a location specified in subdivision (1), (2), or (3) of this subsection on the day as of which property is to be listed is prima facie evidence that it is situated at or commonly used in connection with that location.

(g) Decedents. - The tangible personal property of a decedent whose estate is in the process of administration or has not been distributed is taxable at the place at which it would be taxable if the decedent were still alive and still residing at the place at which the decedent resided at the time of death.

(h) Beneficial Ownership. - Tangible personal property within the jurisdiction of the State held by a resident or nonresident trustee, guardian, or other fiduciary having legal title to the property is taxable in accordance with the following rules:

(1) If any beneficiary is a resident of the State, an amount representing that beneficiary's portion of the property is taxable at the place at which it would be taxable if the beneficiary owned that portion.

(2) If any beneficiary is a nonresident of the State, an amount representing that beneficiary's portion of the property is taxable at the place at which it would be taxable if the fiduciary were the beneficial owner of the property. (1939, c. 310, s. 800; 1947, c. 836; 1951, c. 1102, s. 1; 1955, c. 1012, ss. 2, 3; 1969, c. 940; 1971, c. 806, s. 1; 1973, c. 476, s. 193; c. 1180; 2001-279, s. 1; 2006-30, s. 1; 2011-238, s. 1.)

§ 105-305. Place for listing intangible personal property.

(a) Listing Instructions. - This section applies to all taxable intangible personal property that has a tax situs in this State and is not required by this Subchapter to be appraised originally by the Department of Revenue. The place in this State at which this property is taxable shall be determined as provided in this section. The person whose duty it is to list property shall list it in the county in which the place of taxation is located, indicating on the abstract the information required by G.S. 105-309(d). If the place of taxation lies within a city or town that requires separate listing under G.S. 105-326(a), the person whose duty it is to list shall also list the property for taxation in the city or town.

(b)   Repealed by Session Laws 1997-456, s. 43(a).

(c)   Intangible personal property representing an interest or interests in real property that is situated in this State shall be taxable in the place in which the represented real property is located.

(d), (e) Repealed by Session Laws 1997-456, s. 43(a). (1939, c. 310, s. 801; 1971, c. 806, s. 1; 1973, c. 476, s. 193; 1995, c. 41, s. 8; 1997-456, s. 43(a).)

§ 105-306. In whose name personal property is to be listed.

(a)   Taxable personal property shall be listed in the name of the owner on the day as of which property is to be listed for taxation, and it shall be the duty of the owner to list the property.

(b)   If personal property is listed in the name of a person other than the one in whose name it should be listed, and the name of the proper person is later ascertained, the abstract and tax records shall be corrected to list the property in the name in which it should have been listed. The corrected listing shall have the same force and effect as if the personal property had been listed in the name of the proper person in the first instance.

(c)   For purposes of this Subchapter:

(1)   The owner of the equity of redemption in personal property subject to a chattel mortgage shall be considered the owner of the property.

(2)   The vendee of personal property under a conditional bill of sale, or under any other sale contract through which title to the property is retained by the vender as security for the payment of the purchase price, shall be considered the owner of the property if he has possession of or the right to use the property.

(3)   Personal property owned by a corporation, partnership, or unincorporated association shall be listed in the name of the corporation, partnership, or unincorporated association.

(4) Personal property held in connection with a sole proprietorship shall be listed in the name of the owner, and the name and address of the proprietorship shall be noted on the abstract.

(5) Personal property of which a decedent died possessed, if not under the control of a personal representative, shall be listed in the names of the next of kin or devisees if known, but such property may be listed as property of "the next of kin" or "the devisees" of the decedent, without naming them, until they have given the assessor notice of their names and of the division of the estate. It shall be the duty of a personal representative having control of personal property to list it in the personal representative's fiduciary capacity, as required by subdivision (c)(6), below, until the personal representative is divested of control of the property.

(6) Personal property, the title to which is held by a trustee, guardian, or other fiduciary, shall be listed by the fiduciary in his fiduciary capacity except as otherwise provided in this section.

(7) If personal property is owned by two or more persons who are joint owners, each owner shall list the value of his interest. However, if the joint owners are husband and wife, the property owned jointly shall be listed on a single abstract in the names of both the husband and the wife.

(8) If the person in whose name personal property should be listed is unknown, or if the ownership of the property is in dispute, the property shall be listed in the name of the person in possession of the property, or if there appears to be no person in possession, in the name of "unknown owner." When the name of the owner is later ascertained, the provisions of subsection (b), above, shall apply.

(9) Personal property, owned under a time-sharing arrangement but managed by a homeowners association or other managing entity, shall be listed in the name of the managing entity. (1939, c. 310, s. 802; 1971, c. 806, s. 1; 1983, c. 785, s. 2; 1987, c. 45, s. 1; 2011-284, s. 71.)

§ 105-307. Length of listing period; extension; preliminary work.

(a) Listing Period. - Unless extended as provided in this section, the period during which property is to be listed for taxation each year begins on the first business day of January and ends on January 31.

(b) General Extensions. - The board of county commissioners may, by resolution, extend the time during which property is to be listed for taxation as provided in this subsection. Any action by the board of county commissioners extending the listing period must be recorded in the minutes of the board, and notice of the extensions must be published as required by G.S. 105-296(c). The entire period for listing, including any extension of time granted, is considered the regular listing period for the particular year within the meaning of this Subchapter.

(1) In nonrevaluation years, the listing period may be extended for up to 30 additional days.

(2) In years of octennial appraisal of real property, the listing period may be extended for up to 60 additional days.

(3) If the county has provided for electronic listing of personal property under G.S. 105-310.1, the period for electronic listing of personal property may be extended up to June 1. A resolution that provides a general extension of time for the electronic listing of personal property shall continue in effect until revised or rescinded unless otherwise stated in the resolution.

(c) Individual Extensions. - The board of county commissioners shall grant individual extensions of time for the listing of real and personal property upon written request and for good cause shown. The request must be filed with the assessor no later than the ending date of the regular listing period. The board may delegate the authority to grant extensions to the assessor. Extensions granted under this subsection shall not extend beyond April 15. Notwithstanding the individual extension time limitation in this subsection, if the county has provided for electronic listing of personal property under G.S. 105-310.1, extensions granted for electronic listing of personal property shall not extend beyond June 1.

(d) Preliminary Work. - The assessor may conduct preparatory work before the listing period begins, but may not make a final appraisal of property before the day as of which the value of the property is to be determined under G.S. 105-285. (1939, c. 310, s. 905; 1971, c. 806, s. 1; 1973, cc. 141, 706; 1975, c.

49; 1977, c. 360; 1987, c. 43, s. 5; c. 45, s. 1; 2001-279, s. 2; 2006-30, s. 2; 2011-238, s. 3.)

§ 105-308. Duty to list; penalty for failure.

Every person in whose name any property is to be listed under the terms of this Subchapter shall list the property with the assessor within the time allowed by law on an abstract setting forth the information required by this Subchapter.

In addition to all other penalties prescribed by law, any person whose duty it is to list any property who willfully fails or refuses to list the same within the time prescribed by law shall be guilty of a Class 2 misdemeanor. The failure to list shall be prima facie evidence that the failure was willful.

Any person who willfully attempts, or who willfully aids or abets any person to attempt, in any manner to evade or defeat the taxes imposed under this Subchapter, whether by removal or concealment of property or otherwise, shall be guilty of a Class 2 misdemeanor. (1939, c. 310, s. 901; 1957, c. 848; 1971, c. 806, s. 1; 1977, c. 92; 1987, c. 43, s. 4, c. 45, s. 1; 1993, c. 539, s. 717; 1994, Ex. Sess., c. 24, s. 14(c).)

§ 105-309. What the abstract shall contain.

(a)   Each person whose duty it is to list property for taxation shall file each year with the assessor a tax list or abstract showing, as of the date prescribed by G.S. 105-285(b), the information required by this section. Subject to the provisions of subdivisions (a)(1) and (a)(2), below, each person whose duty it is to list property for taxation shall file a separate abstract.

(1)   Tenants by the entirety shall file a single abstract listing the real property so held, together with all personal property they own jointly.

(2)   Tenants in common shall file a single abstract listing the real property so held, together with all personal property that they own jointly, unless, as provided in G.S. 105-302(c)(9), the assessor allows them to list their undivided interests in the real property on separate abstracts.

(b)   Each abstract shall show the taxpayer's name; residence address; and, if required by the assessor, business address.

(1)   An individual trading under a firm name shall show his name and address and also the name and address of his business firm.

(2)   An unincorporated association shall show both the name and address of the association and the names and addresses of its principal officers.

(3)   A partnership shall show both the name and address of the partnership and the names and addresses of its full partners.

(c)   Each tract, parcel, or lot of real property owned or controlled in the county shall be listed in accordance with the following instructions:

(1)   Real property not divided into lots shall be described by giving:

a.   The township in which located.

b.   The total number of acres in the tract, or, if smaller than one acre, the dimensions of the parcel.

c.   The tract name (if any), the names of at least two adjoining landowners, a reference to the tract's designation on any map maintained in the office of the assessor or on file in the office of the register of deeds, or some other description sufficient to identify and locate the property by parol testimony.

d.   If applicable, the number of acres of:

1.   Cleared land;

2.   Woods and timberland;

3.   Land containing mineral or quarry deposits;

4.   Land susceptible of development for waterpower;

5.   Wasteland.

e.   The portion of the tract or parcel located within the boundaries of any municipality.

(2) Real property divided into lots shall be described by giving:

a. The township in which located.

b. The dimensions of the lot.

c. The location of the lot, including its street number (if any).

d. The lot's designation on any map maintained in the office of the assessor or on file in the office of the register of deeds, or some description sufficient to identify and locate the property by parol testimony.

e. The portion of the lot located within the boundaries of any municipality.

(3) In conjunction with the listing of any real property under subdivisions (c)(1) and (c)(2), above, there shall be given a short description of any buildings and other improvements thereon that belong to the owner of the land.

(4) Buildings and other improvements having a value in excess of one hundred dollars ($100.00) that have been acquired, begun, erected, damaged, or destroyed since the time of the last appraisal of property shall be described.

(5) If some person other than the owner of a tract, parcel, or lot shall own any buildings or other improvements thereon or separate rights (such as mineral, quarry, timber, waterpower, or other rights) therein, that fact shall be specified on the abstract on which the land is listed, together with the name and address of the owner of the buildings, other improvements, or rights.

a. Buildings, other improvements, and separate rights owned by a taxpayer with respect to the lands of another shall be listed separately and identified so as to indicate the name of the owner thereof and the tract, parcel, or lot on which the buildings or other improvements are situated or to which the separate rights appertain.

b. In accordance with the provisions of G.S. 105-302(c)(11), buildings or other improvements or separate rights owned by a taxpayer with respect to the lands of another may be listed either in the name of the owner of the buildings, other improvements, or rights, or in the name of the owner of the land.

(d) Personal property shall be listed to indicate the township and municipality, if any, in which it is taxable and shall be itemized by the taxpayer in such detail as may be prescribed by an abstract form approved by the Department of Revenue. Personal property shall also be listed to indicate which property, if any, is subject to a tax credit under G.S. 105-151.21.

(1) If the assessor considers it necessary to obtain a complete listing of personal property, the assessor may require a taxpayer to submit additional information, inventories, or itemized lists of personal property.

(2) At the request of the assessor, the taxpayer shall furnish any information the taxpayer has with respect to the true value of the personal property the taxpayer is required to list.

(e) At the end of the abstract each person whose duty it is to list property for taxation shall sign the affirmation required by G.S. 105-310.

(f) The assessor must print a homestead tax relief notice on each abstract or on an information sheet distributed with the abstract. The abstract or sheet must include the address and telephone number of the assessor below the notice required by this section. The notice must be in the form required by the Department of Revenue designed to notify the taxpayer of his or her rights and responsibilities under the homestead property tax exclusion provided in G.S. 105-277.1 and the property tax homestead circuit breaker provided in G.S. 105-277.1B.

(g) Any person who fails to give the notice required by G.S. 105-309(f) shall not only be subject to loss of the exemption, but also to the penalties provided by G.S. 105-312, and also if willful to the penalty provided in G.S. 105-310. For the purpose of determining whether a penalty is levied, whenever a taxpayer has received an exemption under G.S. 105-277.1 for one taxable year but the property of taxpayer is not eligible for the exemption the next year, notice given of that fact to the assessor on or before April 15 shall be considered as timely filed. (1939, c. 310, s. 900; 1941, c. 221, s. 1; 1953, c. 970, s. 6; 1955, c. 34; 1971, c. 806, s. 1; 1973, c. 448, s. 2; c. 476, s. 193; 1975, c. 881, s. 3; 1977, c. 666, s. 2; 1979, c. 846, s. 2; 1981, c. 54, ss. 4-6; c. 1052, s. 1; 1985, c. 656, ss. 47, 51; 1985 (Reg. Sess., 1986), c. 947, s. 9; c. 982, s. 23; 1987, c. 43, s. 6; c. 45, s. 1; 1993, c. 360, s. 2; 1996, 2nd Ex. Sess., c. 18, s. 15.1(b); 1998-98, s. 111; 2001-308, s. 2; 2007-484, s. 43.7T(b); 2007-497, s. 2.5.)

§ 105-310. Affirmation; penalty for false affirmation.

There shall be annexed to the abstract on which the taxpayer's property is listed the following affirmation, which shall be signed by an individual qualified under the provisions of G.S. 105-311:

Under penalties prescribed by law, I hereby affirm that to the best of my knowledge and belief this listing, including any accompanying statements, inventories, schedules, and other information, is true and complete. (If this affirmation is signed by an individual other than the taxpayer, he affirms that he is familiar with the extent and true value of all the taxpayer's property subject to taxation in this county and that his affirmation is based on all the information of which he has any knowledge.)

Any individual who willfully makes and subscribes an abstract listing required by this Subchapter which he does not believe to be true and correct as to every material matter shall be guilty of a Class 2 misdemeanor. (1939, c. 310, s. 902; 1971, c. 806, s. 1; 1993, c. 539, s. 718; 1994, Ex. Sess., c. 24, s. 14(c).)

§ 105-310.1. Electronic listing of personal property.

(a)   Personal property may be listed by electronic listing as provided in this section.

(b)   The Department of Revenue may establish, after consultation with the counties, the standards and requirements for electronic listing of personal property, including the minimum requirements that must exist before electronic listing will be allowed in a county.

(c)   The board of county commissioners may, by resolution, provide for electronic listing of personal property in accordance with the standards and requirements prescribed by the Department of Revenue. The board of county commissioners may, by resolution, delegate its authority to provide for electronic listing of personal property to the county assessor.

(d)   Definitions. - The following definitions apply in this section:

(1)   Electronic. - Defined in G.S. 66-312.

(2) Electronic listing. - The filing by electronic means of the abstract required by G.S. 105-309 and the affirmation required by G.S. 105-310. (2011-238, s. 4.)

§ 105-311. Listing and signing affirmation; use of agents, mail, and electronic listing.

(a) Except as otherwise provided in this section, the person whose duty it is to list property for taxation shall file the completed abstract with the assessor for purposes of listing and shall sign the affirmation required by G.S. 105-310 to be annexed to the completed abstract on which the property is listed. The abstract must be filed with the assessor on a form approved by the Department of Revenue.

(1) In the case of an individual taxpayer who is unable to list his property, a guardian, authorized agent, or other person having knowledge of and charged with the care of the person and property of the taxpayer shall file the completed abstract and shall sign the required affirmation in the name of the taxpayer, noting thereon the capacity in which he signs.

(2) In the case of a corporation, partnership, limited liability company, or unincorporated association, a person specified in sub-subdivision a., b., or c. below, shall file the completed abstract and shall sign the required affirmation in the name of the taxpayer, noting thereon the capacity in which he signs, and no other agent shall be permitted to sign the affirmation required on such a taxpayer's abstract:

a. A principal officer of the taxpayer.

b. A full-time employee of the taxpayer who has been officially empowered by a principal officer of the taxpayer in his behalf to list the taxpayer's property for taxation in the county and to sign the affirmation annexed to the abstract or abstracts on which its property is listed.

c. An agent of the taxpayer authorized by a principal officer of the taxpayer in a manner prescribed by the Department of Revenue.

(3) Repealed by Session Laws 2011-238, s. 5, effective June 23, 2011.

(b) Abstracts may be submitted in person or by mail. Additionally, if the county has provided for electronic listing of personal property under G.S. 105-310.1, personal property abstracts may be submitted by electronic listing.

(1) Submission by mail. - In no event shall an abstract submitted by mail be accepted unless the affirmation on the abstract is signed by the individual prescribed in subsection (a) of this section. For the purpose of this Subchapter, abstracts submitted by mail are considered filed as of the date shown on the postmark affixed by the United States Postal Service. If no date is shown on the postmark, or if the postmark is not affixed by the United States Postal Service, the abstract is considered filed when received in the office of the assessor.

(2) Submission by electronic listing. - In no event shall an abstract submitted by electronic listing be accepted unless the affirmation on the abstract is signed by the individual prescribed in subsection (a) of this section. The affirmation may be signed using an electronic signature method approved by the Department of Revenue. For the purpose of this Subchapter, abstracts submitted by electronic listing are considered filed when received in the office of the assessor as denoted by timestamps applied by the receiving equipment or programs.

(c) In any dispute arising under this Subchapter, the burden of proof is on the taxpayer to show that the abstract was timely filed. (1939, c. 310, ss. 901, 903, 904; 1957, c. 848; 1971, c. 806, s. 1; 1973, c. 476, s. 193; 1977, c. 327, s. 1; 1987, c. 43, s. 7; c. 45, s. 1; 2001-279, s. 3; 2001-487, s. 70; 2011-238, s. 5.)

§ 105-312. Discovered property; appraisal; penalty.

(a) Repealed by Session Laws 1991, c. 34, s. 4.

(b) Duty to Discover and Assess Unlisted Property. - It shall be the duty of the assessor to see that all property not properly listed during the regular listing period be listed, assessed and taxed as provided in this Subchapter. The assessor shall file reports of such discoveries with the board of commissioners in such manner as the board may require.

(c) Carrying Forward Real Property. - At the close of the regular listing period each year, the assessor shall compare the tax lists submitted during the listing period just ended with the lists for the preceding year, and he shall carry forward to the lists of the current year all real property that was listed in the preceding year but that was not listed for the current year. When carried forward, the real property shall be listed in the name of the taxpayer who listed it in the preceding year unless, under the provisions of G.S. 105-302, it must be listed in the name of another taxpayer. Real property carried forward in this manner shall be deemed to be discovered property, and the procedures prescribed in subsection (d), below, shall be followed unless the property discovered is listed in the name of the taxpayer who listed it for the preceding year and the property is not subject to appraisal under either G.S. 105-286 or G.S. 105-287 in which case no notice of the listing and valuation need be sent to the taxpayer.

(d)   Procedure for Listing, Appraising, and Assessing Discovered Property. - Subject to the provisions of subsection (c), above, and the presumptions established by subsection (f), below, discovered property shall be listed by the assessor in the name of the person required by G.S. 105-302 or G.S. 105-306. The discovery shall be deemed to be made on the date that the abstract is made or corrected pursuant to subsection (e) of this section. The assessor shall also make a tentative appraisal of the discovered property in accordance with the best information available to him.

When a discovery is made, the assessor shall mail a notice to the person in whose name the discovered property has been listed. The notice shall contain the following information:

(1)   The name and address of the person in whose name the property is listed;

(2)   A brief description of the property;

(3)   A tentative appraisal of the property;

(4)   A statement to the effect that the listing and appraisal will become final unless written exception thereto is filed with the assessor within 30 days from date of the notice.

Upon receipt of a timely exception to the notice of discovery, the assessor shall arrange a conference with the taxpayer to afford him the opportunity to present any evidence or argument he may have regarding the discovery. Within 15 days after the conference, the assessor shall give written notice to the taxpayer of his final decision. Written notice shall not be required, however, if the taxpayer signs an agreement accepting the listing and appraisal. In cases in which agreement is not reached, the taxpayer shall have 15 days from the date of the notice to request review of the decision of the assessor by the board of equalization and review or, if that board is not in session, by the board of commissioners. Unless the request for review by the county board is given at the conference, it shall be made in writing to the assessor. Upon receipt of a timely request for review, the provisions of G.S. 105-322 or G.S. 105-325, as appropriate, shall be followed.

(e) Record of Discovered Property. - When property is discovered, the taxpayer's original abstract (if one was submitted) may be corrected or a new abstract may be prepared to reflect the discovery. If a new abstract is prepared, it may be filed with the abstracts that were submitted during the regular listing period, or it may be filed separately with abstracts designated "Late Listings." Regardless of how filed, the listing shall have the same force and effect as if it had been submitted during the regular listing period.

(f) Presumptions. - When property is discovered and listed to a taxpayer in any year, it shall be presumed that it should have been listed by the same taxpayer for the preceding five years unless the taxpayer shall produce satisfactory evidence that the property was not in existence, that it was actually listed for taxation, or that it was not his duty to list the property during those years or some of them under the provisions of G.S. 105-302 and G.S. 105-306. If it is shown that the property should have been listed by some other taxpayer during some or all of the preceding years, the property shall be listed in the name of the appropriate taxpayer for the proper years, but the discovery shall still be deemed to have been made as of the date that the assessor first listed it.

(g) Taxation of Discovered Property. - When property is discovered, it shall be taxed for the year in which discovered and for any of the preceding five years during which it escaped taxation in accordance with the assessed value it should have been assigned in each of the years for which it is to be taxed and the rate of tax imposed in each such year. The penalties prescribed by subsection (h) of this section shall be computed and imposed regardless of the name in which the discovered property is listed. If the discovery is based upon an understatement of value, quantity, or other measurement rather than an omission from the tax list, the tax shall be computed on the additional valuation fixed upon the property, and the penalties prescribed by subsection (h) of this section shall be computed on the basis of the additional tax.

(h)   Computation of Penalties. - Having computed each year's taxes separately as provided in subsection (g), above, there shall be added a penalty of ten percent (10%) of the amount of the tax for the earliest year in which the property was not listed, plus an additional ten percent (10%) of the same amount for each subsequent listing period that elapsed before the property was discovered. This penalty shall be computed separately for each year in which a failure to list occurred; and the year, the amount of the tax for that year, and the total of penalties for failure to list in that year shall be shown separately on the tax records; but the taxes and penalties for all years in which there was a failure to list shall be then totalled on a single tax receipt.

(h1)   Repealed by Session Laws 1991, c. 624, s. 8.

(i)   Collection. - For purposes of tax collection and foreclosure, the total figure obtained and recorded as provided in subsection (h) of this section shall be deemed to be a tax for the fiscal year beginning on July 1 of the calendar year in which the property was discovered. The schedule of discounts for prepayment and interest for late payment applicable to taxes for the fiscal year referred to in the preceding sentence shall apply when the total figure on the single tax receipt is paid. Notwithstanding the time limitations contained in G.S. 105-381, any property owner who is required to pay taxes on discovered property as herein provided shall be entitled to a refund of any taxes erroneously paid on the same property to other taxing jurisdictions in North Carolina. Claim for refund shall be filed in the county where such tax was erroneously paid as provided by G.S. 105-381.

(j)   Tax Receipts Charged to Collector. - Tax receipts prepared as required by subsections (h) and (i) of this section for the taxes and penalties imposed upon discovered property shall be delivered to the tax collector, and he shall be charged with their collection. Such receipts shall have the same force and effect as if they had been delivered to the collector at the time of the delivery of the regular tax receipts for the current year, and the taxes charged in the receipts shall be a lien upon the property in accordance with the provisions of G.S. 105-355.

(k)   Power to Compromise. - After a tax receipt computed and prepared as required by subsections (g) and (h) of this section has been delivered and charged to the tax collector as prescribed in subsection (j), above, the board of county commissioners, upon the petition of the taxpayer, may compromise, settle, or adjust the county's claim for taxes arising therefrom. The board of commissioners may, by resolution, delegate the authority granted by this subsection to the board of equalization and review, including any board created by resolution pursuant to G.S. 105-322(a) and any special board established by local act.

(l)   Municipal Corporations. - The provisions of this section shall apply to all cities, towns, and other municipal corporations having the power to tax property. Such governmental units shall designate an appropriate municipal officer to exercise the powers and duties assigned by this section to the assessor, and the powers and duties assigned to the board of county commissioners shall be exercised by the governing body of the unit. When the assessor discovers property having a taxable situs in a municipal corporation, he shall send a copy of the notice of discovery required by subsection (d) to the governing body of the municipality together with such other information as may be necessary to enable the municipality to proceed. The governing board of a municipality may, by resolution, delegate the power to compromise, settle, or adjust tax claims granted by this subsection and by subsection (k) of this section to the county board of equalization and review, including any board created by resolution pursuant to G.S. 105-322(a) and any special board established by local act. (1939, c. 310, s. 1109; 1971, c. 806, s. 1; 1973, c. 476, s. 193; c. 787; 1977, c. 864; 1981, c. 623, ss. 1, 2; 1987, c. 45, s. 1; c. 743, ss. 1, 2; 1989, c. 522; 1991, c. 34, s. 4; c. 624, s. 8; 1991 (Reg. Sess., 1992), c. 961, s. 12; 1999-297, s. 2.)

Article 18.

Reports in Aid of Listing.

§ 105-313. Report of property by multi-county business.

A taxpayer who is engaged in business in more than one county in this State and who owns real property or tangible personal property in connection with his multi-county business shall, upon the request of the Department of Revenue or the assessor of a county in which part of this business property is situated, file a report with the Department of Revenue stating, as of the dates specified in G.S. 105-285 of any year, the following information:

(1)   The counties in this State in which the taxpayer's business property is situated;

(2)   The taxpayer's investment, on a county by county basis, in his business property situated in this State, categorized as the Department of Revenue or the assessor may require; and

(3)   The taxpayer's total investment in his business property situated in this State, categorized as the Department of Revenue or the assessor may require.

This report shall be subscribed and sworn to by the owner of the property. If the owner is a corporation, partnership, or unincorporated association, the report shall be subscribed and sworn to by a principal officer of the owner who has knowledge of the facts contained in the report. (1971, c. 806, s. 1; 1973, c. 476, s. 193; 1987, c. 777, s. 3.)

§ 105-314: Repealed by Session Laws 1991, c. 761, s. 37.4.

§ 105-315. Reports by persons having custody of tangible personal property of others.

(a)   As of January 1, every person having custody of taxable tangible personal property that has been entrusted to him by another for storage, sale, renting, or any other business purpose shall furnish the appropriate assessor the reports required by subdivision (a)(2), below:

(1)   Repealed by Session Laws 1987, c. 813, s. 14.

(2)   For all tangible personal property, except inventories exempt under G.S. 105-275(33) and (34), there shall be furnished to the assessor of the county in which the property is situated a statement showing the name of the owner of the property, a description of the property, the quantity of the property, and the amount of money, if any, advanced against the property by the person having custody of it.

(3)   For purposes of illustration, but not by way of limitation, the term "person having custody of taxable tangible personal property" as used in this subsection (a) shall include warehouses, cooperative growers' and marketing associations, consignees, factors, commission merchants, and brokers.

(b) Any person who fails to make the reports required by subsection (a), above, by January 15 in any year shall be liable to the counties in which the property is taxable for a penalty to be measured by any portion of the tax on the property that has not been paid at the time the action to collect this penalty is brought plus two hundred fifty dollars ($250.00). This penalty may be recovered in a civil action in the appropriate division of the General Court of Justice of the county in which the property is taxable. Upon recovery of this penalty, the tax on the property shall be deemed to be paid. (1939, c. 310, ss. 1001, 1002; 1955, c. 1069, ss. 2, 3; 1965, c. 592; 1971, c. 806, s. 1; 1987, c. 45, s. 1; c. 813, s. 14.)

§ 105-316. Reports by house trailer park, marina, and aircraft storage facility operators.

(a) As of January 1 each year:

(1) Every operator of a park or storage lot renting or leasing space for three or more house trailers or mobile homes shall furnish to the assessor of the county in which the park or lot is located the name of the owner of and a description of each house trailer or mobile home situated thereon.

(2) Every operator of a marina or comparable facility renting, leasing, or otherwise providing dockage or storage space for three or more boats, vessels, floating homes, or floating structures shall furnish to the assessor of the county in which the marina or comparable facility is located the name of the owner of and a description of each boat, vessel, floating home, or floating structure for which dockage or storage space is rented, leased, or otherwise provided.

(3) Every operator of a storage facility renting or leasing space for three or more airplanes or other aircraft shall furnish to the assessor of the county in which the storage facility is located the name of the owner of and a description of each airplane or aircraft for which space is rented or leased.

(b) Any person who fails to make any report required by subsection (a), above, by January 15 of any year shall be liable to the county in which the house trailers, mobile homes, boats, vessels, floating homes, floating structures, or airplanes are taxable for a penalty to be measured by any portion of the tax on the personal property that has not been paid at the time the action to collect this penalty is brought, plus two hundred fifty dollars ($250.00). This penalty may be recovered in a civil action in the appropriate division of the General

Court of Justice of the county in which the personal property is taxable. Upon recovery of this penalty, the tax on the personal property shall be deemed to be paid. (1939, c. 310, s. 1002; 1955, c. 1069, s. 3; 1965, c. 592; 1971, c. 806, s. 1; 1985, c. 378, ss. 1, 2; 1987, c. 45, s. 1.)

§ 105-316.1. Tax permit required to move mobile home.

(a)   In order to protect the local taxing units of this State against the nonpayment of ad valorem taxes on mobile homes, it is hereby declared to be unlawful for any person other than a mobile home manufacturer or retailer to remove or cause to be removed any mobile home situated at a premises in this State without first obtaining a tax permit from the tax collector of the county in which the mobile home is situated. The tax permit shall be conspicuously displayed near the license tag on the rear of the mobile home at all times during its transportation. Permits required by G.S. 105-316.1 through 105-316.8 may be obtained at the office of the county tax collector during normal business hours.

(b)   Except as provided in G.S. 105-316.4, manufacturers, retailers and licensed carriers of mobile homes shall not be required to obtain the tax permits required by this section. Persons or firms transporting mobile homes shall, however, be responsible for seeing that a proper license tag, and when required under this section, a tax permit, are properly displayed thereon at all times during their transportation. (1975, c. 881, s. 1; 1977, 2nd Sess., c. 1187, ss. 1, 2.)

§ 105-316.2. Requirements for obtaining permit.

(a)   In order to obtain the permits herein provided, persons other than manufacturers and retailers of mobile homes shall be required to (i) pay all taxes due to be paid by the owner to the county or to any other taxing unit therein; or (ii) show proof to the tax collector that no taxes are due to be paid; or (iii) demonstrate to the tax collector that the removal of the mobile home will not jeopardize the collection of any taxes due or to become due to the county or to any taxing unit therein.

(b) In addition to complying with the provisions of subsection (a) above, owners of mobile homes required to obtain the permits herein provided shall also furnish the following information to the tax collector:

(1) The name and address of the owner,

(2) The address or location of the premises from which the mobile home is to be moved,

(3) The address or location of the place to which the mobile home is to be moved, and

(4) The name and address of the carrier who is to transport the mobile home. (1975, c. 881, s. 1.)

§ 105-316.3. Issuance of permits.

(a) Except as otherwise provided in G.S. 105-316.2 above, no permit required by G.S. 105-316.1 through 105-316.8 shall be issued by the tax collector unless and until all taxes due to be paid by the owner to the county or to any other taxing unit therein, including any penalties or interest thereon, have been paid. Any taxes which have not yet been computed but which will become due during the current calendar year shall be determined as in the case of prepayments.

(b) Upon compliance with the provisions of G.S. 105-316.1 through 105-316.8, the tax collector shall issue, without charge, a permit authorizing the removal of the mobile home. He shall also maintain a record of all permits issued. (1975, c. 881, s. 1.)

§ 105-316.4. Issuance of permits under repossession.

Notwithstanding the provisions of G.S. 105-316.2(a) and 105-316.3(a), above, any person who intends to take possession of a mobile home, whether by judicial or nonjudicial authority, as a holder of a lien on said mobile home shall apply for, and be issued, the permit herein provided without paying all taxes due to be paid by the owner of the mobile home being repossessed, upon notifying the tax collector of the location in North Carolina to which the mobile home is to be taken. At the time of notification the tax collector shall render to the holder of the lien a statement of taxes due against only the mobile home. Within seven days of the issuance of the permit the applicant shall pay to the tax collector the taxes due as set forth in the statement.

Notwithstanding the foregoing, any applicant who is a nonresident of North Carolina must pay the taxes due as set forth above at the time of notification to the tax collector and application for the permit.

Upon issuance of the permit and the payment of any taxes as prescribed herein, the mobile home shall no longer be subject to levy or attachment of any lien for any other taxes then owed by the owner thereof, whether or not previously determined. (1975, c. 881, s. 1; 1977, 2nd Sess., c. 1187, s. 3.)

§ 105-316.5. Form of permit.

The permit shall be in substantially the following form:

TAX PERMIT

County of _____   Permit Number
_____

State of North Carolina   Date of Issuance
_____

Permission is hereby granted to:
_____

(Name & address of owner)

_____
_____

(Name & address of carrier)

to remove the following described mobile home:

_____
_____

(Make, model, size, serial number, etc.)

From:

_____
_____

(Address)

To:

_____
_____

(Address)

This permit is issued in accordance with the provisions of G.S. 105-316.1 through G.S. 105-316.8 of the General Statutes of North Carolina.

(Signed) _____

Tax Collector

(or Deputy Tax Collector)

County of _____

(1975, c. 881, s. 1; 1977, 2nd Sess., c. 1187, s. 1.)

§ 105-316.6. Penalties for violations.

(a) Any person required by G.S. 105-316.1 through 105-316.8 to obtain a tax permit who fails to do so or who fails to properly display same shall be guilty of a Class 3 misdemeanor. This penalty shall be in addition to any penalties imposed for failure to list property for taxation and interest for failure to pay taxes provided by the general laws of this State.

(b) Any manufacturer or retailer of mobile homes who aids or abets any owner covered by G.S. 105-316.1 through 105-316.8 to defeat in any manner the purpose of G.S. 105-316.1 through 105-316.8 shall be guilty of a Class 3 misdemeanor.

(c) Any person who transports a mobile home from a location in this State for an owner other than a manufacturer or retailer of mobile homes without having properly displayed thereon the tax permit required by G.S. 105-316.1 through 105-316.8 shall be guilty of a Class 3 misdemeanor.

(d) Any law-enforcement officer of this State who apprehends any person violating the provisions of G.S. 105-316.1 through 105-316.8 shall detain such person and mobile home until satisfactory arrangements have been made to meet the requirements of G.S. 105-316.1 through 105-316.8. (1975, c. 881, s. 1; 1977, 2nd Sess., c. 1187, ss. 1, 4, 5; 1993, c. 539, s. 719; 1994, Ex. Sess., c. 24, s. 14(c).)

§ 105-316.7. Mobile home defined.

For the purpose of G.S. 105-316.1 through 105-316.8, "mobile home" means a structure that (i) is designed, constructed, and intended for use as a dwelling house, office, place of business, or similar place of habitation and (ii) is capable of being transported from place to place on wheels attached to its frame. It also means a manufactured home as described in G.S. 105-273(13). This definition does not include trailers and vehicles required to be registered annually pursuant to Part 3, Article 3 of Chapter 20 of the General Statutes. (1975, c. 881, s. 1; 1987, c. 805, s. 4.)

§ 105-316.8. Taxable situs not presumed.

Nothing in G.S. 105-316.1 through 105-316.8 shall be interpreted so as to subject to taxation any mobile home which does not have a taxable situs within this State under the general rules of law appropriate to such a determination. (1975, c. 881, s. 1.)

Article 19.

Administration of Real and Personal Property Appraisal.

§ 105-317. Appraisal of real property; adoption of schedules, standards, and rules.

(a) Whenever any real property is appraised it shall be the duty of the persons making appraisals:

(1) In determining the true value of land, to consider as to each tract, parcel, or lot separately listed at least its advantages and disadvantages as to location; zoning; quality of soil; waterpower; water privileges; dedication as a nature preserve; conservation or preservation agreements; mineral, quarry, or other valuable deposits; fertility; adaptability for agricultural, timber-producing, commercial, industrial, or other uses; past income; probable future income; and any other factors that may affect its value except growing crops of a seasonal or annual nature.

(2) In determining the true value of a building or other improvement, to consider at least its location; type of construction; age; replacement cost; cost; adaptability for residence, commercial, industrial, or other uses; past income; probable future income; and any other factors that may affect its value.

(3) To appraise partially completed buildings in accordance with the degree of completion on January 1.

(b) In preparation for each revaluation of real property required by G.S. 105-286, it shall be the duty of the assessor to see that:

(1) Uniform schedules of values, standards, and rules to be used in appraising real property at its true value and at its present-use value are prepared and are sufficiently detailed to enable those making appraisals to adhere to them in appraising real property.

(2) Repealed by Session Laws 1981, c. 678, s. 1.

(3) A separate property record be prepared for each tract, parcel, lot, or group of contiguous lots, which record shall show the information required for compliance with the provisions of G.S. 105-309 insofar as they deal with real property, as well as that required by this section. (The purpose of this subdivision is to require that individual property records be maintained in sufficient detail to enable property owners to ascertain the method, rules, and standards of value by which property is appraised.)

(4) The property characteristics considered in appraising each lot, parcel, tract, building, structure and improvement, in accordance with the schedules of values, standards, and rules, be accurately recorded on the appropriate property record.

(5) Upon the request of the owner, the board of equalization and review, or the board of county commissioners, any particular lot, parcel, tract, building, structure or improvement be actually visited and observed to verify the accuracy of property characteristics on record for that property.

(6) Each lot, parcel, tract, building, structure and improvement be separately appraised by a competent appraiser, either one appointed under the provisions of G.S. 105-296 or one employed under the provisions of G.S. 105-299.

(7) Notice is given in writing to the owner that he is entitled to have an actual visitation and observation of his property to verify the accuracy of property characteristics on record for that property.

(c) The values, standards, and rules required by subdivision (b)(1) shall be reviewed and approved by the board of county commissioners before January 1 of the year they are applied. The board of county commissioners may approve the schedules of values, standards, and rules to be used in appraising real property at its true value and at its present-use value either separately or simultaneously. Notice of the receipt and adoption by the board of county commissioners of either or both the true value and present-use value schedules, standards, and rules, and notice of a property owner's right to comment on and contest the schedules, standards, and rules shall be given as follows:

(1) The assessor shall submit the proposed schedules, standards, and rules to the board of county commissioners not less than 21 days before the meeting

at which they will be considered by the board. On the same day that they are submitted to the board for its consideration, the assessor shall file a copy of the proposed schedules, standards, and rules in his office where they shall remain available for public inspection.

(2)   Upon receipt of the proposed schedules, standards, and rules, the board of commissioners shall publish a statement in a newspaper having general circulation in the county stating:

a.   That the proposed schedules, standards, and rules to be used in appraising real property in the county have been submitted to the board of county commissioners and are available for public inspection in the assessor's office; and

b.   The time and place of a public hearing on the proposed schedules, standards, and rules that shall be held by the board of county commissioners at least seven days before adopting the final schedules, standards, and rules.

(3)   When the board of county commissioners approves the final schedules, standards, and rules, it shall issue an order adopting them. Notice of this order shall be published once a week for four successive weeks in a newspaper having general circulation in the county, with the last publication being not less than seven days before the last day for challenging the validity of the schedules, standards, and rules by appeal to the Property Tax Commission. The notice shall state:

a.   That the schedules, standards, and rules to be used in the next scheduled reappraisal of real property in the county have been adopted and are open to examination in the office of the assessor; and

b.   That a property owner who asserts that the schedules, standards, and rules are invalid may except to the order and appeal therefrom to the Property Tax Commission within 30 days of the date when the notice of the order adopting the schedules, standards, and rules was first published.

(d)   Before the board of county commissioners adopts the schedules of values, standards, and rules, the assessor may collect data needed to apply the schedules, standards, and rules to each parcel in the county. (1939, c. 310, s. 501; 1959, c. 704, s. 4; 1967, c. 944; 1971, c. 806, s. 1; 1973, c. 476, s. 193; c. 695, s. 5; 1981, c. 224; c. 678, s. 1; 1985, c. 216, s. 2; c. 628, s. 4; 1987, c. 45, s. 1; c. 295, s. 1; 1997-226, s. 5.)

§ 105-317.1. Appraisal of personal property; elements to be considered.

(a)   Whenever any personal property is appraised it shall be the duty of the persons making appraisals to consider the following as to each item (or lot of similar items):

(1)   The replacement cost of the property;

(2)   The sale price of similar property;

(3)   The age of the property;

(4)   The physical condition of the property;

(5)   The productivity of the property;

(6)   The remaining life of the property;

(7)   The effect of obsolescence on the property;

(8)   The economic utility of the property, that is, its usability and adaptability for industrial, commercial, or other purposes; and

(9)   Any other factor that may affect the value of the property.

(b)   In determining the true value of taxable tangible personal property held and used in connection with the mercantile, manufacturing, producing, processing, or other business enterprise of any taxpayer, the persons making the appraisal shall consider any information as reflected by the taxpayer's records and as reported by the taxpayer to the North Carolina Department of Revenue and to the Internal Revenue Service for income tax purposes, taking into account the accuracy of the taxpayer's records, the taxpayer's method of accounting, and the level of trade at which the taxpayer does business.

(c)   A taxpayer who owns personal property taxable in the county may appeal the value, situs, or taxability of the property within 30 days after the date of the initial notice of value. If the assessor does not give separate written notice of the value to the taxpayer at the taxpayer's last known address, then the tax bill serves as notice of the value of the personal property. The notice must contain a statement that the taxpayer may appeal the value, situs, or taxability of the property within 30 days after the date of the notice. Upon receipt of a timely appeal, the assessor must arrange a conference with the taxpayer to afford the taxpayer the opportunity to present any evidence or argument regarding the value, situs, or taxability of the property. Within 30 days after the conference, the assessor must give written notice to the taxpayer of the assessor's final decision. Written notice of the decision is not required if the taxpayer signs an agreement accepting the value, situs, or taxability of the property. If an agreement is not reached, the taxpayer has 30 days from the date of the notice of the assessor's final decision to request review of that decision by the board of equalization and review or, if that board is not in session, by the board of county commissioners. Unless the request for review is given at the conference, it must be made in writing to the assessor. Upon receipt of a timely request for review, the provisions of G.S. 105-322 or G.S. 105-325, as appropriate, must be followed. (1971, c. 806, s. 1; 1987, c. 813, s. 15; 2002-156, s. 2.)

§ 105-317.2. Report on transfers of real property.

To facilitate the accurate appraisal of real property for taxation, the information listed in this section must be included in each deed conveying property. The following information is required:

(1)   The name of each grantor and grantee and the mailing address of each grantor and grantee.

(2)   A statement whether the property includes the primary residence of a grantor.

Failure to comply with this section does not affect the validity of a duly recorded deed. This section does not apply to deeds of trust, deeds of release, or similar instruments. (2009-454, s. 1.)

Article 20.

Approval, Preparation, Disposition of Records.

§ 105-318. Forms for listing, appraising, and assessing property.

The Department of Revenue may design and prescribe the books and forms to be used throughout the State in the listing, appraising, and assessing of property for taxation. If the board exercises the authority granted by the preceding sentence, it is authorized to make arrangements for the purchase and distribution of approved books and forms through the Division of Purchase and Contract, the cost thereof to be billed to the counties. If the Department does not exercise the authority granted by the first sentence of this section, each county and municipality shall submit the books and forms it proposes to adopt for these purposes to the Department for approval before they are employed. (1939, c. 310, s. 907; 1971, c. 806, s. 1; 1973, c. 476, s. 193.)

§ 105-319. Tax records; preparation of scroll and tax book.

(a)   For each year there shall be prepared for each county and tax-levying municipality a scroll (showing property valuations) and a tax book (showing the amount of taxes due) or a combined record (showing both property valuation and taxes due). The governing body of the county or municipality shall have authority to determine whether the tax records shall be prepared in combined form or in a separate scroll and tax book. When used in this Subchapter, the term "tax records" shall mean the scroll, tax book, and combined record. No tax records shall be adopted by any county or municipality until they have been approved by the Department of Revenue.

(b)   County tax records shall, unless otherwise authorized by the board of county commissioners, be prepared separately for each township. The tax records of both counties and municipalities shall, unless otherwise authorized by the unit governing body, be divided into two parts:

(1)   Individual taxpayers (including corporate fiduciaries when, in their fiduciary capacity, they list the property of individuals).

(2)   Corporations, partnerships, other business firms, unincorporated associations, and all other taxpayers other than individual persons.

(c)   The tax records shall show at least the following information:

(1)   In alphabetical order, the name of each taxpayer whose property is listed and assessed for taxation.

(2)   The assessment of each taxpayer's real property listed for unit-wide taxation (divided into as many categories as the Department of Revenue may prescribe).

(3)   The assessment of each taxpayer's personal property listed for unit-wide taxation (divided into as many categories as the Department of Revenue may prescribe).

(4)   The total assessed value of each taxpayer's real and personal property listed for unit-wide purposes.

(5)   The amount of ad valorem tax due by each taxpayer for unit-wide purposes.

(6)   The amount of dog license tax due by each taxpayer.

(7)   The total assessed value of each taxpayer's real and personal property listed for taxation in any special district or subdivision of the unit.

(8)   The amount of ad valorem tax due by each taxpayer to any special district or subdivision of the unit.

(9)   The amount of penalties, if any, imposed under the provisions of G.S. 105-312.

(10)   The total amount of all taxes and penalties due by each taxpayer to the unit and to special districts and subdivisions of the unit.

(d)   Listings and assessments and any changes therein made during the period between the close of the regular listing period and the first meeting of the board of equalization and review, as well as those made during the regular listing period, shall be entered on the county tax records, and the county tax records shall be submitted to the board of equalization and review at its first meeting. Additions and changes made by the board of equalization and review shall be entered on the county tax records in accordance with the provisions of G.S. 105-326. Municipal corporations shall be governed by the provisions of G.S. 105-326 through 105-328 with regard to matters dealt with in this subsection (d). (1939, c. 310, s. 1101; 1963, c. 784, s. 1; 1969, c. 1279; 1971, c. 806, s. 1; 1973, c. 476, s. 193.)

§ 105-320. Tax receipts; preparation.

(a) No taxing unit shall adopt a tax receipt form until it has been approved by the Department of Revenue, and no tax receipt form shall be approved unless it shows at least the following information:

(1) The name and mailing address of the taxpayer charged with taxes.

(2) The assessment of the taxpayer's real property listed for unit-wide taxation.

(3) The assessment of the taxpayer's personal property listed for unit-wide taxation.

(4) The total assessed value of the taxpayer's real and personal property listed for unit-wide taxation.

(5) The total assessed value of the taxpayer's real and personal property listed for taxation in any special district or subdivision of the unit.

(6) The rate of tax levied for each unit-wide purpose, the total rate levied for all unit-wide purposes, and the rate levied by or for any special district or subdivision of the unit in which the taxpayer's property is subject to taxation. (In lieu of showing this information on the tax receipt, it may be furnished on a separate sheet of paper, properly identified, at the time the official receipt is delivered upon payment).

(7) The amount of ad valorem tax due by the taxpayer for unit-wide purposes.

(8) The amount of ad valorem tax due by the taxpayer to any special district or subdivision of the unit.

(9) The amount of dog license tax due by the taxpayer.

(10) The amount of penalties, if any, imposed under the provisions of G.S. 105-312.

(11) The total amount of all taxes and penalties due by the taxpayer to the unit and to special districts and subdivisions of the unit.

(12)   The amount of discount allowed for prepayment of taxes under the provisions of G.S. 105-360.

(13)   The amount of interest charged for late payment of taxes under the provisions of G.S. 105-360.

(14)   Repealed by Session Laws 1987, c. 813, s. 16.

(15)   Repealed by 1987 (Regular Session, 1988), c. 1041, s. 1.2.

(16)   The total assessed value of farm machinery, attachments, and repair parts of individual owners and Subchapter S corporations engaged in farming subject to the income tax credit in G.S. 105-151.21 and the amount of ad valorem taxes due by an individual farmer or a Subchapter S corporation engaged in farming on farm machinery, attachments, and repair parts subject to that credit.

(b)   Instead of being shown on the tax receipt, the information required in subdivision (16) of subsection (a) may be shown on a separate sheet furnished to the affected taxpayers.

(c)   The governing body of the county or municipality shall designate the person or persons who shall compute and prepare the tax receipt for all taxes charged upon the tax records. (1939, c. 310, s. 1102; 1961, c. 380; 1971, c. 806, s. 1; 1973, c. 476, s. 193; 1985, c. 656, s. 23; 1985 (Reg. Sess., 1986), c. 947, s. 6; 1987, c. 813, ss. 16, 17; 1987 (Reg. Sess., 1988), c. 1041, ss. 1.2, 1.3; 1991, c. 45, s. 14(c).)

§ 105-321. Disposition of tax records and receipts; order of collection.

(a)   County tax records shall be filed in the office of the assessor unless the board of county commissioners shall require them to be filed in some other public office of the county. City and town tax records shall be filed in some public office of the municipality designated by the governing body of the city or town. In the discretion of the governing body, a duplicate copy of the tax records may be delivered to the tax collector at the time he is charged with the collection of taxes.

(b) Before delivering the tax receipts to the tax collector in any year, the board of county commissioners or municipal governing body shall adopt and enter in its minutes an order directing the tax collector to collect the taxes charged in the tax records and receipts. A copy of this order shall be delivered to the tax collector at the time the tax receipts are delivered to him, but the failure to do so shall not affect the tax collector's rights and duties to employ the means of collecting taxes provided by this Subchapter. The order of collection shall have the force and effect of a judgment and execution against the taxpayers' real and personal property and shall be drawn in substantially the following form:

State of North Carolina

County (or City or Town) of
_____

To the Tax Collector of the County (or City or Town) of
_____

_____:

You are hereby authorized, empowered, and commanded to collect the taxes set forth in the tax records filed in the office of _____ and in the tax receipts herewith delivered to you, in the amounts and from the taxpayers likewise therein set forth. Such taxes are hereby declared to be a first lien upon all real property of the respective taxpayers in the County (or City or Town) of _____ , and this order shall be a full and sufficient authority to direct, require, and enable you to levy on and sell any real or personal property of such taxpayers, for and on account thereof, in accordance with law.

Witness my hand and official seal, this ____ day of _____ ,
_____

_____(Seal)

              Chairman, Board of
Commissioners of

              _____ County

                                                                        (Mayor, City (or Town) of
_____)

Attest:

_____

Clerk of Board of Commissioners of _____ County

(Clerk of the City (or Town) of _____)

(c)   The original tax receipts, together with any duplicate copies that may have been prepared, shall be delivered to the tax collector by the governing body on or before the first day of September each year if the tax collector has made settlement as required by G.S. 105-352. The tax collector shall give his receipt for the tax receipts and duplicates delivered to him for collection.

(d)   Repealed by Session Laws 2006-30, s. 5, effective June 29, 2006.

(e)   The governing body of a taxing unit may contract with a bank or other financial institution for receipt of payment of taxes payable at par and of delinquent taxes and interest for the current tax year. A financial institution may not issue a receipt for any tax payments received by it, however. Discount for early payment of taxes shall be allowed by a financial institution that contracts with a taxing unit pursuant to this subsection to the same extent as allowed by the tax collector. A financial institution that contracts with a taxing unit for receipt of payment of taxes shall furnish a bond to the taxing unit conditioned upon faithful performance of the contract in a form and amount satisfactory to the governing body of the taxing unit. A governing body of a taxing unit that contracts with a financial institution pursuant to this subsection shall publish a timely notice of the institution at which taxpayers may pay their taxes in a newspaper having circulation within the taxing unit. No notice is required, however, if the financial institution receives payments only through the mail.

(f)   Minimal Taxes. - Notwithstanding the provisions of G.S. 105-380, the governing body of a taxing unit that collects its own taxes may, by resolution, direct its assessor and tax collector not to collect minimal taxes charged on the tax records and receipts. Minimal taxes are the combined taxes and fees of the taxing unit and any other units for which it collects taxes, due on a tax receipt prepared pursuant to G.S. 105-320 in a total original principal amount that does not exceed an amount, up to five dollars ($5.00), set by the governing body. The amount set by the governing body should be the estimated cost to the taxing unit of billing the taxpayer for the amounts due on a tax receipt or tax notice. Upon adoption of a resolution pursuant to this subsection, the tax collector shall not bill the taxpayer for, or otherwise collect, minimal taxes but shall keep a record of all minimal taxes by receipt number and amount and shall make a report of the amount of these taxes to the governing body at the time of the settlement. These minimal taxes shall not be a lien on the taxpayer's real property and shall not be collectible under Article 26 of this Subchapter. A resolution adopted pursuant to this subsection must be adopted on or before June 15 preceding the first taxable year to which it applies and remains in effect until amended or repealed by resolution of the taxing unit. A resolution adopted pursuant to this subsection shall not apply to taxes on registered motor vehicles. (1939, c. 310, s. 1103; 1971, c. 806, s. 1; 1973, c. 476, s. 193; c. 615; 1987, c. 45, s. 1; 1989, c. 578, s. 1; 1991, c. 584, s. 1; 1995, c. 24, s. 1; c. 329, ss. 1, 2; 1999-456, s. 59; 2006-30, s. 5; 2012-79, s. 3.1.)

Article 21.

Review and Appeals of Listings and Valuations.

§ 105-322. County board of equalization and review.

(a)   Personnel. - Except as otherwise provided herein, the board of equalization and review of each county shall be composed of the members of the board of county commissioners.

Upon the adoption of a resolution so providing, the board of commissioners is authorized to appoint a special board of equalization and review to carry out the duties imposed under this section. The resolution shall provide for the membership, qualifications, terms of office and the filling of vacancies on the board. The board of commissioners shall also designate the chairman of the special board. The resolution may also authorize a taxpayer to appeal a decision of the special board with respect to the listing or appraisal of his property or the property of others to the board of county commissioners. The resolution shall be adopted not later than the first Monday in March of the year for which it is to be effective and shall continue in effect until revised or rescinded. It shall be entered in the minutes of the meeting of the board of commissioners and a copy thereof shall be forwarded to the Department of Revenue within 15 days after its adoption.

Nothing in this subsection (a) shall be construed as repealing any law creating a special board of equalization and review or creating any board charged with the duties of a board of equalization and review in any county.

(b) Compensation. - The board of county commissioners shall fix the compensation and allowances to be paid members of the board of equalization and review for their services and expenses.

(c) Oath. - Each member of the board of equalization and review shall take the oath required by Article VI, § 7 of the North Carolina Constitution with the following phrase added to it: "that I will not allow my actions as a member of the board of equalization and review to be influenced by personal or political friendships or obligations,". The oath must be filed with the clerk of the board of county commissioners.

(d) Clerk and Minutes. - The assessor shall serve as clerk to the board of equalization and review, shall be present at all meetings, shall maintain accurate minutes of the actions of the board, and shall give to the board such information as he may have or can obtain with respect to the listing and valuation of taxable property in the county.

(e) Time of Meeting. - Each year the board of equalization and review shall hold its first meeting not earlier than the first Monday in April and not later than the first Monday in May. In years in which a county does not conduct a real property revaluation, the board shall complete its duties on or before the third Monday following its first meeting unless, in its opinion, a longer period of time is necessary or expedient to a proper execution of its responsibilities. Except as provided in subdivision (g)(5) of this section, the board may not sit later than July 1 except to hear and determine requests made under the provisions of subdivision (g)(2), below, when such requests are made within the time prescribed by law. In the year in which a county conducts a real property revaluation, the board shall complete its duties on or before December 1, except that it may sit after that date to hear and determine requests made under the provisions of subdivision (g)(2), below, when such requests are made within the time prescribed by law. From the time of its first meeting until its adjournment, the board shall meet at such times as it deems reasonably necessary to perform its statutory duties and to receive requests and hear the appeals of taxpayers under the provisions of subdivision (g)(2), below.

(f)   Notice of Meetings and Adjournment. - A notice of the date, hours, place, and purpose of the first meeting of the board of equalization and review shall be published at least three times in some newspaper having general circulation in the county, the first publication to be at least 10 days prior to the first meeting. The notice shall also state the dates and hours on which the board will meet following its first meeting and the date on which it expects to adjourn; it shall also carry a statement that in the event of earlier or later adjournment, notice to that effect will be published in the same newspaper. Should a notice be required on account of earlier adjournment, it shall be published at least once in the newspaper in which the first notice was published, such publication to be at least five days prior to the date fixed for adjournment. Should a notice be required on account of later adjournment, it shall be published at least once in the newspaper in which the first notice was published, such publication to be prior to the date first announced for adjournment.

(g)   Powers and Duties. - The board of equalization and review has the following powers and duties:

(1)   Duty to Review Tax Lists. - The board shall examine and review the tax lists of the county for the current year to the end that all taxable property shall be listed on the abstracts and tax records of the county and appraised according to the standard required by G.S. 105-283, and the board shall correct the abstracts and tax records to conform to the provisions of this Subchapter. In carrying out its responsibilities under this subdivision (g)(1), the board, on its own motion or on sufficient cause shown by any person, shall:

a.   List, appraise, and assess any taxable real or personal property that has been omitted from the tax lists.

b.   Correct all errors in the names of persons and in the description of properties subject to taxation.

c.   Increase or reduce the appraised value of any property that, in the board's opinion, has been listed and appraised at a figure that is below or above the appraisal required by G.S. 105-283; however, the board shall not change the appraised value of any real property from that at which it was appraised for the preceding year except in accordance with the terms of G.S. 105-286 and 105-287.

d. Cause to be done whatever else is necessary to make the lists and tax records comply with the provisions of this Subchapter.

e. Embody actions taken under the provisions of subdivisions (g)(1)a through (g)(1)d, above, in appropriate orders and have the orders entered in the minutes of the board.

f. Give written notice to the taxpayer at the taxpayer's last known address in the event the board, by appropriate order, increases the appraisal of any property or lists for taxation any property omitted from the tax lists under the provisions of this subdivision (g)(1).

(2) Duty to Hear Taxpayer Appeals. - On request, the board of equalization and review shall hear any taxpayer who owns or controls property taxable in the county with respect to the listing or appraisal of the taxpayer's property or the property of others.

a. A request for a hearing under this subdivision (g)(2) shall be made in writing to or by personal appearance before the board prior to its adjournment. However, if the taxpayer requests review of a decision made by the board under the provisions of subdivision (g)(1), above, notice of which was mailed fewer than 15 days prior to the board's adjournment, the request for a hearing thereon may be made within 15 days after the notice of the board's decision was mailed.

b. Taxpayers may file separate or joint requests for hearings under the provisions of this subdivision (g)(2) at their election.

c. At a hearing under provisions of this subdivision (g)(2), the board, in addition to the powers it may exercise under the provisions of subdivision (g)(3), below, shall hear any evidence offered by the appellant, the assessor, and other county officials that is pertinent to the decision of the appeal. Upon the request of an appellant, the board shall subpoena witnesses or documents if there is a reasonable basis for believing that the witnesses have or the documents contain information pertinent to the decision of the appeal.

d. On the basis of its decision after any hearing conducted under this subdivision (g)(2), the board shall adopt and have entered in its minutes an order reducing, increasing, or confirming the appraisal appealed or listing or removing from the tax lists the property whose omission or listing has been appealed. The board shall notify the appellant by mail as to the action taken on the taxpayer's appeal not later than 30 days after the board's adjournment.

(3) Powers in Carrying Out Duties. - In the performance of its duties under subdivisions (g)(1) and (g)(2), above, the board of equalization and review may exercise the following powers:

a. It may appoint committees composed of its own members or other persons to assist it in making investigations necessary to its work. It may also employ expert appraisers in its discretion. The expense of the employment of committees or appraisers shall be borne by the county. The board may, in its discretion, require the taxpayer to reimburse the county for the cost of any appraisal by experts demanded by the taxpayer if the appraisal does not result in material reduction of the valuation of the property appraised and if the appraisal is not subsequently reduced materially by the board or by the Department of Revenue.

b. The board, in its discretion, may examine any witnesses and documents. It may place any witnesses under oath administered by any member of the board. It may subpoena witnesses or documents on its own motion, and it must do so when a request is made under the provisions of subdivision (g)(2)c, above.

A subpoena issued by the board shall be signed by the chair of the board, directed to the witness or to the person having custody of the document, and served by an officer authorized to serve subpoenas. Any person who willfully fails to appear or to produce documents in response to a subpoena or to testify when appearing in response to a subpoena shall be guilty of a Class 1 misdemeanor.

(4) Power to Submit Reports. - Upon the completion of its other duties, the board may submit to the Department of Revenue a report outlining the quality of the reappraisal, any problems it encountered in the reappraisal process, the number of appeals submitted to the board and to the Property Tax Commission, the success rate of the appeals submitted, and the name of the firm that conducted the reappraisal. A copy of the report should be sent by the board to the firm that conducted the reappraisal.

(5) Duty to Change Abstracts and Records After Adjournment. - Following adjournment upon completion of its duties under subdivisions (g)(1) and (g)(2) of this subsection, the board may continue to meet to carry out the following duties:

a. To hear and decide all appeals relating to discovered property under G.S. 105-312(d) and (k).

b. To hear and decide all appeals relating to the appraisal, situs, and taxability of classified motor vehicles under G.S. 105-330.2(b).

c. To hear and decide all appeals relating to audits conducted under G.S. 105-296(j) and relating to audits conducted under G.S. 105-296(j) and (l) of property classified at present-use value and property exempted or excluded from taxation.

d. To hear and decide all appeals relating to personal property under G.S. 105-317.1(c). (1939, c. 310, s. 1105; 1965, c. 191; 1967, c. 1196, s. 6; 1971, c. 806, s. 1; 1973, c. 476, s. 193; 1977, c. 863; 1987, c. 45, s. 1; 1989, c. 79, s. 3; c. 176, s. 1; c. 196; 1991, c. 110, s. 5; 1991 (Reg. Sess., 1992), c. 1007, s. 22; 1993, c. 539, s. 720; 1994, Ex. Sess., c. 24, s. 14(c); 2001-139, ss. 6, 7; 2002-156, s. 3.)

§ 105-323. Giving effect to decisions of the board of equalization and review.

All changes in listings, names, descriptions, appraisals, and assessments made by the board of equalization and review shall be reflected upon the abstracts and tax records by insertion of rebates given, additional charges made, or any other insertion; by correction; or by any other charge. The tax records shall then be totalled, and at least a majority of the members of the board of equalization and review shall sign the following statement to be inserted at the end of the tax records:

State of North Carolina

County of
_____
_____

We, the undersigned members of the Board of Equalization and Review of _____ County, hereby certify that these tax records constitute the fixed and permanent tax list and assessment roll and record of taxes due for the year _____, subject to only such changes as may be allowed by law.

_____
___

_____
___

Members of the Board of Equalization

and Review of _____ County

The omission of this endorsement shall not affect the validity of the tax records or of any taxes levied on the basis of the assessments appearing in them. (1939, c. 310, s. 1106; 1971, c. 806, s. 1; 1999-456, s. 59.)

§ 105-324. Repealed by Session Laws 1987, c. 295, s. 4.

§ 105-325. Powers of board of county commissioners to change abstracts and tax records after board of equalization and review has adjourned.

(a) After the board of equalization and review has finished its work and the changes it effected or ordered have been entered on the abstracts and tax records as required by G.S. 105-323, the board of county commissioners shall not authorize any changes to be made on the abstracts and tax records except as follows:

(1) To give effect to decisions of the Property Tax Commission on appeals taken under G.S. 105-290.

(2) To add to the tax records any valuation certified by the Department of Revenue for property appraised in the first instance by the Department or to give effect to corrections made in such appraisals by the Department.

(3) Subject to the provisions of subdivisions (a)(3)a and (a)(3)b, below, to correct the name of any taxpayer appearing on the abstract or tax records erroneously; to substitute the name of the person who should have listed property for the name appearing on the abstract or tax records as having listed the property; and to correct an erroneous description of any property appearing on the abstract or tax records.

a. Any correction or substitution made under the provisions of this subdivision (a)(3) shall have the same force and effect as if the name of the taxpayer or description of the property had been correctly listed in the first instance, but the provisions of this subdivision (a)(3)a shall not be construed as a limitation on the taxation and penalization of discovered property required by G.S. 105-312.

b. If a correction or substitution under this subdivision (a)(3) will adversely affect the interests of any taxpayer, he shall be given written notice thereof and an opportunity to be heard before the change is entered on the abstract or tax records.

(4) To correct appraisals, assessments, and amounts of taxes appearing erroneously on the abstracts or tax records as the result of clerical or mathematical errors. (If the clerical or mathematical error was made by the taxpayer, his agent, or an officer of the taxpayer and if the correction demonstrates that the property was listed at a substantial understatement of value, quantity, or other measurement, the provisions of G.S. 105-312 shall apply.)

(5) To add to the tax records and abstracts or to correct the tax records and abstracts to include property discovered under the provisions of G.S. 105-312 or property exempted or excluded from taxation pursuant to G.S. 105-282.1(a)(4).

(6) Subject to the provisions of subdivisions (a)(6)a, (a)(6)b, (a)(6)c, and (a)(6)d, below, to appraise or reappraise property when the assessor reports to the board that, since adjournment of the board of equalization and review, facts have come to his attention that render it advisable to raise or lower the appraisal of some particular property of a given taxpayer in the then current calendar year.

a. The power granted by this subdivision (a)(6) shall not authorize appraisal or reappraisal because of events or circumstances that have taken place or arisen since the day as of which property is to be listed.

b. No appraisal or reappraisal shall be made under the authority of this subdivision (a)(6) unless it could have been made by the board of equalization and review had the same facts been brought to the attention of that board.

c. If a reappraisal made under the provisions of this subdivision (a)(6) demonstrates that the property was listed at a substantial understatement of value, quantity, or other measurement, the provisions of G.S. 105-312 shall apply.

d. If an appraisal or reappraisal made under the provisions of this subdivision (a)(6) will adversely affect the interests of any taxpayer, he shall be given written notice thereof and an opportunity to be heard before the appraisal or reappraisal shall become final.

(7) To give effect to decisions of the board of county commissioners on appeals taken under G.S. 105-322(a).

(b) The board of county commissioners may give the assessor general authority to make any changes authorized by subsection (a), above, except those permitted under subdivision (a)(6), above.

(c) Orders of the board of county commissioners and actions of the assessor upon delegation of authority to him by the board that are made under the provisions of this section may be appealed to the Property Tax Commission under the provisions of G.S. 105-290. (1939, c. 310, s. 1108; 1971, c. 806, s. 1; 1973, c. 476, s. 193; 1987, c. 45, s. 1, c. 295, s, 8, c. 680, s. 6; 1989, c. 176, s. 2.)

§ 105-325.1. Special committee for motor vehicle appeals.

The board of county commissioners may appoint a special committee of its members or other persons to hear and decide appeals arising under G.S. 105-330.2(b). The county shall bear the expense of employing the committee. (1991 (Reg. Sess., 1992), c. 961, s. 9.)

Article 22.

Listing, Appraising, and Assessing by Cities and Towns.

§ 105-326. Listing property for city and town taxation; duty of owner; authority of governing body to obtain lists from county.

(a)   All property subject to ad valorem taxation in any city or town shall be listed annually during the period prescribed by G.S. 105-307 in the city or town in which it is taxable in the name of the person required by G.S. 105-302 and 105-306 on an abstract prepared according to G.S. 105-309 and affirmed as required by G.S. 105-310. In lieu of requiring property owners to list their property with the city or town, the governing body of any city or town may make provision for obtaining from the abstracts and tax records of the county in which the municipality is situated lists of the property subject to taxation by the city or town.

(b)   Regardless of whether a city or town adopts the alternative provided in the second sentence of subsection (a), above, the provisions of G.S. 105-311 and 105-312 shall apply to the listing of property for municipal taxation, as shall the penalties imposed by G.S. 105-308 and 105-312 for failure to list. In the preparation of abstracts, tax records, and tax receipts the city or town shall be governed by the provisions of G.S. 105-318, 105-319, 105-320, and 105-321. The powers and duties assigned to the assessor by the statutes cited as being applicable to municipalities shall be imposed upon and exercised by some official designated by the governing body of the city or town, and the powers and duties assigned therein to the board of county commissioners shall be imposed upon and exercised by the governing body of the city or town. (1939, c. 310, s. 1201; 1971, c. 806, s. 1; 1987, c. 45, s. 1.)

§ 105-327. Appraisal and assessment of property subject to city and town taxation.

For the property it is entitled to tax, a city or town situated in a single county shall accept and adopt the appraisals and assessments fixed by the authorities of that county as modified by the Department of Revenue under the provisions of this Subchapter. However, the requirement of this section shall not be construed to modify the appraisal and assessment authority given cities and towns with respect to discovered property by G.S. 105-312. (1939, c. 310, s. 1201; 1971, c. 806, s. 1; 1973, c. 476, s. 193.)

§ 105-328. Listing, appraisal, and assessment of property subject to taxation by cities and towns situated in more than one county.

(a) For purposes of municipal taxation, all property subject to taxation by a city or town situated in two or more counties may, by resolution of the governing body of the municipality, be listed, appraised, and assessed as provided in G.S. 105-326 and 105-327 if, in such a case, in the opinion of the governing body, the same appraisal and assessment standards will thereby apply uniformly throughout the municipality. However, if, in such a case, the governing body shall determine that adoption of the appraisals and assessments fixed by the counties will not result in uniform appraisals and assessments throughout the municipality, the governing body may, by horizontal adjustments, equalize the appraisal and assessment values fixed by the counties in order to obtain the required uniformity. Taxes levied by the city or town shall be levied uniformly on the assessments so determined.

(b) Should the governing body of a city or town situated in two or more counties not adopt the procedure provided in subsection (a), above, all property subject to taxation by the municipality shall be listed, appraised, and assessed as provided in subdivisions (b)(1) through (b)(6), below.

(1) The governing body of the city or town shall appoint a municipal assessor on or before the first Monday in July in each odd-numbered year. The governing body may remove the municipal assessor from office during his term for good cause after giving him notice in writing and an opportunity to appear and be heard at a public session of the appointing body. Whenever a vacancy occurs in the office, the governing body shall appoint a qualified person to serve as municipal assessor for the period of the unexpired term. A person appointed as a municipal assessor shall meet the qualifications and requirements set for a county assessor under G.S. 105-294. Pursuant to Article VI, Sec. 9, of North Carolina Constitution, the office of municipal assessor is hereby declared to be an office that may be held concurrently with any other appointive office.

(2) With the approval of the governing body, a municipal assessor may employ listers, appraisers, and clerical assistants necessary to carry out the listing, appraisal, assessing, and billing functions required by law.

(3) A municipal assessor and the persons employed by him have the same powers and duties as their county equivalents with respect to property subject to taxation by a city or town.

(4) The governing body shall, with respect to property subject to city or town taxation, be vested with the powers and duties vested by this Subchapter in boards of county commissioners and boards of equalization and review. Appeals may be taken from the municipal board of equalization and review or governing body to the Property Tax Commission in the manner provided in this Subchapter for appeals from county boards of equalization and review and boards of county commissioners.

(5) All expenses incident to the listing, appraisal, and assessment of property for the purpose of city or town taxation shall be borne by the municipality for whose benefit the work is undertaken.

(6) The intent of this subsection (b) is to provide cities and towns that are situated in two or more counties with machinery for listing, appraising, and assessing property for municipal taxation equivalent to that established by this Subchapter for counties. The powers to be exercised by, the duties imposed on, and the possible penalties against municipal governing bodies, boards of equalization and review, assessors, and persons employed by an assessor shall be the same as those provided in this Subchapter by, on, or against county boards of commissioners, boards of equalization and review, assessors, and persons employed by an assessor. (1939, c. 310, s. 1202; 1971, c. 806, s. 1; 1973, c. 476, s. 193; c. 695, s. 13; 1987, c. 43, s. 8; c. 45, s .1; c. 46, s. 2.)

§ 105-329: Repealed by Session Laws 1991 (Regular Session, 1992), c. 961, s. 2.

Article 22A.

Motor Vehicles.

§ 105-330. Definitions.

The following definitions apply in this Article:

(1) Classified motor vehicle. - A motor vehicle classified under this Article.

(1a) Collecting authority. - The Division of Motor Vehicles or an agent contracting with the Division of Motor Vehicles.

(2) Motor vehicle. - Defined in G.S. 20-4.01(23).

(2a) Municipal corporation. - Defined in G.S. 105-273(11).

(3) Public service company. - Defined in G.S. 105-333(14).

(4) Registered classified motor vehicle. - Any of the following:

a. A classified motor vehicle that has a registration plate issued under Article 3 of Chapter 20 of the General Statutes and whose registration is current.

b. A classified motor vehicle transferred to an owner who has applied for a registration plate for the motor vehicle.

(5) Registration fees. - Fees set out in G.S. 20-87 and G.S. 20-88.

(6) Unregistered classified motor vehicle. - A classified motor vehicle that is not a registered classified motor vehicle. (1991, c. 624, s. 1; 2005-294, s. 1; 2006-259, s. 31.5; 2007-527, s. 22(b); 2008-134, s. 65; 2009-445, s. 24(a); 2010-95, s. 22(c); 2011-330, s. 42(a); 2012-79, s. 3.6; 2013-414, s. 70(b), (d).)

§ 105-330.1. Classification of motor vehicles.

(a) Classification. - All motor vehicles other than the motor vehicles listed in subsection (b) of this section are designated a special class of property under Article V, Sec. 2(2) of the North Carolina Constitution and are considered classified motor vehicles. Classified motor vehicles must be listed and assessed as provided in this Article and taxes on classified motor vehicles must be collected as provided in this Article.

(b) Exceptions. - The following motor vehicles are not classified under subsection (a) of this section:

(1) Motor vehicles exempt from registration pursuant to G.S. 20-51.

(2) Manufactured homes, mobile classrooms, and mobile offices.

(3) Semitrailers or trailers registered on a multiyear basis.

(4) Motor vehicles owned or leased by a public service company and appraised under G.S. 105-335.

(5) Repealed by Session Laws 2000, c. 140, s. 75(a), effective July 1, 2000.

(6) Motor vehicles registered under the International Registration Plan.

(7) Motor vehicles issued permanent registration plates under G.S. 20-84.

(8) Self-propelled property-carrying vehicles issued three-month registration plates at the farmer rate under G.S. 20-88.

(9) Motor vehicles owned by participants in the Address Confidentiality Program authorized under Chapter 15C of the General Statutes. (1991, c. 624, s. 1; 1991 (Reg. Sess., 1992), c. 961, s. 3; 1993, c. 485, s. 18; c. 543, s. 4; 1993 (Reg. Sess., 1994), c. 745, s. 1; 2000-140, s. 75(a); 2007-471, s. 6; 2009-445, ss. 24(a), 25(a); 2010-95, s. 22(c), (d); 2013-414, ss. 70(b), (c), 72.)

§ 105-330.2. Appraisal, ownership, and situs.

(a) Determination Date for Registered Vehicle. - The ownership, situs, and taxability of a registered classified motor vehicle is determined annually as of the date on which the vehicle's current registration is renewed, regardless of whether the registration is renewed after it has expired, or on the date an application for a new registration is submitted. The situs of a registered classified motor vehicle may not be changed until the next registration date. The value of a registered classified motor vehicle is determined as follows:

(1) For a registration expiring or an application for a new registration during the period January 1 through August 31, the value is determined as of January 1 of the current year.

(2) For a registration expiring or an application for a new registration during the period September 1 through December 31, the value is determined as of January 1 of the following year.

(3) For a new motor vehicle whose value cannot be determined as of January 1 of the year specified in subdivision (1) or (2) of this subsection, the value is determined as of the date that model of motor vehicle is first offered for sale at retail in this State.

(4) For a motor vehicle whose value cannot be determined as of the date set under any other subdivision in this subsection, the value is determined using the most currently available January 1 retail value of the vehicle.

(a1) Determination Date for Unregistered Vehicle. - The ownership, situs, and taxability of an unregistered classified motor vehicle is determined as of January 1 of the year in which the registration of the motor vehicle expires and is not renewed or the motor vehicle is acquired and the owner does not submit an application for registration. The value of an unregistered classified motor vehicle is determined as of January 1 of the year the vehicle is required to be listed.

(b) Value. - An assessor must appraise a classified motor vehicle at its true value in money as prescribed by G.S. 105-283. The sales price of a classified motor vehicle purchased from a dealer, including all accessories attached to the vehicle when it is delivered to the purchaser, is considered the true value of the vehicle, and the assessor must appraise the vehicle at this value. The sales price excludes the tax imposed under Article 5A of this Chapter. The Property Tax Division of the Department of Revenue must annually adopt a schedule of values, standards, and rules to be used in the valuation of all other classified motor vehicles to ensure equitable statewide valuations, taking into account local market conditions and allowing adjustments for mileage and the condition of the vehicles.

(b1) Valuation Appeal. - The owner of a classified motor vehicle may appeal the appraised value of the vehicle by filing a request for appeal with the assessor within 30 days of the date taxes are due on the vehicle under G.S. 105-330.4. An owner who appeals the appraised value of a classified motor vehicle must pay the tax on the vehicle when due, subject to a full or partial refund if the appeal is decided in the owner's favor.

The combined tax and registration notice or tax receipt for a classified motor vehicle must explain the right to appeal the appraised value of the vehicle. A lessee of a vehicle that is required by the terms of the lease to pay the tax on the vehicle is considered the owner of the vehicle for purposes of filing an appeal under this subsection. Appeals filed under this subsection shall proceed in the manner provided in G.S. 105-312(d).

(b2)   Exemption or Exclusion Appeal. - The owner of a classified motor vehicle may appeal the vehicle's eligibility for an exemption or exclusion by filing a request for appeal with the assessor within 30 days of the assessor's initial decision on the exemption or exclusion application filed by the owner pursuant to G.S. 105-330.3(b). Appeals filed under this subsection shall proceed in the manner provided in G.S. 105-312(d).

(c)   Repealed by Session Laws 2008-134, s. 61, effective July 28, 2008. (1991, c. 624, s. 1; 1991 (Reg. Sess., 1992), c. 961, s. 4; 1995, c. 510, s. 1; 1995 (Reg. Sess., 1996), c. 646, s. 24; 1997-6, s. 10; 1999-353, s. 1; 2005-294, s. 2; 2005-303, s. 1; 2006-259, s. 31.5; 2007-527, s. 22(b); 2008-134, ss. 61, 65; 2009-445, s. 24(a); 2010-95, s. 22(c); 2011-330, s. 42(a); 2012-79, ss. 3.2, 3.6; 2013-414, ss. 70(b), (d), 71(a), (b).)

§ 105-330.3. Listing requirements for classified motor vehicles; application for exempt status.

(a1)   Unregistered Vehicles. - The owner of an unregistered classified motor vehicle must list the vehicle for taxes by filing an abstract with the assessor of the county in which the vehicle is located on or before January 31 following the date the owner acquired the unregistered vehicle or, in the case of a registration that is not renewed, January 31 following the date the registration expires, and on or before January 31 of each succeeding year that the vehicle is unregistered. If a classified motor vehicle required to be listed pursuant to this subsection is registered before the end of the fiscal year for which it was required to be listed, the following applies:

(1)   The vehicle is taxed as a registered vehicle, and the tax assessed pursuant to this subsection for the fiscal year in which the vehicle was required to be listed shall be released and/or refunded.

(2)   For any months for which the vehicle was not taxed between the date the registration expired and the start of the current registered vehicle tax year, the vehicle is taxed as an unregistered vehicle as follows:

a. The value of the motor vehicle is determined as of January 1 of the year in which the registration of the motor vehicle expires.

b. In computing the taxes, the assessor must use the tax rates and any additional motor vehicle taxes of the various taxing units in effect on the date the taxes are computed.

c. The tax on the motor vehicle is the product of a fraction and the number of months for which the vehicle was not taxed between the date the registration expires and the start of the current registered vehicle tax year. The numerator of the fraction is the product of the appraised value of the motor vehicle and the tax rate of the various taxing units. The denominator of the fraction is 12.

d. The taxes are due on the first day of the second month following the month the notice was prepared.

e. Interest accrues on unpaid taxes for these unregistered classified motor vehicles at the rate of five percent (5%) for the remainder of the month following the month the taxes are due. Interest accrues at the rate of three-fourths percent (3/4%) for each following month until the taxes are paid, unless the notice is prepared after the date the taxes are due. In that circumstance, the interest accrues beginning the second month following the date of the notice until the taxes are paid.

(3) A vehicle required to be listed pursuant to this subsection that is not listed by January 31 and is not registered before the end of the fiscal year for which it was required to be listed is subject to discovery pursuant to G.S. 105-312.

(b) Exemption or Exclusion. - The owner of a classified motor vehicle who claims an exemption or exclusion from tax under this Subchapter has the burden of establishing that the vehicle is entitled to the exemption or exclusion. The owner may establish prima facie entitlement to exemption or exclusion of the classified motor vehicle by filing an application for exempt status with the assessor within 30 days of the date taxes on the vehicle are due. When an approved application is on file, the assessor must omit from the tax records the classified motor vehicles described in the application. An application is not required for vehicles qualifying for the exemptions or exclusions listed in G.S. 105-282.1(a)(1). The remaining provisions of G.S. 105-282.1 do not apply to classified motor vehicles.

(c) Duty to report changes. - The owner of a classified motor vehicle that has been omitted from the tax records as provided in subsection (b) of this section must report to the assessor any classified motor vehicle registered in the owner's name or owned by that person but not registered in the person's name that does not qualify for exemption or exclusion for the current year. This report must be made within 30 days after the renewal of registration or initial registration of the vehicle or, for an unregistered vehicle, on or before January 31 of the year in which the vehicle is required to be listed by subsection (a1) of this section. A classified motor vehicle that does not qualify for exemption or exclusion but has been omitted from the tax records as provided in subsection (b) is subject to discovery under the provisions of G.S. 105-312, except that in lieu of the penalties prescribed by G.S. 105-312(h) a penalty of one hundred dollars ($100.00) is assessed for each registration period that elapsed before the disqualification was discovered.

(d) Criminal Sanction. - A person who willfully attempts, or who willfully aids or abets another person to attempt, in any manner to evade or defeat the taxes subject to this Article, whether by removal or concealment of property or otherwise, is guilty of a Class 2 misdemeanor. (1991, c. 624, s. 1; 2008-134, s. 62; 2009-445, s. 24(a); 2010-95, s. 22(c); 2012-79, s. 3.3; 2013-414, ss. 70(b), 71(a), (c).)

§ 105-330.4. Due date, interest, and enforcement remedies.

(a) Due Date. - The registration of a classified motor vehicle may not be issued unless a temporary registration plate is issued for the motor vehicle under G.S. 20-79.1A or the taxes for the motor vehicle's tax year that begins after the issuance of the registration are paid upon registration. A registration of a classified motor vehicle may not be renewed unless the taxes for the motor vehicle's tax year that begins after the registration expires are paid upon registration. If the registration of a classified motor vehicle is renewed earlier than the date the taxes are due, the taxes must be paid as if they were due. Taxes on a classified motor vehicle are due as follows:

(1) For an unregistered classified motor vehicle, the taxes are due on September 1 following the date by which the vehicle was required to be listed.

(2) For a registered classified motor vehicle that is registered under the staggered system, the taxes are due each year on the date the owner applies

for a new registration or the fifteenth day of the month following the month in which the registration renewal sticker expires pursuant to G.S. 20-66(g).

(3)   For a registered classified motor vehicle that is registered under the annual system, taxes are due on the date the owner applies for a new registration or 45 days after the registration expires.

(4)   For a registered classified motor vehicle that has a temporary registration plate issued under G.S. 20-79.1 or a limited registration plate issued under G.S. 20-79.1A, the taxes are due on the last day of the second month following the date the owner applied for the plate.

(a1)   Repealed by Session Laws 2009-445, s. 24(a), effective July 1, 2013, and applicable to combined tax and registration notices issued on or after that date.

(b)   Interest. - Interest accrues on unpaid taxes and unpaid registration fees for registered classified motor vehicles at the rate of five percent (5%) for the remainder of the month the taxes are due under subsection (a) of this section. Interest does not accrue for the first month following the due date. Interest accrues at the rate of three-fourths percent (3/4%) beginning the second month following the due date and for each following month until the taxes and fees are paid. Subject to the provisions of G.S. 105-395.1, interest accrues on delinquent taxes on unregistered classified motor vehicles as provided in G.S. 105-360(a) and the discounts allowed in G.S. 105-360(a) apply to the payment of the taxes.

(c)   Remedies. - The enforcement remedies in this Subchapter apply to unpaid taxes on an unregistered classified motor vehicle and to unpaid taxes on a registered classified motor vehicle for which the tax year begins before October 1, 2013.

(d)   Payments. - Tax payments submitted by mail are deemed to be received as of the date shown on the postmark affixed by the United States Postal Service. If no date is shown on the postmark or if the postmark is not affixed by the United States Postal Service, the tax payment is deemed to be received when the payment is received by the collecting authority. In any dispute arising under this subsection, the burden of proof is on the taxpayer to show that the payment was timely made. (1991, c. 624, s. 1; 1991 (Reg. Sess., 1992), c. 961, s. 5; 1995, c. 510, s. 2; 2001-139, s. 8; 2005-294, ss. 3, 4, 5; 2006-259, s. 31.5; 2007-471, s. 3; 2007-527, s. 22(b); 2008-134, s. 65; 2009-445, ss. 24(a), 25(a);

2010-95, s. 22(c), (d); 2011-330, ss. 40, 42(a); 2012-79, ss. 3.4, 3.6; 2013-414, ss. 70(b)-(d), 71(a), (d).)

§ 105-330.5. Notice required; distribution and collection fees.

(a) Notice for Registered Vehicle. - The Property Tax Division of the Department of Revenue or a third-party contractor selected by the Property Tax Division must prepare a combined tax and registration notice for each registered classified motor vehicle. The combined tax and registration notice must contain all county and municipal corporation taxes and fees due on the motor vehicle as computed by the assessor in the county of registration. If the motor vehicle has a temporary or limited registration plate issued under G.S. 20-79.1 or G.S. 20-79.1A, the combined tax and registration notice must state that the vehicle registration fees for the plate have been paid and that the vehicle's registration becomes valid for the remainder of the year upon payment of the county and municipal corporation taxes and fees that are due. A combined tax and registration notice that sets out the required information on a vehicle issued a limited registration plate constitutes the registration certificate for that vehicle.

In computing the taxes, the assessor must appraise the motor vehicle in accordance with G.S. 105-330.2 and must use the tax rates and any additional motor vehicle taxes of the various taxing units in effect on the date the taxes are computed. The tax on the motor vehicle is the product of a fraction and the number of months in the motor vehicle tax year. The numerator of the fraction is the product of the appraised value of the motor vehicle and the tax rate of the various taxing units. The denominator of the fraction is 12. This procedure constitutes the listing and assessment of each classified motor vehicle for taxation.

The combined tax and registration notice must contain the following:

(1) The appraised value of the motor vehicle.

(2) The tax rate of each taxing unit.

(3) A statement that the appraised value and the taxability of the motor vehicle may be appealed to the assessor in writing within 30 days of the due date.

(4) The registration fee imposed by the Division of Motor Vehicles and any other information required by the Division of Motor Vehicles to comply with the provisions of Chapter 20 of the General Statutes.

(5) Instructions for payment.

(a1) Proration. - When a new registration is obtained for a registered classified motor vehicle that is registered under the annual system, the taxes are prorated for the remainder of the calendar year. The amount of prorated taxes due is the product of the proration fraction and the taxes computed according to subsection (a) of this section. The numerator of the proration fraction is the number of full months remaining in the calendar year following the registration application date and the denominator of the fraction is 12.

(a2) Repealed by Session Laws 2009-445, s. 24(a), effective July 1, 2011, and applicable to combined tax and registration notices issued on or after that date, or when the Division of motor vehicles and the Department of Revenue certify that the integrated computer system or registration renewal and property tax collection for motor vehicles is in operation, whichever occurs first.

(b) Distribution and Collection Fees. - The Property Tax Division of the Department of Revenue or a third-party contractor selected by the Property Tax Division must send a copy of the combined tax and registration notice for a registered classified motor vehicle to the motor vehicle owner, as defined in G.S. 20-4.01. The Department must establish a fee equal to the actual cost of preparing, printing, and sending the notice. The Department may receive a fee for each notice generated for a vehicle registered in a county or municipal corporation from the taxes and fees remitted to the county or municipal corporation in which the vehicle is registered. The collecting authority is responsible for collecting county and municipal taxes and fees assessed under this Article and may receive a fee for collecting these taxes and fees. The amount of this fee must equal at least the applicable amount set under G.S. 20-63(h). The Property Tax Division must establish procedures to ensure that tax payments and fees received pursuant to this Article and Chapter 20 of the General Statutes are properly accounted for and taxes and fees due other taxing units and the Division of Motor Vehicles are remitted at least once each month.

(b1) Repealed by Session Laws 1995, c. 329, s. 2.

(c) Notice for Unregistered Vehicle. - The assessor must prepare and send a tax notice for each unregistered classified motor vehicle before September 1 following the January 31 listing date. The notice must include all county and special district taxes due on the motor vehicle. In computing the taxes, the assessor must use the tax rates of the taxing units in effect for the fiscal year that begins on July 1 following the January 31 listing date. Municipalities must list, assess, and tax unregistered classified motor vehicles as provided in G.S. 105-326, 105-327, and 105-328.

(d) Scope of Levy. - A county must include taxes on registered classified motor vehicles in the tax levy for the fiscal year in which the taxes are collected.

(e) Repealed by Session Laws 2012-79, s. 3.5, effective June 26, 2012. (1991, c. 624, s. 1; 1991 (Reg. Sess., 1992), c. 961, s. 6; 1995, c. 24, s. 1; c. 329, s. 2; c. 510, s. 3; 2005-294, s. 6; 2005-313, s. 8; 2006-259, s. 31.5; 2007-471, ss. 4, 5; 2007-527, s. 22(b); 2008-134, s. 65; 2009-445, ss. 24(a), 25(a); 2010-95, s. 22(c), (d); 2011-330, s. 42(a); 2012-79, ss. 3.5, 3.6; 2013-372, s. 2(b); 2013-414, s. 70(b)-(d).)

§ 105-330.6. Motor vehicle tax year; transfer of plates; surrender of plates.

(a) Tax Year. - The tax year for a classified motor vehicle listed pursuant to G.S. 105-330.3(a)(1) and registered under the staggered system begins on the first day of the first month following the date on which the former registration expires or the new registration is applied for and ends on the last day of the month in which the current registration expires. The tax year for a classified motor vehicle listed pursuant to G.S. 105-330.3(a)(1) and registered under the annual system begins on the first day of the first month following the date on which the registration expires or the new registration is applied for and ends the following December 31. The tax year for a classified motor vehicle listed pursuant to G.S. 105-330.3(a)(2) is the fiscal year that opens in the calendar year in which the vehicle is required to be listed.

(a1) Change in Tax Year. - If the tax year for a classified motor vehicle changes because of a change in its registration for a reason other than the transfer of its registration plates to another classified motor vehicle pursuant to G.S. 20-64, and the new tax year begins before the expiration of the vehicle's original tax year, the taxpayer may receive a credit, in the form of a release, against the taxes on the vehicle for the new tax year. The amount of the credit is equal to a proportion of the taxes paid on the vehicle for the original tax year. The proportion is the number of full calendar months remaining in the original tax year as of the first day of the new tax year, divided by the number of months in the original tax year. To obtain the credit allowed in this subsection, the taxpayer must apply within 30 days after the taxes for the new tax year are due and must provide the county tax collector information establishing the original tax year of the vehicle, the amount of taxes paid on the vehicle for that year, and the reason for the change in registration.

(b) Transfer of Plates. - If the owner of a classified motor vehicle listed pursuant to G.S. 105-330.3(a)(1) transfers the registration plates from the listed vehicle to another classified motor vehicle pursuant to G.S. 20-64 during the listed vehicle's tax year, the vehicle to which the plates are transferred is not required to be listed or taxed until the current registration expires or is renewed.

(c) Surrender of Plates. - If the owner of a classified motor vehicle listed pursuant to G.S. 105-330.3(a)(1) either transfers the motor vehicle to a new owner or moves out-of-state and registers the vehicle in another jurisdiction, and the owner surrenders the registration plates from the listed vehicle to the Division of Motor Vehicles, then the owner may apply for a release or refund of taxes on the vehicle for any full calendar months remaining in the vehicle's tax year after the date of surrender. To apply for a release or refund, the owner must present to the county tax collector within one year after surrendering the plates the receipt received from the Division of Motor Vehicles accepting surrender of the registration plates. The county tax collector shall then multiply the amount of the taxes for the tax year on the vehicle by a fraction, the denominator of which is the number of months in the tax year and the numerator of which is the number of full calendar months remaining in the vehicle's tax year after the date of surrender of the registration plates. The product of the multiplication is the amount of taxes to be released or refunded. If the taxes have not been paid at the date of application, the county tax collector shall make a release of the prorated taxes and credit the owner's tax notice with the amount of the release. If the taxes have been paid at the date of application, the county tax collector shall direct an order for a refund of the prorated taxes to the county finance officer, and the finance officer shall issue a refund to the vehicle owner. (1991, c. 624, s. 1; 1991 (Reg. Sess., 1992), c. 961, s. 7; 1995, c. 510, s. 4; 1998-139, s. 3; 2001-406, s. 1; 2001-497, s. 1(a); 2005-313, s. 9.)

§ 105-330.7. (Repealed for combined tax and registration notices issued on or after July 1, 2013) List of delinquents sent to Division of Motor Vehicles.

On the tenth day of each month the county tax collector shall prepare a list with the name and address of the owner and the vehicle identification number of every classified motor vehicle listed pursuant to G.S. 105-330.3(a)(1) on which taxes remain unpaid on that date and on which taxes became due on the first day of the fourth month preceding that date. The tax collector shall mail that list to the Division of Motor Vehicles. The list shall be in the form and contain the information required by the Division of Motor Vehicles. (1991, c. 624, s. 1; 1991 (Reg. Sess., 1992), c. 961, s. 8; 2005-294, s. 13; 2006-259, s. 31.5; 2007-527, s. 22; 2008-134, s. 65; 2005-294, s. 7; 2011-330, s. 42(a); 2012-79, s. 3.6; 2013-414, ss. 70(b), (d).)

§ 105-330.8. Deadlines not extended.

Except as otherwise provided in this Article, the following sections of the General Statutes do not apply:

(1)   G.S. 105-395.1 and G.S. 103-5.

(2)   G.S. 105-321(f).

(3)   G.S. 105-360. (1991, c. 624, s. 1; 2009-445, s. 24(a); 2010-95, s. 22(c); 2013-414, s. 70(b).)

§ 105-330.9. Antique automobiles.

(a)   Definition. - For the purpose of this section, the term "antique automobile" means a motor vehicle that meets all of the following conditions:

(1)   It is registered with the Division of Motor Vehicles and has an historic vehicle special license plate under G.S. 20-79.4.

(2)   It is maintained primarily for use in exhibitions, club activities, parades, and other public interest functions.

(3) It is used only occasionally for other purposes.

(4) It is owned by an individual.

(5) It is used by the owner for a purpose other than the production of income and is not used in connection with a business.

(b) Classification. - Antique automobiles are designated a special class of property under Article V, Sec. 2(2) of the North Carolina Constitution and must be assessed for taxation in accordance with this section. An antique automobile must be assessed at the lower of its true value or five hundred dollars ($500.00). (1995, c 512, s 2; 2009-445, s. 24(a); 2013-414, s. 70(b).)

§ 105-330.10. Disposition of interest.

The interest collected on unpaid registration fees pursuant to G.S. 105-330.4 shall be transferred on a monthly basis to the North Carolina Highway Fund for technology improvements within the Division of Motor Vehicles. (2005-294, ss. 8, 9; 2006-30, s. 3; 2006-259, s. 31.5; 2007-471, s. 7(a); 2007-527, s. 22(a)-(c); 2008-134, ss. 63, 65, 66, 79; 2009-445, s. 25(b); 2010-95, s. 22(a), (b), (e); 2011-330, s. 42(a)-(c); 2013-414, s. 70(a), (c), (d).)

§ 105-330.11. Memorandum of understanding.

The Department of Revenue, acting through the Property Tax Division, and the Department of Transportation, acting through the Division of Motor Vehicles are directed to enter into a memorandum of understanding concerning the administration of this Article. The memorandum of understanding must include the following:

(1) A procedure for the administration of the listing, appraisal, and assessment of classified motor vehicles.

(2) Information concerning vehicle identification, the name and address of a vehicle's owner, and other information that will be required on a motor vehicle registration form to implement the tax listing and collection provisions of this Article.

(3) A procedure for the business practices, accounting, and costs of carrying out the integrated computer system for registration renewal and property tax collection for motor vehicles once the system has been certified to be in operation by the Department of Revenue and the Department of Transportation. The Departments must consult with the North Carolina Association of County Commissioners, acting on behalf of the counties, and the North Carolina League of Municipalities, acting on behalf of the municipalities, in developing the procedures under this subdivision and obtain their signed endorsements before any part of this procedure is implemented. (2008-134, s. 64; 2009-445, s. 24(a); 2013-414, s. 70(b).)

§§ 105-330.12 through 105-332: Reserved for future codification purposes.

Article 23.

Public Service Companies.

§ 105-333. Definitions.

The following definitions apply in this Article unless the context requires a different meaning:

(1) Airline company. - A company engaged in the business of transporting passengers and property by aircraft for hire within, into, or from this State.

(2) Bus line company. - A company engaged in the business of transporting passengers and property by motor vehicle for hire over the public highways of this State (but not including a bus line company operating primarily upon the public streets within a single local taxing unit), whether the transportation is within, into, or from this State.

(3) Distributable system property. - All real property and personal property owned or used by a railroad company other than nondistributable system property.

(4) Electric membership corporation. - A company organized, reorganized, or domesticated under Chapter 117 of the General Statutes and engaged in the business of supplying electricity for light, heat, or power to consumers in this State.

(5) Electric power company. - A company engaged in the business of supplying electricity for light, heat, or power to consumers in this State.

(6) Repealed by Session Laws 1973, c. 783, s. 5.

(7) Flight equipment. - Aircraft fully equipped for flying and used in any operation within this State.

(8) Gas company. - A company engaged in the business of supplying artificial or natural gas to, from, within, or through this State through pipe or tubing for light, heat, or power to consumers in this State.

(9) Locally assigned rolling stock. - Rolling stock that is owned or leased by a motor freight carrier company, specifically assigned to a terminal or other premises, and regularly used at the premises to which assigned.

(10) Motor freight carrier company. - A company engaged in the business of transporting property by motor vehicle for hire over the public highways of this State as provided in this subdivision:

a. As to interstate carrier companies domiciled in North Carolina, this term includes carriers who regularly transport property by tractor trailer to or from one or more terminals owned or leased by the carrier outside this State or two or more terminals inside this State. For purposes of appraisal and allocation only, the term also includes a North Carolina interstate carrier that does not have a terminal outside this State but whose operations outside the State are sufficient to require the payment of ad valorem taxes on a portion of the value of the rolling stock of the carrier to taxing units in one or more other states.

b. As to interstate carrier companies domiciled outside this State, this term includes carriers who regularly transport property by tractor trailer to or from one or more terminals owned or leased by the carrier inside this State.

c. As to intrastate carrier companies, this term includes only those carriers that are engaged in the transportation of property by tractor trailer to or from two or more terminals owned or leased by the carrier in this State.

(11) Nondistributable system property. - The following properties owned by a railroad company: land other than right-of-way, depots, machine shops, warehouses, office buildings, other structures, and the contents of the structures listed in this subdivision.

(12) Nonsystem property. - The real and tangible personal property owned by a public service company but not used in its public service activities.

(13) Pipeline company. - A company engaged in the business of transporting natural gas, petroleum products, or other products through pipelines to, from, within, or through this State, or having control of pipelines for such a purpose.

(14) Public service company. - A railroad company, a pipeline company, a gas company, an electric power company, an electric membership corporation, a telephone company, a telegraph company, a bus line company, an airline company, or a motor freight carrier company. The term also includes any company performing a public service that is regulated by the United States Department of Energy, the United States Department of Transportation, the Federal Communications Commission, the Federal Aviation Agency, or the North Carolina Utilities Commission, except that the term does not include a water company, providers of mobile telecommunications service as defined in G.S. 105-164.3, a cable television company, or a radio or television broadcasting company.

(15) Railroad company. - A company engaged in the business of operating a railroad to, from, within or through this State on rights-of-way owned or leased by the company. It also means a company operating a passenger service on the lines of any railroad located wholly or partly in this State.

(16) Rolling stock. - Motor vehicles, railroad locomotives, and railroad cars that are propelled by mechanical or electrical power and used upon the highways or, in the case of railroad vehicles, upon tracks.

(17) System property. - The real property and personal property used by a public service company in its public service activities. The term also includes public service company property under construction on the day as of which property is assessed which when completed will be used by the owner in its public service activities.

(18) Telegraph company. - A company engaged in the business of transmitting telegraph messages to, from, within, or through the State.

(19)   Telephone company. - A company engaged in the business of transmitting telephone messages and conversations to, from, within, or through this State.

(20)   Repealed by Session Laws 1973, c. 783, s. 5.

(21)   Terminal. - A motor freight carrier facility that includes buildings for the handling and temporary storage of freight pending transfer between locations. The term also includes a facility that handles truckloads only and typically consists of a wide, open space where rolling stock is parked and a building for offices and maintenance of rolling stock. (1939, c. 310, ss. 1600-1605; 1943, c. 634, s. 3; 1965, c. 287, s. 17; 1971, c. 806, s. 1; c. 1121, s. 4; 1973, c. 198; c. 783, ss. 1-5; c. 1180; 1991 (Reg. Sess., 1992), c. 961, s. 1; 1995, c. 350, ss. 1, 2; 1995 (Reg. Sess., 1996), c. 646, s. 18; 1997-23, ss. 6, 7; 1998-98, s. 25; 2010-95, ss. 19, 20; 2011-330, s. 41.)

§ 105-334. Duty to file report; penalty for failure to file.

(a)   Every public service company, whether incorporated under the laws of this State or any other state or any foreign nation, whose property is subject to taxation in this State, shall prepare and deliver to the Department of Revenue each year a report showing (as of January 1) such information with regard to the property it owns and the system property it leases as the Department of Revenue may by regulation prescribe. This report shall be filed on or before the last day of March, and the following affirmation, which shall be annexed to the report, shall be signed by a principal officer of the public service company making the report:

Under penalties prescribed by law, I hereby affirm that to the best of my knowledge and belief this report, including any accompanying statements, inventories, schedules, and other information is true and complete.

(b)   Any individual who willfully subscribes a report required by this section which he does not believe to be true and correct as to every material matter shall be guilty of a Class 2 misdemeanor.

(c)   For good cause the Department may grant reasonable extensions of time for filing the required reports.

(d) The Department may require any additional reports or information it deems necessary to properly carry out its duties under this Article.

(e) The provisions of G.S. 105-291 and 105-312 are made specifically applicable to all proceedings taken under this Article. (1939, c. 310, ss. 1600-1606; 1943, c. 634, s. 3; 1965, c. 287, s. 17; 1971, c. 806, s. 1; 1973, c. 476, s. 193; 1993, c. 539, s. 721; 1994, Ex. Sess., c. 24, s. 14(c).)

§ 105-335. Appraisal of property of public service companies.

(a) Duty to Appraise. - In accordance with the provisions of subsection (b), below, the Department of Revenue shall appraise for taxation the true value of each public service company (other than bus line, motor freight carrier, and airline companies) as a system (both inside and outside this State). Certain specified properties of bus line, motor freight carrier, and airline companies shall be appraised by the Department in accordance with the provisions of subsection (c), below, and all other properties of such companies shall be listed, appraised, and assessed in the manner prescribed by this Subchapter for the properties of taxpayers other than public service companies.

(b) Property of Public Service Companies Other Than Those Noted in Subsection (c). -

(1) System Property. - Each year, as of January 1, the Department of Revenue shall appraise at its true value (as defined in G.S. 105-283) the system property used by each public service company both inside and outside this State. Property leased by a public service company shall be included in appraising the value of its system property if necessary to ascertain the true value of the company's system property.

(2) Nonsystem Personal Property. - Each year as of January 1, the Department shall appraise at its true value (as defined in G.S. 105-283) each public service company's nonsystem tangible personal property subject to taxation in this State.

(3) Nonsystem Real Property. - In accordance with the county in which the public service company's nonsystem real property is located and the schedules set out in G.S. 105-286 and 105-287, the Department of Revenue shall appraise

at its true value (as defined in G.S. 105-283) each public service company's nonsystem real property subject to taxation in this State.

(c) Property of Bus Line, Motor Freight Carrier, and Airline Companies. -

(1) Bus Company Rolling Stock. - Each year as of January 1, the Department shall appraise at its true value (as defined in G.S. 105-283) the rolling stock owned or leased by or operated under the control of each bus line company, which bus line company is domiciled in this State or which is regularly engaged in business in this State.

(2) Motor Freight Carrier Company Rolling Stock. - Each year as of January 1, the Department shall appraise at its true value (as defined in G.S. 105-283) the rolling stock owned by a motor freight carrier company or leased by a motor freight carrier company and operated by its employees which motor freight carrier company is domiciled in this State or is regularly engaged in business in this State at a terminal owned or leased by the carrier.

(3) Flight Equipment. - Each year, as of January 1, the Department shall appraise at its true value (as defined in G.S. 105-283) the flight equipment owned or leased by or operated under the control of each airline company that is domiciled in the State or that is regularly engaged in business at some airport in this State. (1939, c. 310, s. 1608; 1971, c. 806, s. 1; 1973, c. 476, s. 193; c. 783, s. 6; c. 1180.)

§ 105-336. Methods of appraising certain properties of public service companies.

(a) Appraising System Property of Public Service Companies Other Than Those Noted in Subsection (b). - In determining the true value of each public service company (other than one covered by subsection (b), below) as a system the Department of Revenue shall give consideration to the following:

(1) The market value of the company's capital stock and debt, taking into account the influence of any nonsystem property.

(2) The book value of the company's system property as reflected in the books of account kept under the regulations of the appropriate federal or State

regulatory agency and what it would cost to replace or reproduce the system property, less a reasonable allowance for depreciation.

(3)   The gross receipts and operating income of the company.

(4)   Any other factor or information that in the judgment of the Department has a bearing on the true value of the company's system property.

(b)   Appraising Rolling Stock and Flight Equipment. - In determining the true value of the rolling stock of bus line and motor freight carrier companies and the flight equipment of airline companies, the Department of Revenue shall consider the book value of the property as reflected in the books of account kept under the regulations of the appropriate federal or State regulatory agency and what it would cost to replace or reproduce the property in its existing condition. (1939, c. 310, s. 1608; 1971, c. 806, s. 1; 1973, c. 476, s. 193.)

§ 105-337. Apportionment of taxable values to this State.

With respect to any public service company operating both inside and outside this State, it shall be the duty of the Department of Revenue to apportion for taxation in this State a fair and reasonable share of the value of the company as a system or its rolling stock or flight equipment as appraised under the provisions of G.S. 105-336. Thus, when the Department has determined true value in accordance with the provisions of G.S. 105-336(a) or G.S. 105-336(b), it shall ascertain the portion of the total value subject to taxation in this State by applying property, business, and mileage factors thereto in accordance with the ratio that the company's property, business, or mileage in this State bears to its total property, business, or mileage. In its discretion, the Department may use one or more of the factors listed in the preceding sentence in order to achieve a fair and accurate result in the apportionment of the value of the property of any public service company. As used in this section,

(1)   The term "business factor" means data that reflect the use of the company's property, such as gross revenue, net income, tons of freight carried, revenue ton miles, passenger miles, car miles, ground hours, and comparable data.

(2)   The term "mileage factor" means factual information as to the linear miles of the company's track, wire, lines, pipes, routes, and similar operational

routes and factual information as to the miles traveled by the company's rolling stock.

(3) The term "property factor" means investment in property; it may be either gross or net investment or any other reasonable figure reflecting the company's investment in property. (1939, c. 310, s. 1609; 1971, c. 806, s. 1; 1973, c. 476, s. 193.)

§ 105-338. Allocation of appraised valuation of system property among local taxing units.

(a) State Board's Duty. - For purposes of taxation by local taxing units in this State, the Department of Revenue shall allocate the valuations of public service company property among the local taxing units in accordance with the provisions of this section.

(b) System Valuation of Companies Other Than Those Noted in Subsection (c). -

(1) System Property of Railroad Companies. - The appraised valuation of the distributable system property of a railroad shall be allocated for taxation to the local taxing units in accordance with the ratio of the miles of all the company's tracks in the local taxing unit to the total miles of all the company's tracks in this State, adjusted to reflect density of traffic in the local taxing unit.

(2) System Property of Telephone Companies. -

a. The Department of Revenue shall divide each telephone company's system property in this State into the following two classes and shall determine the original cost of that property and the percentage thereof represented by the property in each of the two classes.

- Class 1: Property located in this State that is identified under the applicable uniform system of accounts as central office equipment, large P.B.X. equipment, motor vehicles, tools and work equipment, office furniture and equipment, materials and supplies, and land and buildings (including towers and other structures).

- Class 2: Property located in this State that does not come within Class 1.

The Department of Revenue shall then apply the percentages obtained in accordance with this subdivision to the appraised valuation of the company's system property in this State and thereby derive the proportions of appraised valuation to be allocated as Class 1 and Class 2 valuations to local taxing units in accordance with subdivision (b)(2)b, below.

b. Having made the division required by subdivision (b)(2)a, above, the Department of Revenue shall allocate the appraised valuation of the properties in each class among the local taxing units of the State as follows:

- Class 1: The appraised valuations of property in this class shall be allocated among the local taxing units in which such property of the company is situated on January 1 in the proportion that the original cost of such property in the taxing unit bears to the original cost of all such property in this State.

- Class 2: The appraised valuations of property in this class shall be allocated among the local taxing units in which the company operates in the proportion that the miles of the company's single aerial wire and single wire in cable (including single tube in coaxial cable) in the taxing unit bears to the total of such wire miles of the company in this State.

(3) System Property of Other Companies Appraised by the Department of Revenue. -

a. The provisions of this subdivision (b)(3) shall govern the allocation of the property of all companies appraised by the Department of Revenue except railroad, telephone, bus line, motor freight carrier, and airline companies.

b. The appraised valuation of the system property of such a company shall be allocated for taxation to the local taxing units in which the company operates in the proportion that the original cost of the taxable system property in the local taxing unit on January 1 bears to the original cost of all the taxable system property in this State. If in any local taxing unit the company owns system property acquired prior to January 1, 1972, for which the original cost cannot be definitely ascertained, a reasonable estimate of the original cost of that property shall be made by the company, and this estimate shall be used by the Department of Revenue for allocation purposes as if it were the actual original cost of the property.

(c) Property of Bus Line, Motor Freight Carrier, and Airline Companies. -

(1) The appraised valuation of a bus line company's rolling stock shall be allocated for taxation to each local taxing unit according to the ratio of the company's scheduled miles during the calendar year preceding January 1 in each such unit to the company's total scheduled miles in this State for the same period. In no event, however, shall the State Board make an allocation to a taxing unit if, when computed, the valuation for that taxing unit amounts to less than five hundred dollars ($500.00).

(2) The appraised valuation of the rolling stock (other than locally assigned rolling stock) owned or leased by a motor freight carrier company shall be allocated for taxation to each local taxing unit in which the company has a terminal according to the ratio of the tons of freight handled in the calendar year preceding January 1 at the company's terminals within the taxing unit to the total tons of freight handled by the company in this State in the same period. If a North Carolina interstate motor freight carrier company has no terminal outside this State, but has been required to pay ad valorem tax to one or more taxing units outside this State, there shall be allowed a reduction in the North Carolina valuation measured by the ratio of the rolling stock subject to ad valorem taxation outside the State to all of the carrier's rolling stock.

(3) The appraised valuation of an airline company's flight equipment shall be allocated for taxation to each local taxing unit in which an airport used by the company is situated according to the ratio obtained by averaging the following two ratios: the ratio of the company's ground hours in the taxing unit in the year preceding January 1 to the company's ground hours in the State in the same period, and the ratio of the company's gross revenue in the taxing unit in the year preceding January 1 to the company's gross revenue in the State in the same period. (1939, c. 310, s. 1610; 1971, c. 806, s. 1; 1973, c. 476, s. 193; c. 1180; 1997-456, s. 27.)

§ 105-339. Certification of appraised valuations of nonsystem property and locally assigned rolling stock.

Having determined the appraised valuations of the nonsystem properties of public service companies in accordance with subdivisions (b)(2) and (b)(3) of G.S. 105-335 and the appraised valuations of locally assigned rolling stock in accordance with subdivision (c)(1) of G.S. 105-335, the Department of Revenue shall assign those appraised valuations to the taxing units in which such properties are situated by certifying the valuations to the appropriate counties and municipalities. Each local taxing unit receiving such certified valuations shall assess them at the figures certified and shall tax the assessed valuations at the rate of tax levied against other property subject to taxation therein. (1939, c. 310, s. 1610; 1971, c. 806, s. 1; 1973, c. 476, s. 193; c. 695, s. 18.)

§ 105-340. Certification of appraised valuations of railroad companies.

(a) Having determined the appraised valuation of the "nondistributable" system property of a railroad company, the Department of Revenue shall assign the valuations for taxation to the local taxing units in which such property is situated in the same manner as is provided for nonsystem property in G.S. 105-339.

(b) Having determined the appraised valuation of the "distributable" system property of a railroad company and having allocated the valuations in accordance with G.S. 105-338(b)(1), the Department of Revenue shall then certify the amounts of those allocations to the local taxing units to which such amounts are due in accordance with the provisions of G.S. 105-341.

(c) Each local taxing unit receiving certified valuations in accordance with this section shall assess them at the figures certified and shall tax the assessed valuations at the rate of tax levied against other property subject to taxation therein. (1939, c. 310, s. 1620; 1971, c. 806, s. 1; 1973, c. 476, s. 193; c. 695, s. 19.)

§ 105-341. Certification of public service company system appraised valuations.

Having determined the appraised valuations of public service company system property in accordance with subdivision (b)(1) of G.S. 105-335 and having allocated the valuations in accordance with G.S. 105-338(b)(2) and (3), the Department of Revenue shall assign each local taxing unit's appraised valuations by certifying them to the appropriate counties and municipalities. Each local taxing unit receiving such certified valuations shall assess them at the figures certified and shall tax the assessed valuations at the rate of tax levied against other property subject to taxation therein. (1939, c. 310, s. 1610; 1971, c. 806, s. 1; 1973, c. 476, s. 193; c. 695, s. 20.)

§ 105-342. Notice, hearing, and appeal.

(a) Right to Information. - Upon written request to the Department of Revenue, any public service company whose property values are subject to appraisal, apportionment, and allocation for purposes of taxation under this Article shall be entitled to be informed of the elements that the Department considered in the appraisal of the company's property, the result in dollars produced by each element (including the methods and mathematical calculations used in determining those results), the specific factors and ratios the Department used in apportioning the appraised valuation of the company's property to this State, and the factors and the specific mathematical calculations the Department used in allocating the company's valuation among the local taxing units of this State. Upon written request to the Department of Revenue, any local taxing unit in this State shall be entitled to the same information with regard to any public service company whose property values are subject to appraisal, apportionment, and allocation for purposes of taxation under this Article.

(b) Appraisal and Apportionment Review. - The appraised valuation of public service company's property and the share thereof apportioned for taxation in this State under G.S. 105-335, 105-336, and 105-337 shall be deemed tentative figures until the provisions of this subsection (b) have been complied with. As soon as practicable after the tentative figures referred to in the preceding sentence have been determined, the Department of Revenue shall give the taxpayer written notice of the proposed figures and shall state in the notice that the taxpayer shall have 20 days after the date on which the notice was mailed in which to submit a written request to the Property Tax Commission for a hearing on the tentative appraisal or apportionment or both. If a timely request for a hearing is not made, the tentative figures shall become final and conclusive at the close of the twentieth day after the notice was mailed. If a timely request is made, the Property Tax Commission shall fix a date and place for the requested hearing and give the taxpayer at least 20 days' written notice thereof. The hearing shall be conducted under the provisions of subsection (d), below.

(c) Repealed by Session Laws 1985, c. 601, s. 4.

(d) Hearing and Appeal. - At any hearing under this section, the Property Tax Commission shall hear all evidence and affidavits offered by the taxpayer and may exercise the authority granted by G.S. 105-290(d) to obtain information pertinent to decision of the issue. The Commission shall make findings of fact and conclusions of law and issue an order embodying its decision. As soon as practicable thereafter, the Commission shall serve a written copy of its decision upon the taxpayer by personal service or by registered or certified mail, return receipt requested. (1971, c. 806, s. 1; 1973, c. 476, s. 193; 1979, c. 584, s. 2; c. 665, s. 1; 1985, c. 601, s. 4; 1987 (Reg. Sess., 1988), c. 1052, s. 1.)

§ 105-343. Penalty for failure to make required reports.

Any public service company which fails or refuses to prepare and deliver to the Department of Revenue any report required by this Article shall forfeit and pay to the State of North Carolina one hundred dollars ($100.00) for each day the report is delayed beyond the date on which it is required to be submitted. This penalty may be recovered in an action in the appropriate division of the General Court of Justice of Wake County in the name of the State on the relation of the Secretary of Revenue. When collected, the penalty shall be paid into the general fund of the State. The Secretary shall have the power to reduce or waive the penalty provided in this section for good cause. (1939, c. 310, s. 1606; 1971, c. 806, s. 1; 1973, c. 476, s. 193.)

§ 105-344. Failure to pay tax; remedies; penalty.

If any public service company fails or refuses to pay any taxes imposed on its property by any taxing unit of this State, the taxing unit may bring an action in the appropriate division of the General Court of Justice of the county in which the taxing unit is located for the recovery of the tax. Not less than 15 days before such an action is instituted, the taxing unit shall notify the taxpayer by registered or certified mail of its intention to bring the action. The judgment rendered in such an action shall include the tax imposed and unpaid and, as an additional tax, a penalty of fifty percent (50%) of the amount of the tax with interest on the sum of these taxes at the rate of nine percent (9%) per annum from the date the tax was due to be paid, plus reasonable attorneys' fees for the prosecution of the action to be fixed by the court. (The awarding of attorneys' fees by the court shall not prevent the taxing unit from paying its attorney an additional fee pursuant to contract, nor shall it prevent the taxing unit from requiring that the attorneys' fees awarded by the court be paid into the general fund of the taxing unit in accordance with any arrangement between the taxing unit and its attorneys.) The judgment rendered by the court may include a mandamus ordering the payment of the judgment, penalty, interest, and costs including the attorneys' fees as part of the costs.

If, during the pendency of an action brought under this section, additional or subsequent taxes shall accrue, those taxes, together with penalties and interest, may be included in the judgment if, prior to rendition of the judgment, the tax collector of the taxing unit files with the court a certificate of the additional taxes, penalties, and interest.

In any action brought under this section, the appraised valuation of the taxpayer's property as determined, allocated, and certified to the taxing unit by the Department of Revenue shall be conclusive and shall not be subject to collateral attack. (1939, c. 310, s. 1611; 1971, c. 806, s. 1; c. 931, s. 1; 1973, c. 476, s. 193.)

Article 24.

Review and Enforcement of Orders.

§ 105-345. Right of appeal; filing of exceptions.

(a) No party to a proceeding before the Property Tax Commission may appeal from any final order or decision of the Commission unless within 30 days after the entry of such final order or decision the party aggrieved by such decision or order shall file with the Commission notice of appeal and exceptions which shall set forth specifically the ground or grounds on which the aggrieved party considers said decision or order to be unlawful, unjust, unreasonable or unwarranted, and including errors alleged to have been committed by the Commission.

(b) Any party may appeal from all or any portion of any final order or decision of the Commission in the manner herein provided. Copy of the notice of appeal shall be mailed by the appealing party at the time of filing with the Commission, to each party to the proceeding to the addresses as they appear in the files of the Commission in the proceeding. The failure of any party, other than the Commission, to be served with or to receive a copy of the notice of appeal shall not affect the validity or regularity of the appeal.

(c)   The Commission may on motion of any party to the proceeding or on its own motion set the exceptions to the final order upon which such appeal is based for further hearing before the Commission.

(d)   The appeal shall lie to the Court of Appeals as provided in G.S. 7A-29. The procedure for the appeal shall be as provided by the rules of appellate procedure.

(e)   The Court of Appeals shall hear and determine all matters arising on such appeal, as in this Article provided, and may in the exercise of its discretion assign the hearing of said appeal to any panel of the Court of Appeals. (1979, c. 584, s. 3; 1983, c. 565.)

§ 105-345.1. No evidence admitted on appeal; remission for further evidence.

No evidence shall be received at the hearing on appeal to the Court of Appeals but if any party shall satisfy the court that evidence has been discovered since the hearing before the Property Tax Commission that could not have been obtained for use at that hearing by the exercise of reasonable diligence, and will materially affect the merits of the case, the court may, in its discretion, remand the record and proceedings to the Commission with directions to take such subsequently discovered evidence, and after consideration thereof, to make such order as the Commission may deem proper, from which order an appeal shall lie as in the case of any other final order from which an appeal may be taken as provided in G.S. 105-345. (1979, c. 584, s. 3.)

§ 105-345.2. Record on appeal; extent of review.

(a)   On appeal the court shall review the record and the exceptions and assignments of error in accordance with the rules of appellate procedure, and any alleged irregularities in procedures before the Property Tax Commission, not shown in the record, shall be considered under the rules of appellate procedure.

(b) So far as necessary to the decision and where presented, the court shall decide all relevant questions of law, interpret constitutional and statutory provisions, and determine the meaning and applicability of the terms of any Commission action. The court may affirm or reverse the decision of the Commission, declare the same null and void, or remand the case for further proceedings; or it may reverse or modify the decision if the substantial rights of the appellants have been prejudiced because the Commission's findings, inferences, conclusions or decisions are:

(1) In violation of constitutional provisions; or

(2) In excess of statutory authority or jurisdiction of the Commission; or

(3) Made upon unlawful proceedings; or

(4) Affected by other errors of law; or

(5) Unsupported by competent, material and substantial evidence in view of the entire record as submitted; or

(6) Arbitrary or capricious.

(c) In making the foregoing determinations, the court shall review the whole record or such portions thereof as may be cited by any party and due account shall be taken of the rule of prejudicial error. The appellant shall not be permitted to rely upon any grounds for relief on appeal which were not set forth specifically in his notice of appeal filed with the Commission. (1979, c. 584, s. 3.)

§ 105-345.3. Relief pending review on appeal.

Pending judicial review, the Property Tax Commission is authorized, where it finds that justice so requires, to postpone the effective date of any action taken by it. Upon such conditions as may be required and to the extent necessary to prevent irreparable injury, a judge of the Court of Appeals is authorized to issue all necessary and appropriate process to postpone the effective date of any action by the Commission or take such action as may be necessary to preserve status or rights of any of the parties pending conclusion of the proceedings on appeal. The court may require the applicant for such stay to post adequate bond as required by the court. (1979, c. 584, s. 3.)

§ 105-345.4. Appeal to Supreme Court.

In all appeals heard in the Court of Appeals, any party may file a motion for review in the Supreme Court of the decision of the Court of Appeals under G.S. 7A-31, and in cases entitled to be appealed as a matter of right under G.S. 7A-30(3) any party may appeal to the Supreme Court from the decision of the Court of Appeals under the same rules and regulations as are prescribed by law for appeals, and such court may advance the cause on its docket. (1979, c. 584, s. 3.)

§ 105-345.5. Judgment on appeal enforced by mandamus.

In all cases in which, upon appeal, an order or decision of the Property Tax Commission is affirmed, in whole or in part, the appellate court may include in its decree a mandamus to the appropriate party to put said order in force, or so much thereof as shall be affirmed, or the appellate court may make such other order as it deems appropriate. (1979, c. 584, s. 3.)

§ 105-346. Peremptory mandamus to enforce order when no appeal.

(a) If no appeal is taken from an order or decision of the Property Tax Commission within the time prescribed by law and the person to which the order or decision is directed fails to put the same in operation, as therein required, the Commission may apply to the judge regularly assigned to the superior court district which includes Wake County, or to the resident judge of said district at chambers upon 10 days' notice, for a peremptory mandamus upon said person for the putting in force of said order or decision; and if said judge shall find that the order of said Commission was valid and within the scope of its powers, he shall issue such peremptory mandamus.

(b) An appeal shall lie to the Court of Appeals in behalf of the Commission, or the defendant, from the refusal or the granting of such peremptory mandamus. The remedy prescribed in this section for enforcement of orders of the Commission is in addition to other remedies prescribed by law. (1979, c. 584, s. 3.)

Article 25.

Levy of Taxes and Presumption of Notice.

§ 105-347. Levy of property taxes.

Each year - not later than the date prescribed by applicable law or, in the absence of specific statutory provisions, not later than the first day of August - the tax levying authorities of counties and municipalities shall levy on property rates of taxes, not exceeding any constitutional or statutory limits, necessary to meet the general and other legally authorized expenses of the taxing units. (1939, c. 310, s. 1400; 1971, c. 806, s. 1.)

§ 105-348. All interested persons charged with notice of taxes.

All persons who have or who may acquire any interest in any real or personal property that may be or may become subject to a lien for taxes are hereby charged with notice that such property is or should be listed for taxation, that taxes are or may become a lien thereon, and that if taxes are not paid the proceedings allowed by law may be taken against such property. This notice shall be conclusively presumed, whether or not such persons have actual notice. (1939, c. 310, s. 1705; 1971, c. 806, s. 1.)

Article 26.

Collection and Foreclosure of Taxes.

§ 105-349. Appointment, term, qualifications, and bond of tax collectors and deputies.

(a) Appointment and Term. - The governing body of each county and municipality shall appoint a tax collector on or before July 1, 1971, to serve for a term to be determined by the appointing body and until his successor has been appointed and qualified. Until the first such appointments are made, county and municipal taxes shall be collected by the tax collectors presently serving under prior provisions of law. The governing body may remove the tax collector from office during his term for good cause after giving him notice in writing and an opportunity to appear and be heard at a public session of the governing body. No hearing shall be required, however, if the tax collector is removed for failing to meet the prerequisites prescribed by G.S. 105-352(b) for delivery of the tax receipts. Unless otherwise provided by G.S. 105-373, whenever any vacancy occurs in this office, the governing body shall appoint a qualified person to serve as tax collector for the period of the unexpired term.

(b) Qualifications. - The governing body shall appoint as tax collector a person of character and integrity whose experience in business and collection work is satisfactory to the governing body.

(c) Bond. - No tax collector shall be allowed to begin his duties until he shall have furnished bond conditioned upon his honesty and faithful performance in such amount as the governing body may prescribe. A tax collector shall not be permitted to collect any taxes not covered by his bond, nor shall a tax collector be permitted to continue collecting taxes after his bond has expired without renewal.

(d) Compensation. - The compensation and expense allowances of the tax collector shall be fixed by the governing body.

(e) Alternative to Separate Office of Tax Collector. - Pursuant to Article VI, Sec. 9, of the North Carolina Constitution, the office of tax collector is hereby declared to be an office that may be held concurrently with any appointive or elective office other than those hereinafter designated, and the governing body may appoint as tax collector any appointive or elective officer who meets the personal and bonding requirements established by this section. A member of the governing body of a taxing unit may not be appointed tax collector, nor may the duties of the office be conferred upon him. A person appointed or elected as the treasurer or chief accounting officer of a taxing unit may not be appointed tax collector, nor may the duties of the office of tax collector be conferred upon him except with the written permission of the secretary of the Local Government Commission who, before giving his permission, shall satisfy himself that the unit's internal control procedures are sufficient to prevent improper handling of public funds.

(f)   Deputy Tax Collectors. - The governing body of a county or municipality is authorized to appoint one or more deputy tax collectors and to establish their terms of office, compensation, and bonding requirements. A deputy tax collector shall have authority to perform, under the direction of the tax collector, any act that the tax collector may perform unless the governing body appointing the deputy specifically limits the scope of the deputy's authority.

(g)   Oath. - Every tax collector and deputy tax collector, as the holder of an office, shall take the oath required by Article VI, § 7 of the North Carolina Constitution with the following phrase added to it: "that I will not allow my actions as tax collector to be influenced by personal or political friendships or obligations,". The oath must be filed with the clerk of the governing body of the taxing unit. (1939, c. 310, ss. 1701, 1702; 1957, c. 537; 1971, c. 806, s. 1; 1991, c. 110, s. 6; 1991 (Reg. Sess., 1992), c. 1007, s. 23.)

§ 105-350. General duties of tax collectors.

It shall be the duty of each tax collector:

(1)   To employ all lawful means to collect all property, dog, license, privilege, and franchise taxes with which he is charged by the governing body.

(2)   To give such bond as may be required of him by the governing body under the provisions of G.S. 105-349.

(3)   To perform such duties in connection with the preparation of the tax records and tax receipts as the governing body may direct under the provisions of G.S. 105-319 and 105-320.

(4)   To keep adequate records of all collections he makes.

(5)   To account for all moneys coming into his hands in such form and detail as may be required by the chief accounting officer of the taxing unit.

(6)   To make settlement at the times required by G.S. 105-373 and at any other time the governing body may require him to do so.

(7) To submit to the governing body at each of its regular meetings a report of the amount he has collected on each year's taxes with which he is charged, the amount remaining uncollected, and the steps he is taking to encourage or enforce payment of uncollected taxes.

(8) To send bills or notices of taxes due to taxpayers if instructed to do so by the governing body.

(9) To visit delinquent taxpayers to encourage payment of taxes if instructed to do so by the governing body. (1939, c. 310, s. 1703; 1971, c. 806, s. 1.)

§ 105-351. Authority of successor collector.

The successor in office of any tax collector may continue and complete any legally authorized process or proceeding begun by his predecessor for the collection of taxes. (1939, c. 310, s. 1703; 1971, c. 806, s. 1.)

§ 105-352. Delivery of tax receipts to tax collector; prerequisites; procedure upon default.

(a) Time of Delivery. - As provided in G.S. 105-321, upon order of the governing body, the tax receipts shall be delivered to the tax collector on or before the first day of September.

(b) Settlement, Bond, and Prepayments. - Before the tax receipts for the current year are delivered to the tax collector, he shall have:

(1) Delivered to the chief accounting officer of the taxing unit the duplicate receipts issued for prepayments received by the tax collector.

(2) Demonstrated to the satisfaction of the chief accounting officer that all moneys received by the tax collector as prepayments have been deposited to the credit of the taxing unit.

(3) Made his annual settlement (as defined in G.S. 105-373) for all taxes in his hands for collection.

(4) Provided bond or bonds as required by G.S. 105-349(c) for taxes for the current year and all prior years in his hands for collection. (In no event shall the governing body accept a bond of lesser amount than that prescribed by any local act applying to the taxing unit.)

In the event prepayments have been received by a person other than the regular tax collector, that person shall, before the tax receipts are delivered to the tax collector, deliver the prepayment receipt duplicates to the chief accounting officer and demonstrate to the satisfaction of that officer that all moneys received by him as prepayments have been deposited to the credit of the taxing unit. If the chief accounting officer has accepted prepayments, he shall not later than the day on which the tax receipts are delivered to the tax collector, make settlement with the governing body in such manner and form as the governing body may prescribe.

(c) Procedure upon Default. - If, when the tax receipts for the current year have been computed and prepared, the regular tax collector shall not have met the requirements of subsection (b), above, the governing body shall immediately appoint a special tax collector and, after he has given satisfactory bond for the full amount of the taxes as required by G.S. 105-349(c), deliver to him the tax receipts for the current year and order him to make collections as provided in G.S. 105-321. In the discretion of the governing body, the cost of the special tax collector's bond and compensation may be deducted from the compensation of the regular tax collector. If the regular tax collector shall thereafter meet the requirements of subsection (b), above, the special collector shall make full settlement (in the manner provided in G.S. 105-373 for tax collectors retiring from office), and the governing body, as provided in G.S. 105-321, shall deliver the tax receipts for the current year to the regular tax collector and order their collection.

(d) Civil and Criminal Penalties. -

(1) Any member of the governing body who shall vote to deliver the tax receipts to a tax collector before the tax collector has met the requirements prescribed by this section shall be individually liable for the amount of taxes charged against the tax collector for which he has not made satisfactory settlement; and any member of the governing body who so votes, or who willfully fails to perform any duty imposed by this section, shall be guilty of a Class 1 misdemeanor.

(2) Any tax collector or other official who fails to account for prepayments as prescribed by this section shall be guilty of a Class 1 misdemeanor. (1939, c. 310, s. 1707; 1971, c. 806, s. 1; 1993, c. 539, s. 722; 1994, Ex. Sess., c. 24, s. 14(c).)

§ 105-353. Place for collection of taxes.

Taxes shall be payable at the office of the tax collector or at a financial institution with which the taxing unit has contracted for receipt of payment of taxes. For the convenience of taxpayers, the governing body may require the tax collector to be present to collect taxes in person or by deputy at other designated places within the taxing unit at times prescribed by the governing body. If the governing body exercises this authority, the tax collector shall give timely notice of the places and times at which he will be present for collection; this notice shall be published in a newspaper having general circulation in the taxing unit and posted at three or more public places within the taxing unit. (1939, c. 310, s. 1712; 1971, c. 806, s. 1; 1989, c. 578, s. 2.)

§ 105-354. Collections for districts and other units of local government.

Whenever a taxing unit collects taxes for some district or other unit of local government, those taxes, for collection and foreclosure purposes, shall be treated as taxes of the taxing unit making the collection. (1971, c. 806, s. 1.)

§ 105-355. Creation of tax lien; date as of which lien attaches.

(a) Lien on Real Property. - Regardless of the time at which liability for a tax for a given fiscal year may arise or the exact amount thereof be determined, the lien for taxes levied on a parcel of real property shall attach to the parcel taxed on the date as of which property is to be listed under G.S. 105-285, and the lien for taxes levied on personal property shall attach to all real property of the taxpayer in the taxing unit on the same date. All penalties, interest, and costs allowed by law shall be added to the amount of the lien and shall be regarded as attaching at the same time as the lien for the principal amount of the taxes. For purposes of this subsection (a):

(1) Taxes levied on real property listed in the name of a life tenant under G.S. 105-302 (c)(8) shall be a lien on the fee as well as the life estate.

(2) Taxes levied on improvements on or separate rights in real property owned by one other than the owner of the land, whether or not listed separately from the land under G.S. 105-302 (c)(11), shall be a lien on both the improvements or rights and on the land.

(b) Lien on Personal Property. - Taxes levied on real and personal property (including penalties, interest, and costs allowed by law) shall be a lien on personal property from and after levy or attachment and garnishment of the personal property levied upon or attached. (1939, c. 310, s. 1704; 1971, c. 806, s. 1; 1973, c. 564, s. 4.)

§ 105-356. Priority of tax liens.

(a) On Real Property. - The lien of taxes imposed on real and personal property shall attach to real property at the time prescribed in G.S. 105-355(a). The priority of that lien shall be determined in accordance with the following rules:

(1) Subject to the provisions of the Revenue Act prescribing the priority of the lien for State taxes, the lien of taxes imposed under the provisions of this Subchapter shall be superior to all other liens, assessments, charges, rights, and claims of any and every kind in and to the real property to which the lien for taxes attaches regardless of the claimant and regardless of whether acquired prior or subsequent to the attachment of the lien for taxes.

(2) The liens of taxes of all taxing units shall be of equal dignity.

(3) The priority of the lien for taxes shall not be affected by transfer of title to the real property after the lien has attached, nor shall it be affected by the death, receivership, or bankruptcy of the owner of the real property to which the lien attaches.

(b) On Personal Property. - The lien of taxes on real and personal property shall attach to personal property at the time prescribed in G.S. 105-355(b). The priority of that lien shall be determined in accordance with the following rules:

(1) The tax lien, when it attaches to personal property, shall, insofar as it represents taxes imposed upon the property to which the lien attaches, be superior to all other liens and rights whether such other liens and rights are prior or subsequent to the tax lien in point of time.

(2) The tax lien, when it attaches to personal property, shall, insofar as it represents taxes imposed upon property other than that to which the lien attaches, be inferior to prior valid liens and perfected security interests and superior to all subsequent liens and security interests.

(3) As between the tax liens of different taxing units, the tax lien first attaching shall be superior. (1939, c. 310, s. 1704; 1971, c. 806, s. 1.)

§ 105-357. Payment of taxes.

(a) Medium of Payment. - Taxes shall be payable in existing national currency. Deeds to real property, notes of the taxpayer or others, bonds or notes of the taxing unit, and payments in kind shall not be accepted in payment of taxes. A taxing unit may not permit the payment of taxes by offset of any bill, claim, judgment, or other obligation owed to the taxpayer by the taxing unit. The prohibition against payment of taxes by offset does not apply to offset of an obligation arising from a lease or another contract entered into between the taxpayer and the taxing unit before July 1 of the fiscal year for which the unpaid taxes were levied.

(b) Acceptance of Checks and Electronic Payment. - The tax collector may accept checks and electronic payments, as defined in G.S. 147-86.20, in payment of taxes, as authorized by G.S. 159-32.1. Acceptance of a check or electronic payment is at the tax collector's own risk. A tax collector who accepts electronic payment of taxes may add a fee to each electronic payment transaction to offset the service charge the taxing unit pays for electronic payment service. A tax collector who accepts electronic payment or check in payment of taxes may issue the tax receipt immediately or withhold the receipt until the check has been collected or the electronic payment invoice has been honored by the issuer.

If a tax collector accepts a check or an electronic payment and issues a tax receipt and the check is returned unpaid (without negligence on the part of the tax collector in presenting the check for payment) or the electronic payment invoice is not honored by the issuer, the taxes for which the check or electronic payment was given shall be deemed unpaid; the tax collector shall immediately correct the copy of the tax receipt and other appropriate records to show the fact of nonpayment, and shall give written notice by certified or registered mail to the person to whom the tax receipt was issued to return it to the tax collector. After correcting the records to show the fact of nonpayment, the tax collector shall proceed to collect the taxes by the use of any remedies allowed for the collection of taxes or by bringing a civil action on the check or electronic payment.

A financial institution with which a taxing unit has contracted for receipt of payment of taxes may accept a check in payment of taxes. If the check is honored, the financial institution shall so notify the tax collector, who shall, upon request of the taxpayer, issue a receipt for payment of the taxes. If the check is returned unpaid, the financial institution shall so notify the tax collector, who shall proceed to collect the taxes by use of any remedy allowed for collection of taxes or by bringing a civil action on the check.

(1)   Effect on Tax Lien. - If the tax collector accepts a check or electronic payment in payment of taxes on real property and issues the receipt, and the check is later returned unpaid or the electronic payment invoice is not honored by the issuer, the taxing unit's lien for taxes on the real property shall be inferior to the rights of purchasers for value and of persons acquiring liens of record for value if the purchasers or lienholders acquire their rights in good faith and without actual knowledge that the check has not been collected or the electronic payment invoice has not been honored, after examination of the copy of the tax receipt in the tax collector's office during the time that record showed the taxes as paid or after examination of the official receipt issued to the taxpayer prior to the date on which the tax collector notified the taxpayer to return the receipt.

(2)   Penalty. - In addition to interest for nonpayment of taxes provided by G.S. 105-360 and in addition to any criminal penalties provided by law, the penalty for presenting in payment of taxes a check or electronic funds transfer that is returned or not completed because of insufficient funds or nonexistence of an account of the drawer or transferor is twenty-five dollars ($25.00) or ten percent (10%) of the amount of the check or electronic invoice, whichever is greater, subject to a maximum of one thousand dollars ($1,000). This penalty does not apply if the tax collector finds that, when the check or electronic funds transfer was presented for payment, the drawer of the check or transferor of funds had sufficient funds in an account at a financial institution in this State to make the payment and, by inadvertence, the drawer of the check or transferor

of the funds failed to draw the check or initiate a transfer on the account that had sufficient funds. This penalty shall be added to and collected in the same manner as the taxes for which the check or electronic payment was given.

(c) Small Underpayments and Overpayments. - The governing body of a taxing unit may, by resolution, permit its tax collector to treat small underpayments of taxes as fully paid and to not refund small overpayments of taxes unless the taxpayer requests a refund before the end of the fiscal year in which the small overpayment is made. A "small underpayment" is a payment made, other than in person, that is no more than one dollar ($1.00) less than the taxes due on a tax receipt. A "small overpayment" is a payment made, other than in person, that is no more than one dollar ($1.00) greater than the taxes due on a tax receipt.

The tax collector shall keep records of all underpayments and overpayments of taxes by receipt number and amount and shall report these payments to the governing body as part of his settlement.

A resolution authorizing adjustments of underpayments and overpayments as provided in this subsection shall:

(1) Be adopted on or before June 15 of the year to which it is to apply;

(2) Apply to taxes levied for all previous fiscal years; and

(3) Continue in effect until repealed or amended by resolution of the taxing unit. (1939, c. 310, s. 1710; 1971, c. 806, s. 1; 1987, c. 661; 1989, c. 578, s. 3; 1989 (Reg. Sess., 1990), c. 1005, s. 8; 1991, c. 584, s. 2; 1999-434, s. 6; 2001-487, s. 25; 2002-156, s. 1; 2005-134, s. 1; 2005-313, s. 10.)

§ 105-358. Waiver of penalties; partial payments.

(a) Waiver. - A tax collector may, upon making a record of the reasons therefor, reduce or waive the penalty imposed on giving a worthless check under G.S. 105-357(b)(2).

(b) Partial Payments. - Unless otherwise directed by the governing body, the tax collector shall accept partial payments on taxes and issue partial payment receipts therefor.

When a payment is made on the tax for any year or on any installment, it shall first be applied to accrued penalties, interest, and costs and then to the principal amount of the tax or installment. In its discretion, the governing body may prescribe by uniform regulation the minimum amount or percentage of tax liability that may be accepted as a partial payment. (1939, c. 310, ss. 1708, 1709; 1971, c. 806, s. 1; 2002-156, s. 1.2; 2003-416, s. 10.)

§ 105-359. Prepayments.

(a) To Whom Made. - Payments of taxes made before the tax receipts have been delivered to the tax collector, herein referred to as prepayments, shall be made to the regular tax collector unless the governing body shall have designated some other person to receive them. The regular tax collector or person named to receive prepayments shall give bond satisfactory to the governing body.

(b) When Accepted. - No taxing unit shall be required to accept any tender of prepayment until the annual budget estimate has been filed as required by law.

(c) Estimation of Liability; Overpayment and Underpayment. - If the tax rate has not been finally fixed or if the assessed valuation of the taxpayer's property has not been finally determined at the time a prepayment is tendered, the tax collector shall compute the amount of the tax liability on the basis of the best information available to him. If it is later ascertained that there has been an overpayment, the excess (without interest) shall be refunded by the taxing unit. If it is later ascertained that there was an underpayment, the unpaid balance of the tax shall be due, and the balance due shall be allowed the discount or charged the interest in effect with respect to taxes for the same year at the time the balance is paid.

(d) Receipts. - A receipt issued for a prepayment made on the basis of an estimate of the tax rate or assessed valuation shall so state, and such a receipt shall not release property from the tax lien created by G.S. 105-355(a). An official and final receipt shall be made available to the taxpayer as soon as possible after determination that the tax has been fully paid.

(e) Duties of Chief Accounting Officer. - It shall be the duty of the chief accounting officer of the taxing unit to:

(1)   Secure and retain in his office, available to taxpayers upon request, the official receipts for taxes paid in full by prepayment.

(2)   Credit on the tax receipts to be delivered to the tax collector all taxes that have been paid in full or in part by prepayment.

(3)   Prepare and deliver refunds for overpayments made by way of prepayment.

(4)   Reduce the charge to be made against the tax collector by deducting from the total amount of taxes levied so much of the amount received as prepayments as is not required to be refunded under the provisions of subsection (c), above.

Any chief accounting officer who fails to perform the duties imposed upon him by this subsection (e) shall be guilty of a Class 1 misdemeanor. (1939, c. 310, ss. 1706, 1707; 1969, c. 921, s. 2; 1971, c. 806, s. 1; 1993, c. 539, s. 723; 1994, Ex. Sess., c. 24, s. 14(c).)

§ 105-360. Due date; interest for nonpayment of taxes; discounts for prepayment; interest on overpayment of tax.

(a)   Taxes levied under this Subchapter by a taxing unit are due and payable on September 1 of the fiscal year for which the taxes are levied. Taxes are payable at par or face amount if paid before January 6 following the due date. Taxes paid on or after January 6 following the due date are subject to interest charges. Interest accrues on taxes paid on or after January 6 as follows:

(1)   For the period January 6 to February 1, interest accrues at the rate of two percent (2%).

(2)   For the period February 1 until the principal amount of the taxes, the accrued interest, and any penalties are paid, interest accrues at the rate of three-fourths of one percent (3/4%) a month or fraction thereof.

(b)   Repealed by Session Laws 1987, c. 93, s. 2.

(c)   Under the conditions established by this subsection (c), the governing body of any county or municipality levying taxes under the provisions of this

Subchapter shall have authority to establish a schedule of discounts to be applied to taxes paid prior to the due date prescribed in subsection (a) above. To exercise this authority, the governing body shall:

(1) Not later than the first day of May preceding the due date of the taxes to which it first applies, adopt a resolution or ordinance specifying the amounts of the discounts and the periods of time during which they are to be applicable.

(2) Submit the resolution or ordinance to the Department of Revenue for approval.

(3) Upon approval by the Department of Revenue, publish the discount schedule at least once in some newspaper having general circulation in the taxing unit.

When such a resolution or ordinance is submitted to the Department of Revenue, the Department may approve it or disapprove it in whole or in part if, in the opinion of the Department, the discounts or the periods of time for which discounts are allowed are excessive or unreasonable. Such a resolution or ordinance, once adopted and approved by the Department of Revenue, shall continue in effect until repealed. Nothing in this subsection (c) shall prevent the governing body of any taxing unit from providing by resolution that the schedule of discounts for prepayment of taxes in effect in the taxing unit on June 30, 1971, shall continue in effect through November 1, 1971, but no longer.

(d) For the purposes of computing discounts and interest, tax payments submitted by mail shall be deemed to be received as of the date shown on the postmark affixed by the United States Postal Service. If no date is shown on the postmark or if the postmark is not affixed by the United States Postal Service, the tax payment shall be deemed to be received when the payment is received in the office of the tax collector. In any dispute arising under this subsection, the burden of proof shall be on the taxpayer to show that the payment was timely made.

(e) (Effective for taxable years beginning on or after January 1, 2011) When an order of the county board of equalization and review reduces the valuation of property or removes the property from the tax lists and, based on the order, the taxpayer has paid more tax than is due on the property, the taxpayer is entitled to receive interest on the overpayment in accordance with this subdivision. An overpayment of tax bears interest at the rate set under subsection (a) of this section from the date the interest begins to accrue until a refund is paid. Interest accrues from the later of the date the tax was paid and the date the tax would have been considered delinquent under G.S. 105-360. A refund is considered paid on a date determined by the governing body of the taxing unit that is no sooner than five days after a refund check is mailed. (1939, c. 310, s. 1403; 1943, c. 667; 1945, c. 247, s. 3; c. 1041; 1947, c. 888, s. 1; 1969, c. 921, s. 1; 1971, c. 806, s. 1; 1973, c. 476, s. 193; 1977, c. 327, s. 2; c. 630; 1979, c. 233, ss. 1, 2; 1987, c. 93, ss. 1, 2; 2008-35, s. 2.7; 2011-3, s. 3(a).)

§ 105-361. Statement of amount of taxes due.

(a)   Duty to Furnish a Certificate. - On the request of a person who is listed in subdivision (1) of this subsection and who complies with subdivision (2) of this subsection, the tax collector must give the person a written certificate stating the amount of any taxes and special assessments owed for the current year and for any prior year and the amount of any deferred taxes and interest that would become due if a disqualifying event occurred.

(1)   Who may make request. - Any of the following persons may request the certificate:

a.   An owner of the real property.

b.   An occupant of the real property.

c.   A person having a lien on the real property.

d.   A person having a legal interest or estate in the real property.

e.   A person or firm having a contract to purchase or lease the property or a person or firm having contracted to make a loan secured by the real property.

f.   The authorized agent or attorney of any person described in this subdivision.

(2)   Identification of property. - A person requesting a certificate with respect to taxes must specify the name of the person who listed the real property for taxation for each year for which the information is sought. A person requesting a certificate with respect to assessments must identify the real estate in the manner required by the tax collector.

(b) Reliance on the Certificate. - When a certificate has been issued as provided in subsection (a), above, all taxes and special assessments that have accrued against the property for the period covered by the certificate shall cease to be a lien against the property, except to the extent of taxes and special assessments stated to be due in the certificate, as to all persons, firms, and corporations obtaining such a certificate and their successors in interest who rely on the certificate:

(1) By paying the amount of taxes and assessments stated therein to be a lien on the real property;

(2) By purchasing or leasing the real property; or

(3) By lending money secured by the real property.

The tax collector shall be liable on his bond for any loss to the taxing unit arising from an understatement of the tax and special assessment obligations in the preparation of a certificate furnished under this section.

(c) Penalty. - Any tax collector who fails or refuses to furnish a certificate when requested under the conditions prescribed in this section shall be liable for a penalty of fifty dollars ($50.00) recoverable in a civil action by the person who made the request.

(d) Oral Statements. - An oral statement made by the tax collector as to the amount of taxes, special assessments, penalties, interest, and costs due on any real or personal property shall bind neither the tax collector nor the taxing unit.

(e) Internet. - If the taxing unit maintains an Internet web site on which current information on the amount of taxes, special assessments, penalties, interest, and costs due on any real or personal property is available, the governing body of the taxing unit may adopt an ordinance to allow a person to rely on information obtained from the web site as if it were a certificate issued pursuant to subsection (a) of this section. The ordinance may provide for disclaimers to be posted on the web site containing language notifying the person relying on the information contained in the web site about matters relevant to the information, such as the date on which the information was posted, the date as of which the information is current, and any special instructions and procedures for accessing the complete and accurate information. The ordinance may also provide for appropriate procedural provisions by which the tax collector may ensure full and accurate payment of all taxes, assessments, and obligations certified under this subsection.

A person who relies on the web site information must keep and present a copy of the information as necessary or appropriate, as if the copy were a certificate issued under subsection (a) of this section. The tax collector shall be liable on the tax collector's bond for any loss to the taxing unit arising from an understatement of the tax and special assessment obligations contained in the information available on the web site unless the taxing unit's ordinance provides the disclaimers authorized by this subsection. (1939, c. 310, s. 1711; 1971, c. 806, s. 1; 1973, c. 604; c. 1340; 2003-399, s. 1; 2009-445, s. 26.)

§ 105-362. Discharge of lien on real property.

(a) General Rule. - The tax lien on real property shall continue until the principal amount of the taxes plus penalties, interest, and costs allowed by law have been fully paid.

(b) Release of Separate Parcels from Tax Lien. -

(1) When the lien of taxes of any taxing unit for any year attaches to two or more parcels of real property owned by the same taxpayer, the lien may be discharged as to any parcel at any time prior to advertisement of tax foreclosure sale in accordance with either subdivision (b)(1)a or subdivision (b)(1)b:

a. Upon payment, by or on behalf of the listing taxpayer, of the taxes for the year on the parcel or parcels to be released, of the taxes for the year on the parcel or parcels to be released, plus all personal property taxes owed by the listing taxpayer for the same year.

b. Upon payment, by or on behalf of any person (other than the listing taxpayer) who has a legal interest in the parcel or parcels to be released, of the taxes for the year on the parcel or parcels to be released, plus a proportionate part of personal property taxes owed by the listing taxpayer for the same year. The proportionate part shall be a percentage of the personal property taxes equal to the percentage of the total assessed valuation of the taxpayer's real property in the taxing unit represented by the assessed valuation of the parcel or parcels to be released.

(2)   When real property listed as one parcel is divided, a part thereof may be released as provided in subdivision (b)(1), above, after the assessed valuation of the part to be released has been determined and certified to the tax collector by the tax supervisor.

(3)   It shall be the duty of the tax collector accepting a payment made under this subsection (b) for the purpose of releasing the tax lien from less than all of the taxpayer's real property:

a.   To give the person making the payment a receipt setting forth a description of the real property released from the tax lien and bearing a statement that such property is being released from the tax lien.

b.   To indicate on the tax receipts, tax records, and other official records of his office what real property has been released from the tax lien.

If the tax collector fails to issue the receipt or make the record entries required by this subdivision (3), the omission may be supplied at any time.

(4)   When any parcel of real property has been released under the provisions of this subsection (b) from the lien of taxes of any taxing unit for any year, the property shall not thereafter be subject to the lien of any other regularly levied taxes of the same taxing unit for the same year, whether such other taxes be levied against the listing owner of the property or against some other person acquiring title thereto. No tax foreclosure judgment for such other taxes shall become a lien on the released property; and, upon appropriate request and satisfactory proof of the release by any interested person, the clerk of the superior court shall indicate on the judgment docket that the judgment is not a lien on the released property. However, the failure to make such an entry shall not have the effect of making the judgment a lien on the released property. (1939, c. 310, s. 1704; 1971, c. 806, s. 1.)

§ 105-363. Remedies of cotenants and joint owners of real property.

(a)   Payment of Taxes on Share of One Cotenant. - Any one of several tenants in common or joint tenants (other than copartners) of real property may pay that portion of the taxes, interest, and costs that are a lien upon his undivided share of the property and thereby release the tax lien from his share. Thereafter, in any partition sale of the property the share of the joint owner who has paid his portion of the taxes shall be set apart free from the tax lien, and his share of the proceeds of any sale shall not be diminished by disbursements to pay any taxes, interest, or costs. In the event the tax lien is foreclosed and the property is sold for failure to pay taxes, the share of any joint owner who has paid his portion of the taxes shall be excepted from the advertisement and sale.

(b) Payment of Entire Amount of Taxes by One Cotenant. - Any one of several tenants in common or joint tenants (other than copartners) of real property may pay the entire amount of the taxes, interest, and costs constituting a lien on the property, and any amount so paid that is in excess of his share of the taxes, interest, and costs and that was not paid through agreement with or on behalf of the other joint owners shall constitute a lien in his favor upon the shares of the other joint owners. Such a lien may be enforced in a proceeding for actual partition, a proceeding for partition and sale, or by any other appropriate judicial proceeding. (1901, c. 558, ss. 13, 14, 47; Rev., s. 2860; C.S., s. 7983; 1971, c. 806, s. 1.)

§ 105-364. Collection of taxes outside the taxing unit.

(a) Duty of Governing Body. - It shall be the duty of the governing body of each taxing unit to require reports from the tax collector at such times as it may prescribe (but not less frequently than in connection with the tax collector's annual settlement) concerning the efforts he has made to locate taxpayers who have removed from the taxing unit, the efforts he has made to locate personal property in other taxing units belonging to delinquent taxpayers, and the efforts he has made under the provisions of this section to collect taxes.

(b) Duty to Certify Unpaid Taxes. - If a taxpayer has no personal property or real property subject to the tax lien in the taxing unit but does have personal property in some other taxing unit in this State, or if a taxpayer has removed from the taxing unit, leaving no personal property or real property subject to the tax lien there, and is known to be in some other taxing unit in this State, the tax collector shall forward the tax receipt (with a certificate stating that the taxes are unpaid) for collection to the tax collector of the taxing unit in which the taxpayer is known to have personal property or in which he is known to be. The tax collector may not, however, certify an unpaid tax receipt to another taxing unit if 10 years have elapsed since the date the unpaid taxes became due.

(c) Effect of Certificate; Duty of Receiving Tax Collector. - In the hands of the tax collector receiving them, the copy of the tax receipt and the certificate of nonpayment shall have the force and effect of an unpaid tax receipt of his own taxing unit, and it shall be the receiving tax collector's duty to proceed immediately to collect the taxes by any means by which he could lawfully collect taxes of his own taxing unit. Within 30 days after receiving such a tax receipt and certificate, the collector receiving them shall report to the tax collector that sent them that he has collected the tax, that he has begun proceedings to collect the tax, or that he is unable to collect it. If the tax collector reports that he has begun proceedings to collect the tax, he shall, not later than 90 days after so reporting, make a final report to the tax collector who certified the tax receipt stating that he has collected the tax or that he is unable to collect it.

(1) In acting on a tax receipt and certificate under the provisions of this section, the tax collector receiving them shall, in addition to collecting the amount of taxes certified as due, also impose a fee equal to ten percent (10%) of the amount of taxes certified as unpaid, to be paid into the general fund of his taxing unit.

(2) Within five days after making a collection under the provisions of this section, the tax collector receiving the tax receipt and certificate shall remit the funds collected, less the fee provided for in subdivision (c)(1), above, to the tax collector of the taxing unit that levied the tax.

(3) If the tax collector receiving the tax receipt and certificate reports that he is unable to collect the tax, he shall make his report under oath and shall state therein that he has used due diligence and is unable to collect the tax by levy, attachment and garnishment, or any other legal means.

(d) Liability on Bond. - A tax collector who receives a tax receipt and certificate from the tax collector of another taxing unit under the provisions of subsection (b), above, shall be liable on his bond to the taxing unit that levied the tax for the amount of the taxes certified if:

(1) The tax collector receiving the certified tax receipt fails to make any report to the certifying tax collector within 30 days after receiving the certified tax receipt.

(2) The tax collector receiving the certified tax receipt fails to swear to any report stating that he is unable to collect the certified tax.

(3) Having reported that he has begun proceedings to collect a certified tax, the tax collector receiving the certified tax receipt fails to make a final report within 90 days after reporting that he has begun proceedings for collection. (1939, c. 310, s. 1714; 1955, c. 909; 1963, c. 132; 1971, c. 806, s. 1; 1973, c. 231.)

§ 105-365. Preference accorded taxes in liquidation of debtors' estates.

In all cases in which a taxpayer's assets are in the hands of a receiver or assignee for the benefit of creditors or are otherwise being liquidated or managed for the benefit of creditors, the taxes owed by the debtor (together with interest, penalties, and costs) shall be a preferred claim, second only to administration expenses and specific liens. The provisions of this section shall not be construed to modify or reduce the priority given by G.S. 105-356 to tax liens on real and personal property or to alter or preclude the exercise of any remedies against personal property provided for in G.S. 105-366. (1939, c. 310, s. 1704; 1971, c. 806, s. 1.)

§ 105-365.1. When and against whom collection remedies may be used.

(a) Date of Delinquency. - A tax collector may collect a tax using the remedies provided in G.S. 105-366 through G.S. 105-375 on or after the date the tax is delinquent. A tax is delinquent on the following date:

(1) For a tax that is not a deferred tax, the date the tax accrues interest.

(2) For a deferred tax, other than a tax described in subdivision (3) of this subsection, the date a disqualifying event occurs.

(3) For a deferred tax under G.S. 105-277.1B that lost its eligibility for deferral due to the death of the owner, the first day of the ninth month following the date of death.

(b) Enforced Collection. - For purposes of using the collection remedies provided in G.S. 105-366 through G.S. 105-375 to collect delinquent taxes, the taxing unit shall proceed against property of the following taxpayer:

(1) To collect delinquent taxes assessed on real property, the owner of record of property on which tax is due as of the date of delinquency and any subsequent owner of record of the property.

(2) To collect delinquent taxes assessed on personal property, the owner of record as of January 1 of the calendar year in which the fiscal year of taxation begins.

(3) To collect delinquent taxes assessed on a registered motor vehicle, the owner of record as of the date on which the current vehicle registration is renewed or the date on which a new registration is applied for. (2008-35, s. 2.8.)

§ 105-366. Remedies against personal property.

(a) Authority to Proceed against Personal Property; Relation between Remedies against Personal Property and Remedies against Real Property. - All tax collectors shall have authority to proceed against personal property to enforce the collection of taxes as provided in this section and in G.S. 105-367 and 105-368. Any tax collector may, in his discretion, proceed first against personal property before employing the remedies for enforcing the lien for taxes against real property, and he shall proceed first against personal property:

(1) When directed to do so by the governing body of the taxing unit; or

(2) When requested to do so by the taxpayer or by a mortgagee or other person holding a lien upon the real property subject to the lien for taxes if the person making the request furnishes the tax collector with a written statement describing the personal property to be proceeded against and giving its location.

No foreclosure of a tax lien on real property may be attacked as invalid on the ground that payment of the tax should have been procured from personal property.

(b) Remedies after Taxes Are Delinquent. - At any time after taxes are delinquent and before the filing of a tax foreclosure complaint under G.S. 105-374 or the docketing of a judgment for taxes under G.S. 105-375, and subject to the provisions of G.S. 105-356 governing the priority of liens, the tax collector may levy upon and sell or attach the following property for failure to pay taxes:

(1) Any personal property owned by the taxpayer, regardless of the time at which it was acquired and regardless of the existence or date of creation of mortgages or other liens thereon.

(2) Any personal property transferred by the taxpayer to a relative (which shall mean any parent, grandparent, child, grandchild, brother, sister, aunt, uncle, niece, or nephew, or their spouses, of the taxpayer or his spouse).

(3) Personal property in the hands of a receiver for the taxpayer. (It shall not be necessary for the tax collector to apply for an order of the court directing payment or authorizing the levy or attachment, but he may proceed as though the property were not in the hands of the receiver, and the tax collector's filing of a claim in a receivership proceeding shall not preclude him from proceeding to levy under G.S. 105-367 or to attach under G.S. 105-368.)

(4) Personal property of a deceased taxpayer if the levy or attachment is made before final settlement of the estate.

(5) The stock of goods or fixtures of a wholesale merchant or retailer, as defined in G.S. 105-164.3, in the hands of a purchaser or transferee thereof, or any other personal property of the purchaser or transferee of the property, if the taxes on the goods or fixtures remain unpaid 30 days after the date of the sale or transfer. In the case of other personal property of the purchaser or transferee, the levy or attachment must be made within six months of the sale or transfer.

(6) Personal property of the taxpayer that has been repossessed by one having a security interest therein so long as the property remains in the hands of the person who has repossessed it or the person to whom it has been transferred other than by bona fide sale for value.

(7) Personal property due the taxpayer or to become due to him within the calendar year.

(8) Personal property of a partner in satisfaction of taxes on partnership property, but only after the tax collector:

a. Has sold the taxing unit's lien for taxes against the partnership real property, if any; and

b. Exhausted the partnership's personal property through the use of levy and attachment and garnishment; and

c. Exercised the authority granted him by G.S. 105-364 in an effort to collect the tax due on the partnership's property.

(9) Personal property transferred by the taxpayer by any type of transfer other than those mentioned in this subsection (b) and other than by bona fide sale for value if the levy or attachment is made within six months of the transfer.

(c) Remedies Before Taxes Are Delinquent. - If between the date as of which property is to be listed and January 6 of the fiscal year for which the taxes are imposed the tax collector has reasonable grounds for believing that the taxpayer is about to remove his property from the taxing unit or transfer it to another person or is in imminent danger of becoming insolvent, the tax collector may levy on or attach that property or any other personal property of the taxpayer, in the manner provided in G.S. 105-367 and 105-368. If the amount of taxes collected under this subsection has not yet been determined, these taxes shall be computed in accordance with G.S. 105-359 and any applicable discount shall be allowed.

(d) Remedies against Sellers and Purchasers of Stocks of Goods or Fixtures of Wholesale Merchants or Retailers. -

(1) Any wholesale merchant or retailer, as defined in G.S. 105-164.3, who sells or transfers the major part of its stock of goods, materials, supplies, or fixtures, other than in the ordinary course of business, or who goes out of business, must take the following actions:

a. At least 48 hours prior to the date of the pending sale, transfer, or termination of business, give notice to the assessors and tax collectors of the taxing units in which the business is located.

b. Within 30 days of the sale, transfer, or termination of business, pay all taxes due or to become due on the transferred property on the first day of September of the current calendar year.

(2) Any person to whom the major part of the stock of goods, materials, supplies, or fixtures of a wholesale merchant or retailer is sold or transferred, other than in the ordinary course of business, or who becomes the successor in business of a wholesale merchant or retailer shall withhold from the purchase money paid to the merchant an amount sufficient to pay the taxes due or to become due on the transferred property on the first day of September of the current calendar year until the former owner or seller produces either a receipt

from the tax collector showing that the taxes have been paid or a certificate that no taxes are due. If the purchaser or successor in business fails to withhold a sufficient amount of the purchase money to pay the taxes as required by this subsection and the taxes remain unpaid after the 30-day period allowed, the purchaser or successor is personally liable for the amount of the taxes unpaid. This liability may be enforced by means of a civil action brought in the name of the taxing unit against the purchaser or successor in an appropriate trial division of the General Court of Justice in the county in which the taxing unit is located.

(3)   Whenever any wholesale merchant or retailer sells or transfers the major part of its stock of goods, materials, supplies, or fixtures, other than in the ordinary course of business, or goes out of business and the taxes due or to become due on the transferred property on the first day of September of the current calendar year are unpaid, the tax collector, to enforce collection of the unpaid taxes, may do any of the following:

a.   Levy on or attach any personal property of the seller.

b.   If the taxes remain unpaid 30 days after the date of the transfer or termination of business, levy on or attach any of the property transferred in the hands of the transferee or successor in business, or any other personal property of the transferee or successor in business, but in either case the levy or attachment must be made within six months of the transfer or termination of business.

(4)   In using the remedies provided in this subsection, the amount of taxes not yet determined shall be computed in accordance with G.S. 105-359, and any applicable discount shall be allowed. (1939, c. 310, s. 1713; 1951, c. 1141, s. 1; 1955, cc. 1263, 1264; 1957, c. 1414, ss. 2-4; 1969, c. 305, c. 1029, s. 1; 1971, c. 806, s. 1; 1973, c. 564, s. 1; 1987, c. 45, s. 1; c. 93, s. 3; 1998-98, ss. 112, 113.)

§ 105-367. Procedure for levy.

(a)   The levy upon the sale of tangible personal property for tax collection purposes (including levy and sale fees) shall be governed by the laws regulating levy and sale under execution except as otherwise provided in this section.

(b) The tax collector or any duly appointed deputy tax collector shall make the levy and conduct the sale; it shall not be necessary for the sheriff to make the levy or conduct the sale. However, upon the authorization of the governing body of the taxing unit, the tax collector may direct an execution against personal property for taxes to the sheriff in the case of county or municipal taxes or to a municipal policeman in the case of municipal taxes. In either case the officer to whom the execution is directed shall proceed to levy on and sell the personal property subject to levy in the manner and with the powers and authority normally exercised by sheriffs in levying upon and selling personal property under execution.

(c) In addition to the notice of sale required by the laws governing sale of property levied upon under execution, the tax collector may advertise the sale in any reasonable manner and for any reasonable period of time he deems necessary to produce an adequate bid for the property. The taxing unit shall advance the cost of all advertising.

(d) Levy and sale fees, plus actual advertising costs, shall be added to and collected in the same manner as taxes. The advertising costs, when collected, shall be used to reimburse the taxing unit for advertising costs it has advanced. Levy and sale fees, when collected, shall be treated in the same manner as other fees received by the collecting official. (1939, c. 310, s. 1713; 1951, c. 1141, s. 1; 1955, cc. 1263, 1264; 1957, c. 1414, ss. 2-4; 1969, c. 305; c. 1029, s. 1; 1971, c. 806, s. 1.)

§ 105-368. Procedure for attachment and garnishment.

(a) Subject to the provisions of G.S. 105-356 governing the priority of the lien acquired, the tax collector may attach wages and other compensation, rents, bank deposits, the proceeds of property subject to levy, or any other intangible personal property, including property held in the Escheat Fund, in the circumstances and to the extent prescribed in G.S. 105-366(b), (c), and (d).

In the case of property due the taxpayer or to become due to him within the current calendar year, the person owing the property to the taxpayer or having the property in his possession shall be liable for the taxes to the extent of the amount he owes or has in his possession. However, when wages or other compensation for personal services is attached, the garnishee shall not pay to the tax collector more than ten percent (10%) of such compensation for any one pay period.

(b)   To proceed under this section, the tax collector shall serve or cause to be served upon the taxpayer and the person owing or having in his possession the wages, rents, debts or other property sought to be attached a notice as provided by this subsection. The notice may be personally served by any deputy or employee of the tax collector or by any officer having authority to serve summonses, or may be served in any manner provided in Rule 4 of the North Carolina Rules of Civil Procedure. The notice shall contain:

(1)   The name of the taxpayer, and if known his Social Security number or federal tax identification number and his address.

(2)   The amount of the taxes, penalties, interest, and costs (including the fees allowed by this section) and the year or years for which the taxes were imposed.

(3)   The name of the taxing unit or units by which the taxes were levied.

(4)   A brief description of the property sought to be attached.

(5)   A copy of the applicable law, that is, G.S. 105-366 and 105-368. Notices concerning two or more taxpayers may be combined if they are to be served upon the same garnishee, but the taxes, penalties, interest, and costs charged against each taxpayer must be set forth separately.

(c)   If the garnishee has no defense to offer or no setoff against the taxpayer, he shall within 10 days after service of the notice answer it by sending to the tax collector by registered or certified mail a statement to that effect, and if the amount demanded by the tax collector is then due to the taxpayer or subject to his demand, the garnishee shall remit it to the tax collector with his statement; but if the amount due to the taxpayer or subject to his demand is to mature in the future, the garnishee's statement shall set forth that fact, and the demand shall be paid to the tax collector upon maturity. Any payment by the garnishee under the provisions of this subsection (c) shall completely satisfy any liability therefor on his part to the taxpayer.

(d)   If the garnishee has a defense or setoff against the taxpayer, he shall state it in writing under oath, and, within 10 days after service of the garnishment notice, he shall send two copies of his statement to the tax collector by registered or certified mail. If the tax collector admits the defense or setoff, he shall so advise the garnishee in writing within 10 days after receipt of the garnishee's statement, and the attachment or garnishment shall thereupon be discharged to the amount required by the defense or setoff, and any amount attached or garnished which is not affected by the defense or setoff shall be remitted to the tax collector as provided in subsection (c), above.

If the tax collector does not admit the defense or setoff, he shall set forth in writing his objections thereto and send a copy thereof to the garnishee within 10 days after receipt of the garnishee's statement, or within such further time as may be agreed on by the garnishee, and at the same time the tax collector shall file a copy of the notice of garnishment, a copy of the garnishee's statement, and a copy of the tax collector's objections thereto in the appropriate division of the General Court of Justice of the county in which the garnishee resides or does business, where the issues made shall be tried as in civil actions.

(e) If the garnishee has not responded to the notice of garnishment as required by subsections (c) and (d), above, within 15 days after service of the notice, the tax collector may file in the appropriate division of the General Court of Justice of the county in which the garnishee resides a copy of the notice of garnishment, accompanied by a written statement that the garnishee has not responded thereto and a request for judgment, and the issues shall be tried as in civil actions.

(f) The taxpayer may raise any defenses to the attachment or garnishment that he may have in the manner provided in subsection (d), above, for the garnishee.

(g) The fee for serving a notice of garnishment shall be the same as that charged in a civil action. If judgment is entered in favor of the taxing unit by default or after hearing, the garnishee shall become liable for the taxes, penalties, and interest due by the taxpayer, plus the fees and costs of the action, but payment shall not be required from amounts which are not to become due to the taxpayer until they actually come due. The garnishee may satisfy the judgment upon paying the amount thereof, and if he fails to do so, execution may issue as provided by law. From any judgment or order entered, either the taxing unit or the garnishee may appeal as provided by law. If, before or after judgment, adequate security is filed for the payment of the taxes, penalties, interest, and costs, the tax collector may release the attachment or garnishment, or execution may be stayed at the request of the tax collector pending appeal, but the final judgment shall be paid or enforced as above provided. If judgment is rendered against the taxing unit, it shall pay the fees and costs of the action. All fees collected by officers shall be disposed of in the same manner as other fees collected by such officers.

(h) Tax collectors may proceed against the wages, salary, or other compensation of officials and employees of this State and its agencies, instrumentalities, and political subdivisions in the manner provided in this section. If the taxpayer is an employee of the State, the notice of attachment shall be served upon him and upon the head or chief fiscal officer of the department, agency, instrumentality, or institution by which he is employed. If the taxpayer is an employee of a political subdivision of the State (county, municipality, etc.), the notice of attachment shall be served upon him and upon the officer charged with making up the payrolls of the political subdivision by which he is employed. All deductions from the wages or salary of a taxpayer made pursuant to this subsection (h) and remitted to the tax collector shall, pro tanto, constitute a satisfaction of the salary or wages due the taxpayer.

(i) (1) Any person who, after written demand therefor, refuses to give the tax collector or assessor a list of the names and addresses of all of his employees who may be liable for taxes, shall be guilty of a Class 1 misdemeanor.

(2) Any tax collector or assessor who receives, upon his written demand, any list of employees may not release or furnish that list or any copy thereof, or disclose any name or information thereon, to any other person, and may not use that list in any manner or for any purpose not directly related to and in furtherance of the collection and foreclosure of taxes. Any tax collector or assessor who violates or allows the violation of this subdivision (i)(2) shall be guilty of a Class 1 misdemeanor. (1939, c. 310, s. 1713; 1951, c. 1141, s. 1; 1955, cc. 1263, 1264; 1957, c. 1414, ss. 2-4; 1969, c. 305, c. 1029, s. 1; 1971, c. 806, s. 1; 1979, c. 103, ss. 3, 4; 1979, 2nd Sess., c. 1085, s. 2; 1981, c. 76, s. 1; 1987, c. 45, s. 1; 1989, c. 580, s. 2; 1993, c. 539, s. 724; 1994, Ex. Sess., c. 24, s. 14(c).)

§ 105-369. Advertisement of tax liens on real property for failure to pay taxes.

(a) Report of Unpaid Taxes That Are Liens on Real Property. - In February of each year, the tax collector must report to the governing body the total amount of unpaid taxes for the current fiscal year that are liens on real property.

A county tax collector's report is due the first Monday in February, and a municipal tax collector's report is due the second Monday in February. Upon receipt of the report, the governing body must order the tax collector to advertise the tax liens. For purposes of this section, district taxes collected by county tax collectors shall be regarded as county taxes and district taxes collected by municipal tax collectors shall be regarded as municipal taxes.

(b)   Repealed by Session Laws 1983 (Regular Session, 1984), c. 1013.

(b1)   Notice to Owner. - After the governing body orders the tax collector to advertise the tax liens, the tax collector must send a notice to the record owner of each affected parcel of property, as determined as of the date the taxes became delinquent. The notice must be sent to the owner's last known address by first-class mail at least 30 days before the date the advertisement is to be published. The notice must state the principal amount of unpaid taxes that are a lien on the parcel to be advertised and inform the owner that the name of the record owner as of the date the taxes became delinquent will appear in a newspaper advertisement of delinquent taxes if the taxes are not paid before the publication date. Failure to mail the notice required by this section to the correct record owner does not affect the validity of the tax lien or of any foreclosure action.

(c)   Time and Contents of Advertisement. - A tax collector's failure to comply with this subsection does not affect the validity of the taxes or tax liens. The county tax collector shall advertise county tax liens by posting a notice of the liens at the county courthouse and by publishing each lien at least one time in one or more newspapers having general circulation in the taxing unit. The municipal tax collector shall advertise municipal tax liens by posting a notice of the liens at the city or town hall and by publishing each lien at least one time in one or more newspapers having general circulation in the taxing unit. Advertisements of tax liens shall be made during the period March 1 through June 30. The costs of newspaper advertising shall be paid by the taxing unit. If the taxes of two or more taxing units are collected by the same tax collector, the tax liens of each unit shall be advertised separately unless, under the provisions of a special act or contractual agreement between the taxing units, joint advertisement is permitted.

The posted notice and newspaper advertisement shall set forth the following information:

(1) Repealed by Session Laws 2006-106, s. 2, effective for taxes imposed for taxable years beginning on or after July 1, 2006.

(1a) The name of the record owner as of the date the taxes became delinquent for each parcel on which the taxing unit has a lien for unpaid taxes, in alphabetical order.

(1b) After the information required by subdivision (1a) of this subsection for each parcel, a brief description of each parcel of land to which a lien has attached and a statement of the principal amount of the taxes constituting a lien against the parcel.

(2) A statement that the amounts advertised will be increased by interest and costs and that the omission of interest and costs from the amounts advertised will not constitute waiver of the taxing unit's claim for those items.

(3) In the event the list of tax liens has been divided for purposes of advertisement in more than one newspaper, a statement of the names of all newspapers in which advertisements will appear and the dates on which they will be published.

(4) A statement that the taxing unit may foreclose the tax liens and sell the real property subject to the liens in satisfaction of its claim for taxes.

(d) Costs. - Each parcel of real property advertised pursuant to this section shall be assessed an advertising fee to cover the actual cost of the advertisement. Actual advertising costs per parcel shall be determined by the tax collector on any reasonable basis. Advertising costs assessed pursuant to this subsection are taxes.

(e) Payments during Advertising Period. - At any time during the advertisement period, any parcel may be withdrawn from the list by payment of the taxes plus interest that has accrued to the time of payment and a proportionate part of the advertising fee to be determined by the tax collector. Thereafter, the tax collector shall delete that parcel from any subsequent advertisement, but the tax collector is not liable for failure to make the deletion.

(f) Listing and Advertising in Wrong Name. - No tax lien is void because the real property to which the lien attached was listed or advertised in the name of a person other than the person in whose name the property should have been listed for taxation if the property was in other respects correctly described on the abstract or in the advertisement.

(g) Wrongful Advertisement. - Any tax collector or deputy tax collector who willfully advertises any tax lien knowing that the property is not subject to taxation or that the taxes advertised have been paid is guilty of a Class 3 misdemeanor, and shall be required to pay the injured party all damages sustained in consequence. (1939, c. 310, s. 1715; 1955, c. 993; 1971, c. 806, s. 1; 1983, c. 808, s. 1; 1983 (Reg. Sess., 1984), c. 1013; 1993, c. 539, s. 725; 1994, Ex. Sess., c. 24, s. 14(c); 1999-439, s. 1; 2000-140, s. 73; 2006-106, s. 2.)

§§ 105-370 through 105-372: Repealed by Session Laws 1983, c. 808, ss. 2-4.

§ 105-373. Settlements.

(a) Annual Settlement of Tax Collector. -

(1) Preliminary Report. - After July 1 and before he is charged with taxes for the current fiscal year, the tax collector shall make a sworn report to the governing body of the taxing unit showing:

a. A list of the persons owning real property whose taxes for the preceding fiscal year remain unpaid and the principal amount owed by each person; and

b. A list of the persons not owning real property whose personal property taxes for the preceding fiscal year remain unpaid and the principal amount owed by each person. (To this list the tax collector shall append his statement under oath that he has made diligent efforts to collect the taxes due from the persons listed out of their personal property and by other means available to him for collection, and he shall report such other information concerning these taxpayers as may be of interest to or required by the governing body, including a report of his efforts to make collection outside the taxing unit under the provisions of G.S. 105-364.) The governing body of the taxing unit may publish this list in any newspaper in the taxing unit. The cost of publishing this list shall be paid by the taxing unit.

(2) Insolvents. - Upon receiving the report required by subdivision (a)(1), above the governing body of the taxing unit shall enter upon its minutes the names of persons owing taxes (but who listed no real property) whom it finds to be insolvent, and it shall by resolution designate the list entered in its minutes as the insolvent list to be credited to the tax collector in his settlement.

(3) Settlement for Current Taxes. - After July 1 and before he is charged with taxes for the current fiscal year, the tax collector shall make full settlement with the governing body of the taxing unit for all taxes in his hands for collection for the preceding fiscal year.

a. In the settlement the tax collector shall be charged with:

1. The total amount of all taxes in his hands for collection for the year, including amounts originally charged to him and all amounts subsequently charged on account of discoveries;

2. All penalties, interest, and costs collected by him in connection with taxes for the current year; and

3. All other sums collected by him.

b. The tax collector shall be credited with:

1. All sums representing taxes for the year deposited by him to the credit of the taxing unit or receipted for by a proper official of the unit;

2. Releases duly allowed by the governing body;

3. The principal amount of taxes constituting liens on real property;

4. The principal amount of taxes included in the insolvent list determined in accordance with subdivision (a)(2), above;

5. Discounts allowed by law;

6. Commissions (if any) lawfully payable to the tax collector as compensation; and

7. The principal amount of taxes for any assessment appealed to the Property Tax Commission when the appeal has not been finally adjudicated.

The tax collector shall be liable on his bond for both honesty and faithful performance of duty; for any deficiencies; and, in addition, for all criminal penalties provided by law.

The settlement, together with the action of the governing body with respect thereto, shall be entered in full upon the minutes of the governing body.

(4) Disposition of Tax Receipts after Settlement. - Uncollected taxes allowed as credits in the settlement prescribed in subdivision (a)(3), above, whether represented by tax liens held by the taxing unit or included in the list of insolvents, shall, for purposes of collection, be recharged to the tax collector or charged to some other person designated by the governing body of the taxing unit under statutory authority. The person charged with uncollected taxes shall:

a. Give bond satisfactory to the governing body;

b. Receive the tax receipts and tax records representing the uncollected taxes;

c. Have and exercise all powers and duties conferred or imposed by law upon tax collectors; and

d. Receive compensation as determined by the governing body.

(b) Settlements for Delinquent Taxes. - Annually, at the time prescribed for the settlement provided in subdivision (a)(3), above, all persons having in their hands for collection any taxes for years prior to the year involved in the settlement shall settle with the governing body of the taxing unit for collections made on each such year's taxes. The settlement for the taxes for prior years shall be made in whatever form is satisfactory to the chief accounting officer and the governing body of the taxing unit, and it shall be entered in full upon the minutes of the governing body.

(c) Settlement at End of Term. - Whenever any tax collector fails to succeed himself at the end of his term of office, he shall, on the last business day of his term, make full and complete settlement for all taxes (current or delinquent) in his hands and deliver the tax records, tax receipts, tax sale certificates, and accounts to his successor in office. The settlement shall be made in whatever form is satisfactory to the chief accounting officer and the governing body of the taxing unit, and it shall be entered in full upon the minutes of the governing body.

(d) Settlement upon Vacancy during Term. - When a tax collector voluntarily resigns, he shall, upon his last day in office, make full settlement (in the manner provided in subsection (c), above) for all taxes in his hands for collection. In default of such a settlement, or in case of a vacancy occurring during a term for any reason, it shall be the duty of the chief accounting officer or, in the discretion of the governing body, of some other qualified person appointed by it immediately to prepare and submit to the governing body a report in the nature of a settlement made on behalf of the former tax collector. The report, together with the governing body's action with respect thereto, shall be entered in full upon the minutes of the governing body. Whenever a settlement must be made in behalf of a former tax collector, as provided in this subsection (d), the governing body may deliver the tax receipts, tax records, and tax sale certificates to a successor collector immediately upon the occurrence of the vacancy, or it may make whatever temporary arrangements for the collection of taxes as may be expedient, but in no event shall any person be permitted to collect taxes until he has given bond satisfactory to the governing body.

(e) Effect of Approval of Settlement. - Approval of any settlement by the governing body does not relieve the tax collector or his bondsmen of liability for any shortage actually existing at the time of the settlement and thereafter discovered; nor does it relieve the collector of any criminal liability.

(f) Penalties. - In addition to any other civil or criminal penalties provided by law, any member of a governing body of a taxing unit, tax collector, or chief accounting officer who fails to perform any duty imposed upon him by this section shall be guilty of a Class 1 misdemeanor.

(g) Relief from Collecting Insolvents. - The governing body of any taxing unit may, in its discretion, relieve the tax collector of the charge of taxes owed by persons on the insolvent list that are five or more years past due when it appears to the governing body that such taxes are uncollectible.

(h) Relief from Collecting Taxes on Classified Motor Vehicles. The board of county commissioners may, in its discretion, relieve the tax collector of the charge of taxes on classified motor vehicles listed pursuant to G.S. 105-330.3(a)(1) that are one year or more past due when it appears to the board that the taxes are uncollectible. This relief, when granted, shall include municipal and special district taxes charged to the collector. (1939, c. 310, s. 1719; 1945, c. 635; 1947, c. 484, ss. 3, 4; 1951, c. 300, s. 1; c. 1036, s. 1; 1953, c. 176, s. 2; 1955, c. 908; 1967, c. 705, s. 1; 1971, c. 806, s. 1; 1983, c. 670, s. 22; c. 808, ss. 5-7; 1987, c. 16; 1991, c. 624, s. 3; 1991 (Reg. Sess., 1992), c. 961, s. 10;

1993, c. 539, s. 726; 1994, Ex. Sess., c. 24, s. 14(c); 1997-456, s. 27; 2006-30, s. 7.)

§ 105-374. Foreclosure of tax lien by action in nature of action to foreclose a mortgage.

(a) General Nature of Action. - The foreclosure action authorized by this section shall be instituted in the appropriate division of the General Court of Justice in the county in which the real property is situated and shall be an action in the nature of an action to foreclose a mortgage.

(b) Taxing units may proceed under this section, either on the original tax lien created by G.S. 105-355(a) or on the lien acquired at a tax lien sale held under former G.S. 105-369 before July 1, 1983, with or without a lien sale certificate; and the amount of recovery in either case shall be the same. To this end, it is hereby declared that the original attachment of the tax lien under G.S. 105-355(a) is sufficient to support a tax foreclosure action by a taxing unit, that the issuance of a lien sale certificate to the taxing unit for lien sales held before July 1, 1983, is a matter of convenience in record keeping within the discretion of the governing body of the taxing unit, and that issuance of such certificates is not a prerequisite to perfection of the tax lien.

(c) Parties; Summonses. - The owner of record as of the date the taxes became delinquent and spouse (if any), any subsequent owner, all other taxing units having tax liens, all other lienholders of record, and all persons who would be entitled to be made parties to a court action (in which no deficiency judgment is sought) to foreclose a mortgage on such property, shall be made parties and served with summonses in the manner provided by G.S. 1A-1, Rule 4.

The fact that the owner of record as of the date the taxes became delinquent, any subsequent owner, or any other defendant is a minor, is incompetent, or is under any other disability shall not prevent or delay the tax lien sale or the foreclosure of the tax lien; and all such persons shall be made parties and served with summons in the same manner as in other civil actions.

Persons who have disappeared or who cannot be located and persons whose names and whereabouts are unknown, and all possible heirs or assignees of such persons, may be served by publication; and such persons, their heirs, and assignees may be designated by general description or by fictitious names in such an action.

(c1)   Lienholders Separately Designated. - The word "lienholder" shall appear immediately after the name of each lienholder (including trustees and beneficiaries in deeds of trust, and holders of judgment liens) whose name appears in the caption of any action instituted under the provisions of this section. Such designation is intended to make clear to the public the capacity of such persons which necessitated their having been made parties to such action. Failure to add such designation to captions shall not constitute grounds for attacking the validity of actions brought under this section, or titles to real property derived from such actions.

(d)   Complaint as Lis Pendens. - The complaint in an action brought under this section shall, from the time it is filed in the office of the clerk of superior court, serve as notice of the pendency of the foreclosure action, and every person whose interest in the real property is subsequently acquired or whose interest therein is subsequently registered or recorded shall be bound by all proceedings taken in the foreclosure action after the filing of the complaint in the same manner as if those persons had been made parties to the action. It shall not be necessary to have the complaint cross-indexed as a notice of action pending to have the effect prescribed by this subsection (d).

(e)   Subsequent Taxes. - The complaint in a tax foreclosure action brought under this section by a taxing unit shall, in addition to alleging the tax lien on which the action is based, include a general allegation of subsequent taxes which are or may become a lien on the same real property in favor of the plaintiff unit. Thereafter it shall not be necessary to amend the complaint to incorporate the subsequent taxes by specific allegation. In case of redemption before confirmation of the foreclosure sale, the person redeeming shall be required to pay, before the foreclosure action is discontinued, at least all taxes on the real property which have at the time of discontinuance become due to the plaintiff unit, plus penalties, interest, and costs thereon. Immediately prior to judgment ordering sale in a foreclosure action (if there has been no redemption prior to that time), the tax collector or the attorney for the plaintiff unit shall file in the action a certificate setting forth all taxes which are a lien on the real property in favor of the plaintiff unit (other than taxes the amount of which has not been definitely determined).

Any plaintiff in a tax foreclosure action (other than a taxing unit) may include in his complaint, originally or by amendment, all other taxes and special assessments paid by him which were liens on the same real property.

(f) Joinder of Parcels. - All real property within the taxing unit subject to liens for taxes levied against the same taxpayer for the first year involved in the foreclosure action may be joined in one action. However, if real property is transferred by the listing taxpayer subsequent to the first year involved in the foreclosure action, all subsequent taxes, penalties, interest, and costs (for which the property is ordered sold under the terms of this Subchapter) shall be prorated to such property in the same manner as if payments were being made to release such property from the tax lien under the provisions of G.S. 105-356(b).

(g) Special Benefit Assessments. - A cause of action for the foreclosure of the lien of any special benefit assessments may be included in any complaint filed under this section.

(h) Joint Foreclosure by Two or More Taxing Units. - Liens of different taxing units on the same parcel of real property, representing taxes in the hands of the same tax collector, shall be foreclosed in one action. Liens of different taxing units on the same parcel of real property, representing taxes in the hands of different tax collectors, may be foreclosed in one action in the discretion of the governing bodies of the taxing units.

The lien of any taxing unit made a party defendant in any foreclosure action shall be alleged in an answer filed by the taxing unit, and the tax collector of each answering unit shall, prior to judgment ordering sale, file a certificate of subsequent taxes similar to that filed by the tax collector of the plaintiff unit, and the taxes of each answering unit shall be of equal dignity with the taxes of the plaintiff unit. Any answering unit may, in case of payment of the plaintiff unit's taxes, continue the foreclosure action until all taxes due to it have been paid, and it shall not be necessary for any answering unit to file a separate foreclosure action or to proceed under G.S. 105-375 with respect to any such taxes.

If a taxing unit properly served as a party defendant in a foreclosure action fails to answer and file the certificate provided for in the preceding paragraph, all of its taxes shall be barred by the judgment of sale except to the extent that the purchase price at the foreclosure sale (after payment of costs and of the liens of all taxing units whose liens are properly alleged by complaint or answer and certificates) may be sufficient to pay such taxes. However, if a defendant taxing unit is plaintiff in another foreclosure action pending against the same property, or if it has begun a proceeding under G.S. 105-375, its answer may allege that fact in lieu of alleging its liens, and the court, in its discretion, may order consolidation of such actions or such other disposition thereof (and such disposition of the costs therein) as it may deem advisable. Any such order may be made by the clerk of the superior court, subject to appeal as provided in G.S. 1-301.1.

(i) Costs. - Subject to the provisions of this subsection (i), costs may be taxed in any foreclosure action brought under this section in the same manner as in other civil actions. When costs are collected, either by payment prior to the sale or upon payment of the purchase price at the foreclosure sale, the fees allowed officers shall be paid to those entitled to receive them. In foreclosure actions in which the plaintiff is a taxing unit, no prosecution bond shall be required.

The word "costs," as used in this subsection (i), shall be construed to include one reasonable attorney's fee for the plaintiff in such amount as the court shall, in its discretion, determine and allow. When a taxing unit is made a party defendant in a tax foreclosure action and files answer therein, there may be included in the costs an attorney's fee for the defendant unit in such amount as the court shall, in its discretion, determine and allow. The governing body of any taxing unit may, in its discretion, pay a smaller or greater sum than that allowed as costs to its attorney as a suit fee, and the governing body may allow a reasonable commission to its attorney on taxes collected by him after they have been placed in his hands; or the governing body may arrange with its attorney for the handling of tax foreclosure suits on a salary basis or may make any other reasonable agreement with its attorney or attorneys. Any arrangement made between a taxing unit and its attorney may provide that attorneys' fees collected as costs in foreclosure actions be collected for the use of the taxing unit.

In any foreclosure action in which real property is actually sold after judgment, costs shall include a commissioner's fee to be fixed by the court, not exceeding five percent (5%) of the purchase price; and in case of redemption between the date of sale and the order of confirmation, the fee shall be added to the amount otherwise necessary for redemption. In case more than one sale is made of the same property in any action, the commissioner's fee may be based on the highest amount bid, but the commissioner shall not be allowed a separate fee for each such sale. The governing body of any plaintiff unit may request the court to appoint as commissioner a salaried official, attorney, or employee of the unit and, when the requested appointment is made, may require that the commissioner's fees, when collected, be paid to the plaintiff unit for its use.

(j) Contested Actions. - Any action brought under this section in which an answer raising an issue requiring trial is filed within the time allowed by law shall be entitled to a preference as to time of trial over all other civil actions.

(k) Judgment of Sale. - Any judgment in favor of the plaintiff or any defendant taxing unit in an action brought under this section shall order the sale of the real property or as much as may be necessary for the satisfaction of all of the following:

(1) Taxes adjudged to be liens in favor of the plaintiff (other than taxes the amount of which has not been definitely determined) together with penalties, interest, and costs thereon.

(2) Taxes adjudged to be liens in favor of other taxing units (other than taxes the amount of which has not yet been definitely determined) if those taxes have been alleged in answers filed by the other taxing units, together with penalties, interest, and costs thereon.

The judgment shall appoint a commissioner to conduct the sale and shall order that the property be sold in fee simple, free and clear of all interests, rights, claims, and liens whatever except that the sale shall be subject to taxes the amount of which cannot be definitely determined at the time of the judgment, taxes and special assessments of taxing units which are not parties to the action, and, in the discretion of the court, taxes alleged in other tax foreclosure actions or proceedings pending against the same real property.

In all cases in which no answer is filed within the time allowed by law, and in cases in which answers filed do not seek to prevent sale of said property, the clerk of the superior court may enter the judgment, subject to appeal as provided in G.S. 1-301.1.

(l) Advertisement of Sale. - The sale shall be advertised, and all necessary resales shall be advertised, in the manner provided by Article 29A of Chapter 1 of the General Statutes or by any statute enacted in substitution therefor.

(m) Sale. - The sale shall be by public auction to the highest bidder and shall, in accordance with the judgment, be held at the courthouse door on any day of the week except a Sunday or legal holiday when the courthouse is closed for transactions. (In actions brought by a municipality that is not a county seat, the court may, in its discretion, direct that the sale be held at the city or town hall door.) The commissioner conducting the sale may, in his discretion, require from any successful bidder a deposit equal to not more than twenty percent (20%) of his bid, which deposit, in the event that the bidder refuses to take title and a resale becomes necessary, shall be applied to pay the costs of sale and any loss resulting. (However, this provision shall not deprive the commissioner of his right to sue for specific performance of the contract.) No deposit shall be required of a taxing unit that has made the highest bid at the foreclosure sale.

(n) Report of Sale. - Within three days following the foreclosure sale the commissioner shall report the sale to the court giving full particulars thereof.

(o) Exceptions and Increased Bids. - At any time within 10 days after the commissioner files his report of the foreclosure sale, any person having an interest in the real property may file exceptions to the report, and at any time within that 10-day period an increased bid may be filed in the amount specified by and subject to the provisions (other than provisions in conflict herewith) of Article 29A of Chapter 1 of the General Statutes or the provisions (other than provisions in conflict herewith) of any law enacted in substitution therefor. In the absence of exceptions or increased bids, the court may, whenever it deems such action necessary for the best interests of the parties, order resale of the property.

(p) Judgment of Confirmation. - At any time after the expiration of 10 days from the time the commissioner files his report, if no exception or increased bid has been filed, the commissioner may apply for judgment of confirmation, and in like manner he may apply for such a judgment after the court has passed upon exceptions filed, or after any necessary resales have been held and reported and 10 days have elapsed. The judgment of confirmation shall direct the commissioner to deliver the deed upon payment of the purchase price. This judgment may be entered by the clerk of superior court subject to appeal as provided in G.S. 1-301.1.

(q) Application of Proceeds; Commissioner's Final Report. - After delivery of the deed and collection of the purchase price, the commissioner shall apply the proceeds as follows:

(1) First, to payment of all costs of the action, including the commissioner's fee and the attorney's fee, which costs shall be paid to the officials or funds entitled thereto;

(2) Then to the payment of taxes, penalties, and interest for which the real property was ordered to be sold, and in case the funds remaining are insufficient for this purpose, they shall be distributed pro rata to the various taxing units for whose taxes the property was ordered sold;

(3) Then pro rata to the payment of any special benefit assessments for which the property was ordered sold, together with interest and costs thereon;

(4) Then pro rata to payment of taxes, penalties, interest, and costs of taxing units that were parties to the foreclosure action but which filed no answers therein;

(5) Then pro rata to payment of special benefit assessments of taxing units that were parties to the foreclosure action but which filed no answers therein, together with interest and costs thereon;

(6) And any balance then remaining shall be paid in accordance with any directions given by the court and, in the absence of such directions, shall be paid into court for the benefit of the persons entitled thereto. (If the clerk is in doubt as to who is entitled to the surplus or if any adverse claims are asserted thereto, the clerk shall hold the surplus until rights thereto are established in a special proceeding pursuant to G.S. 1-339.71.)

Within five days after delivering the deed, the commissioner shall make a full report to the court showing delivery of the deed, receipt of the purchase price, and the disbursement of the proceeds, accompanied by receipts evidencing all such disbursements.

(r) Purchase and Resale by Taxing Unit. - The rights of a taxing unit to purchase real property at a foreclosure sale and resell it are governed by G.S. 105-376. (1939, c. 310, s. 1719; 1945, c. 635; 1947, c. 484, ss. 3, 4; 1951, c. 300, s. 1; c. 1036, s. 1; 1953, c. 176, s. 2; 1955, c. 908; 1967, c. 705, s. 1; 1971, c. 806, s. 1; 1973, c. 788, s. 1; 1981, c. 580; 1983, c. 808, s. 8; 1999-216, ss. 14-16; 2003-337, s. 11; 2006-106, s. 3.)

§ 105-375. In rem method of foreclosure.

(a) Intent of Section. - It is hereby declared to be the intention of this section that proceedings brought under it shall be strictly in rem. It is further declared to be the intention of this section to provide, as an alternative to G.S. 105-374, a simple and inexpensive method of enforcing payment of taxes necessarily levied, to the knowledge of all persons, for the requirements of local governments in this State; and to recognize, in authorizing this proceeding, that all persons owning interests in real property know or should know that the tax lien on their real property may be foreclosed and the property sold for failure to pay taxes.

(b) Docketing Certificate of Taxes as Judgment. - In lieu of following the procedure set forth in G.S. 105-374, the governing body of any taxing unit may direct the tax collector to file with the clerk of superior court, no earlier than 30 days after the tax liens were advertised, a certificate showing the following: the name of the taxpayer as defined in G.S. 105-273(17), for each parcel on which the taxing unit has a lien for unpaid taxes, together with the amount of taxes, penalties, interest, and costs that are a lien thereon; the year or years for which the taxes are due; and a description of the property sufficient to permit its identification by parol testimony. The fees for docketing and indexing the certificate shall be payable to the clerk of superior court at the time the taxes are collected or the property is sold.

(c) Notice to Taxpayer and Others. -

(1) Notice required. - The tax collector filing the certificate provided for in subsection (b) of this section, shall, at least 30 days prior to docketing the judgment, send notice of the tax lien foreclosure to the taxpayer, as defined in G.S. 105-273(17), at the taxpayer's last known address, and to all lienholders of record who have a lien against the taxpayer (including any liens referred to in the conveyance of the property to the taxpayer).

(2) Contents of notice. - All notice required by this subsection shall state that a judgment will be docketed and the proposed date of the docketing, that execution will be issued as provided by law, a brief description of the real property affected, and that the lien may be satisfied prior to judgment being entered.

(3) Service of notice. - The notice required by this subsection shall be sent to the taxpayer by registered or certified mail, return receipt requested.

(4) Additional efforts may be required. - If within 10 days following the mailing of the notice, a return receipt has not been received by the tax collector

indicating receipt of the notice, then the tax collector shall do both of the following:

a. Make reasonable efforts to locate and notify the taxpayer and all lienholders of record prior to the docketing of the judgment and the issuance of the execution. Reasonable efforts may include posting the notice in a conspicuous place on the property, or, if the property has an address to which mail may be delivered, mailing the notice by first-class mail to the attention of the occupant.

b. Have a notice published in a newspaper of general circulation in the county once a week for two consecutive weeks directed to, and naming, all unnotified lienholders and the taxpayer that a judgment will be docketed against the taxpayer.

(5) Costs of notice added to lien. - All costs of mailing and publication, plus a charge of two hundred fifty dollars ($250.00) to defray administrative costs, shall be added to the amount of taxes that are a lien on the real property and shall be paid by the taxpayer to the taxing unit at the time the taxes are collected or the property is sold.

(d) Effect of Docketing Certificate of Taxes Due. - Immediately upon the docketing and indexing of a certificate as provided in subsection (b), above, the taxes, penalties, interest, and costs shall constitute a valid judgment against the real property described therein, with the priority provided for tax liens in G.S. 105-356. The judgment, except as expressly provided in this section, shall have the same force and effect as a duly rendered judgment of the superior court directing sale of the property for the satisfaction of the tax lien, and it shall bear interest at an annual rate of eight percent (8%).

(e) Special Assessments. - Street, sidewalk, and other special assessments may be included in any judgment for taxes taken under this section, or the special assessments may be included in a separate judgment docketed under this section. The tax collector may use such a judgment as a method of foreclosing the lien of special assessments. When used to foreclose the lien of special assessments, the procedure may be instituted at any time after the assessment or installment falls due and remains unpaid; the waiting period required by subsection (b) of this section does not apply to the foreclosure of special assessments.

(f) Motion to Set Aside. - At any time prior to the issuance of execution, any person having an interest in the real property to be foreclosed may appear before the clerk of superior court and move to set aside the judgment on the ground that the tax has been paid or that the tax lien on which the judgment is based is invalid.

(g) Cancellation upon Payment. - Upon payment in full of any judgment docketed under this section, together with interest thereon and costs accrued to the date of payment, the tax collector receiving payment shall certify the fact thereof to the clerk of superior court and cancel the judgment.

(h) Relationship between G.S. 105-374 and This Section. - If, before the issuance of execution on the judgment under subsection (i), below, the taxing unit is made a defendant in a foreclosure action brought against the property under G.S. 105-374, it shall file an answer in that proceeding and thereafter all proceedings shall be governed by order of the court in accordance with that section.

(i) Issuance of Execution. - At any time after three months and before two years from the indexing of the judgment as provided in subsection (b), above, execution shall be issued at the request of the tax collector in the same manner as executions are issued upon other judgments of the superior court, and the real property shall be sold by the sheriff in the same manner as other real property is sold under execution with the following exceptions:

(1) No debtor's exemption shall be allowed.

(2) In lieu of personal service of notice on the taxpayer, the sheriff shall send notice by registered or certified mail, return receipt requested, to the taxpayer at the taxpayer's last known address at least 30 days prior to the day fixed for the sale. If within 10 days following the mailing of the notice, a return receipt has not been received by the sheriff indicating receipt of the notice, then the sheriff shall make additional efforts to locate and notify the taxpayer and all lienholders of record of the sale under execution in accordance with subdivision (4) of subsection (c) of this section.

(3) The sheriff shall add to the amount of the judgment as costs of the sale any postage expenses incurred by the tax collector and the sheriff in foreclosing under this section.

(4) In any advertisement or posted notice of sale under execution, the sheriff may (and at the request of the governing body shall) combine the advertisements or notices for properties to be sold under executions against the properties of different taxpayers in favor of the same taxing unit or group of units; however, the property included in each judgment shall be separately described and the name of the taxpayer specified in connection with each.

The purchaser at the execution sale shall acquire title to the property in fee simple free and clear of all claims, rights, interests, and liens except the liens of other taxes or special assessments not paid from the purchase price and not included in the judgment.

(j) Attorney's Fee. - The governing body of the taxing unit may make whatever arrangement it deems satisfactory for compensating an attorney rendering assistance or advice in foreclosure proceedings brought under this section, but the attorney's fee shall not be added to the judgment as part of the costs of the action.

(k) Consolidation of Liens. - By agreement between the governing bodies, two or more taxing units may consolidate their tax liens for the purpose of docketing a judgment, or may have one execution issued for separate judgments, against the same property. In like manner, one execution may issue for separate judgments in favor of one or more taxing units against the same property for different years' taxes.

(l) Purchase and Resale by Taxing Unit. - The rights of a taxing unit to purchase real property at a foreclosure sale and resell it are governed by G.S. 105-376.

(m) Procedure if Section Declared Unconstitutional. - If any provisions of this section are declared invalid or unconstitutional by the Supreme Court of North Carolina, a United States district court of three judges, the United States Circuit Court of Appeals, or the United States Supreme Court, all taxing units that have proceeded under this section shall have five years from the date of the filing of the opinion (or, in the case of appeal, from the date of the filing of the opinion on appeal) in which to institute foreclosure actions under G.S. 105-374 for all taxes included in judgments taken under this section and for subsequent taxes due or which, but for purchase of the property by the taxing unit, would have become due; and such judicial decision shall not have the effect of invalidating the tax lien or disturbing its priority. (1939, c. 310, s. 1720; 1945, c. 646; 1957, cc. 91, 1262; 1971, c. 806, s. 1; 1973, c. 108, s. 52; c. 681, ss. 1, 2; 1983, c. 808, s. 9;

c. 855, ss. 1, 2; 1987, c. 450; 1989, c. 37, s. 7; c. 682; 1999-439, ss. 2, 3; 2001-139, s. 9; 2006-106, ss. 4-6; 2011-352, s. 1.)

§ 105-376. Taxing unit as purchaser at foreclosure sale; payment of purchase price; resale of property acquired by taxing unit.

(a) Taxing Unit as Purchaser. - Any taxing unit (or two or more taxing units jointly) may bid at a foreclosure sale conducted under G.S. 105-374 or G.S. 105-375, and any taxing unit that becomes the successful bidder may assign its bid at any time by private sale for not less than the amount of the bid.

(b) Payment of Purchase Price by Taxing Units; Status of Property Purchased by Taxing Units. - Any taxing unit that becomes the purchaser at a tax foreclosure sale may, in the discretion of its governing body, pay only that part of the purchase price that would not be distributed to it and other taxing units on account of taxes, penalties, interest, and such costs as accrued prior to the initiation of the foreclosure action under G.S. 105-374 or docketing of a judgment under G.S. 105-375. Thereafter, in such a case, the purchasing taxing unit shall hold the property for the benefit of all taxing units that have an interest in the property as defined in this subsection (b). All net income from real property so acquired and the proceeds thereof, when resold, shall be first used to reimburse the purchasing unit for disbursements actually made by it in connection with the foreclosure action and the purchase of the property, and any balance remaining shall be distributed to the taxing units having an interest therein in proportion to their interests. The total interest of each taxing unit, including the purchasing unit, shall be determined by adding:

(1) The taxes of the unit, with penalties, interest, and costs (other than costs already reimbursed to the purchasing unit) to satisfy which the property was ordered sold;

(2) Other taxes of the unit, with penalties, interest, and costs which would have been paid in full from the purchase price had the purchase price been paid in full;

(3) Taxes of the unit, with penalties, interest, and costs to which the foreclosure sale was made subject; and

(4)   The principal amount of all taxes which became liens on the property after purchase at the foreclosure sale or which would have become liens thereon but for the purchase, but no amount shall be included for taxes for years in which (on the day as of which property was to be listed for taxation) the property was being used by the purchasing unit for a public purpose.

If the amount of net income and proceeds of resale distributable exceeds the total interests of all taxing units defined in this subsection (b), the remainder shall be applied to any special benefit assessments to satisfy which the sale was ordered or to which the sale was made subject, and any balance remaining shall accrue to the purchasing unit.

When any real property that has been purchased as provided in this section is permanently dedicated to use for a public purpose, the purchasing unit shall make settlement with other taxing units having an interest in the property (as defined in this subsection) in such manner and in such amount as may be agreed upon by the governing bodies; and if no agreement can be reached, the amount to be paid shall be determined by a resident judge of the superior court in the district in which the property is situated.

Nothing in this section shall be construed as requiring the purchasing unit to secure the approval of other interested taxing units before reselling the property or as requiring the purchasing unit to pay other interested taxing units in full if the net income and resale price are insufficient to make such payments.

Any taxing unit purchasing property at a foreclosure sale may, in the discretion of its governing body, instead of following the foregoing provisions of this section, make full payment of the purchase price, and thereafter it shall hold the property as sole owner in the same manner as it holds other real property, subject only to taxes and special assessments, with penalties, interest, and costs, to which the sale was made subject.

(c)   Resale of Real Property Purchased by Taxing Units. - Real property purchased at a tax foreclosure sale by a taxing unit may be resold at any time (for such price as the governing body of the taxing unit may approve) at a sale conducted in the manner provided by law for sales of other real property of the taxing unit. However, a purchasing taxing unit, in the discretion of its governing body, may resell such property to the former owner or to any other person formerly having an interest in the property at private sale for an amount not less than the taxing unit's interest therein if it holds the property as sole owner or for an amount not less than the total interests of all taxing units (other than special assessments due the taxing unit holding title) if it holds the property for the benefit of all such units. (1939, c. 310, s. 1719; 1945, c. 635; 1947, c. 484, ss. 3, 4; 1951, c. 300, s. 1; c. 1036, s. 1; 1953, c. 176, s. 2; 1955, c. 908; 1967, c. 705, s. 1; 1971, c. 806, s. 1.)

§ 105-377. Time for contesting validity of tax foreclosure title.

Notwithstanding any other provisions of law prescribing the period for commencing an action, no action or proceeding shall be brought to contest the validity of any title to real property acquired by a taxing unit or by a private purchaser in any tax foreclosure action or proceeding authorized by this Subchapter or by other laws of this State in force at the time the title was acquired, nor shall any motion to reopen or set aside the judgment in any such tax foreclosure action or proceeding be entertained after one year from the date on which the deed is recorded. (1939, c. 310, s. 1721; 1971, c. 806, s. 1; 1977, c. 886, s. 2.)

§ 105-378. Limitation on use of remedies.

(a) Use of Remedies Barred. - No county or municipality may maintain an action or procedure to enforce any remedy provided by law for the collection of taxes or the enforcement of any tax liens (whether the taxes or tax liens are evidenced by the original tax receipts, tax sales certificates, or otherwise) unless the action or procedure is instituted within 10 years from the date the taxes became due.

(b) Not Applicable to Special Assessments. - The provisions of subsection (a), above, shall not be construed to apply to the lien of special assessments.

(c) Repealed by Session Laws 1998-98, s. 26, effective August 14, 1998.

(d) Enforcement and Collection Delayed Pending Appeal. - When the board of county commissioners or municipal governing body delivers a tax receipt to a tax collector for any assessment that has been or is subsequently appealed to the county board of equalization and review or the Property Tax Commission, the tax collector may not seek collection of taxes or enforcement of a tax lien resulting from the assessment until the appeal has been finally adjudicated. The tax collector, however, may send an initial bill or notice to the taxpayer. (1933, c. 181, s. 7; c. 399; 1945, c. 832; 1947, c. 1065, s. 1; 1949, cc. 60, 269, 735; 1951, cc. 71, 306, 572; 1953, cc. 381, 427, 538, 645, 656, 752, 775, 1008; 1955, c. 1087; 1957, cc. 53, 678, 1123; 1959, cc. 373, 608; 1961, cc. 542, 695, 885; 1965, cc. 129, 294; 1967, c. 242; c. 321, s. 1; c. 422, s. 1; 1969, c. 96; 1971, c. 806, s. 1; 1998-98, s. 26; 2006-30, s. 6; 2011-3, s. 3(b).)

Article 27.

Refunds and Remedies.

§ 105-379. Restriction on use of injunction and claim and delivery.

(a) Grounds for Injunction. - No court may enjoin the collection of any tax, the sale of any tax lien, or the sale of any property for nonpayment of any tax imposed under the authority of this Subchapter except upon a showing that the tax (or some part thereof) is illegal or levied for an illegal or unauthorized purpose.

(b) No Order in Claim and Delivery. - No court may issue any order in claim and delivery proceedings or otherwise for the taking of any personal property levied on or attached by the tax collector under the authority of this Subchapter. (1901, c. 558, s. 30; Rev., s. 2855; C.S., s. 7979; 1971, c. 806, s. 1.)

§ 105-380. No taxes to be released, refunded, or compromised.

(a) The governing body of a taxing unit is prohibited from releasing, refunding, or compromising all or any portion of the taxes levied against any property within its jurisdiction except as expressly provided in this Subchapter.

(b) Taxes that have been released, refunded, or compromised in violation of this section shall be deemed to be unpaid and shall be collectible by any means provided by this Subchapter, and the existence and priority of any tax lien on property shall not be affected by the unauthorized release, refund, or compromise of the tax liability.

(c) Any tax that has been released, refunded, or compromised in violation of this section may be recovered from any member or members of the governing body who voted for the release, refund, or compromise by civil action instituted by any resident of the taxing unit, and when collected, the recovered tax shall be paid to the treasurer of the taxing unit. The costs of bringing the action, including reasonable attorneys' fees, shall be allowed the plaintiff in the event the tax is recovered.

(d) The provisions of this section are not intended to restrict or abrogate the powers of a board of equalization and review or any agency exercising the powers of such a board.

(e) (Expires July 1, 2016) The governing body of a municipality shall release any tax levied under this Subchapter, without application from the taxpayer being required, on property that was within the corporate limits of the municipality for six months or less prior to deannexation from the municipality, and for which no notice of the tax has yet been sent to the taxpayer. The release shall be made in accordance with the provisions of this Article. (1901, c. 558, s. 31; Rev., s. 2854; C.S., s. 7976; 1971, c. 806, s. 1; 1973, c. 564, s. 2; 2013-19, s. 1.)

§ 105-381. Taxpayer's remedies.

(a) Statement of Defense. - Any taxpayer asserting a valid defense to the enforcement of the collection of a tax assessed upon his property shall proceed as hereinafter provided.

(1) For the purpose of this subsection, a valid defense shall include the following:

a. A tax imposed through clerical error;

b. An illegal tax;

c. A tax levied for an illegal purpose.

(2) If a tax has not been paid, the taxpayer may make a demand for the release of the tax claim by submitting to the governing body of the taxing unit a

written statement of his defense to payment or enforcement of the tax and a request for release of the tax at any time prior to payment of the tax.

(3) If a tax has been paid, the taxpayer, at any time within five years after said tax first became due or within six months from the date of payment of such tax, whichever is the later date, may make a demand for a refund of the tax paid by submitting to the governing body of the taxing unit a written statement of his defense and a request for refund thereof.

(b) Action of Governing Body. - Upon receiving a taxpayer's written statement of defense and request for release or refund, the governing body of the taxing unit shall within 90 days after receipt of such request determine whether the taxpayer has a valid defense to the tax imposed or any part thereof and shall either release or refund that portion of the amount that is determined to be in excess of the correct tax liability or notify the taxpayer in writing that no release or refund will be made. The governing body may, by resolution, delegate its authority to determine requests for a release or refund of tax of less than one hundred dollars ($100.00) to the finance officer, manager, or attorney of the taxing unit. A finance officer, manager, or attorney to whom this authority is delegated shall monthly report to the governing body the actions taken by him on requests for release or refund. All actions taken by the governing body or finance officer, manager, or attorney on requests for release or refund shall be recorded in the minutes of the governing body. If a release is granted or refund made, the tax collector shall be credited with the amount released or refunded in his annual settlement.

(c) Suit for Recovery of Property Taxes. -

(1) Request for Release before Payment. - If within 90 days after receiving a taxpayer's request for release of an unpaid tax claim under (a) above, the governing body of the taxing unit has failed to grant the release, has notified the taxpayer that no release will be granted, or has taken no action on the request, the taxpayer shall pay the tax. He may then within three years from the date of payment bring a civil action against the taxing unit for the amount claimed.

(2) Request for Refund. - If within 90 days after receiving a taxpayer's request for refund under (a) above, the governing body has failed to refund the full amount requested by the taxpayer, has notified the taxpayer that no refund will be made, or has taken no action on the request, the taxpayer may bring a civil action against the taxing unit for the amount claimed. Such action may be

brought at any time within three years from the expiration of the period in which the governing body is required to act.

(d)   Civil Actions. - Civil actions brought pursuant to subsection (c) above shall be brought in the appropriate division of the general court of justice of the county in which the taxing unit is located. If, upon the trial, it is determined that the tax or any part of it was illegal or levied for an illegal purpose, or excessive as the result of a clerical error, judgment shall be rendered therefor with interest thereon at six percent (6%) per annum, plus costs, and the judgment shall be collected as in other civil actions. (1901, c. 558, s. 30; Rev., s. 2855; C. S., s. 7979; 1971, c. 806, s. 1; 1973, c. 564, s. 3; 1977, c. 946, s. 2; 1985, c. 150, s. 1; 1987, c. 127.)

§ 105-382. Repealed by Session Laws 1977, c. 946, s. 3.

Article 28.

Special Duties to Pay Taxes.

§ 105-383. Fiduciaries to pay taxes.

(a)   Duty to Pay. - It shall be the duty of every guardian, executor, administrator, agent, trustee, receiver, or other fiduciary having care or control of any real or personal property to pay the taxes thereon out of the trust funds in his hands.

(b)   Liability for Failure to Pay. - Any fiduciary who fails to pay the taxes on property in his care or control when trust funds are available to him for that purpose shall be personally liable for the taxes. This liability may be enforced by a civil action brought in the name of the tax collector of the taxing unit to which the taxes are owed against the fiduciary in an appropriate division of the General Court of Justice of the county in which the taxing unit is located.

(c)   Liability for Sale of Property. - Any fiduciary who suffers property in his care or control to be sold by reason of his negligence in failing to pay the taxes thereon when available funds were in his hands shall be liable to his ward, principal, or cestui que trust for all actual damages incurred as a result of his neglect.

(d)   Effect of Section. - This section shall not have the effect of relieving property and estates held in trust or under the control of fiduciaries from the lien of property taxes. (1762, c. 69, s. 14; R.C., c. 54, s. 27; 1868-9, c. 201, s. 32; 1879, c. 71, s. 53; Code, ss. 1595, 3698; Rev., s. 2862; C.S., s. 7985; 1971, c. 806, s. 1.)

§ 105-384. Duties and liabilities of life tenant.

(a)   If real or personal property is held by a tenant for life or by a tenant for the life of another, it shall be the duty of the life tenant to pay the taxes imposed on the property.

(b)   Any remainderman or reversioner of real or personal property who pays the taxes thereon may recover the money so paid in an action against the life tenant of the property; in the case of real property, the action may be brought only in the appropriate division of the General Court of Justice of the county in which the real property is located.

(c)   Any tenant for life of real or personal property who suffers the property to be foreclosed and sold or sold under levy for failure to pay the taxes thereon shall be liable to the remainderman or to the reversioner for any damages incurred. (1879, c. 71, ss. 53, 54; Code, ss. 3698, 3699; 1901, c. 558, s. 45; Rev., s. 2859; C.S., s. 7982; 1971, c. 806, s. 1.)

§ 105-385. Duty to pay taxes on real property; judicial sales; sales under powers; governmental purchasers.

(a)   Judicial Sales. - In all civil actions and special proceedings in which the sale of any real property is ordered, the judgment shall provide for the payment of all taxes then constituting a lien upon the property and all special assessments or installments thereof then due, and the tax liens and special assessments shall be satisfied from the proceeds of the sale before the proceeds are disbursed. The judgment in such a civil action or special proceeding shall adjust the disbursements for taxes and special assessments between the parties to the action or special proceeding in accordance with their respective rights.

(b)   Sales under Powers. - Any person who sells real property under a power of sale conferred upon him by a deed, will, power of attorney, mortgage, deed of trust, or assignment for the benefit of creditors shall from the proceeds of the sale first satisfy all taxes constituting a lien upon the real property and all special assessments or installments thereof then due unless the notice of sale provided that the property would be sold subject to tax liens and special assessments, and it was so sold.

(c)   Governmental Purchasers. - Any agency, department, or institution of the State of North Carolina and any county or municipal corporation that purchases real property shall satisfy all taxes constituting a lien upon the property purchased and all special assessments or installments thereof then due by deducting the amount of the taxes and special assessments from the purchase price and paying it to the proper taxing unit or units. Any agency, department, or institution of the State and any county or municipal corporation that fails to make the deductions and payments required by this subsection (c) shall be liable to the taxing unit or units to which the taxes and special assessments are owed for the amount thereof. This liability may be enforced in a civil action brought by the taxing unit or units to which the taxes and special assessments are owed in the appropriate trial division of the General Court of Justice of the county in which the property is located; this remedy shall be in addition to any remedies the taxing unit may have against the grantor of the property. (1901, c. 558, s. 47; Rev., s. 2857; C.S., s. 7980; 1929, c. 231, s. 1; 1951, c. 252, s. 1; 1971, c. 806, s. 1.)

§ 105-386. Tax paid by holder of lien; remedy.

If any person having a lien or encumbrance of any kind upon real property shall pay the taxes that constitute a lien upon the real property:

(1)   He shall thereby acquire a lien upon the real property from the time of payment, which lien shall be superior to all other liens and which may be enforced by an action in the appropriate division of the General Court of Justice of the county in which the real property is situated.

(2) He may, by an action for moneys paid to the use of the owner of the real property at the time of payment, recover the amount paid. (1879, c. 71, s. 55; Code, s. 3700; 1901, c. 558, s. 46; Rev., s. 2858; C.S., s. 7981; 1971, c. 806, s. 1.)

Article 29.

Validations.

§§ 105-387 through 105-392: Recodified as §§ 47-108.21 to 47-108.26 by Session Laws 1987, c. 777, s. 4(1).

§ 105-393. Repealed by Session Laws 1987, c. 777, s. 4(2).

Article 30.

General Provisions.

§ 105-394. Immaterial irregularities.

Immaterial irregularities in the listing, appraisal, or assessment of property for taxation or in the levy or collection of the property tax or in any other proceeding or requirement of this Subchapter shall not invalidate the tax imposed upon any property or any process of listing, appraisal, assessment, levy, collection, or any other proceeding under this Subchapter.

The following are examples of immaterial irregularities:

(1) The failure of list takers, tax supervisors, or members of boards of equalization and review to take and subscribe the oaths required of them.

(2) The failure to sign the affirmation required on the abstract.

(3) The failure to list, appraise, or assess any property for taxation or to levy any tax within the time prescribed by law.

(4) The failure of the board of equalization and review to meet or to adjourn within the time prescribed by law or to give any required notice of its meetings and adjournment.

(5) Any defect in the description upon any abstract, tax receipt, tax record, notice, advertisement, or other document, of real or personal property, if the description be sufficient to enable the tax collector or any person interested to determine what property is meant by the description. (In such cases the tax supervisor or tax collector may correct the description on the documents bearing the defective description, and the correct description shall be used in any documents later issued in tax foreclosure proceedings authorized by this Subchapter.)

(6) The failure of the collector to advertise any tax lien.

(7) Repealed by Session Laws 1983, c. 808, s. 11.

(8) Any irregularity or informality in the order or manner in which tax liens on real property are offered for sale.

(9) The failure to make or serve any notice mentioned in this Subchapter.

(10) The omission of a dollar mark or other designation descriptive of the value of figures upon any document required by this Subchapter.

(11) Any other immaterial informality, omission, or defect on the part of any person in any proceeding or requirement of this Subchapter. (1939, c. 310, s. 1715; 1965, c. 192, ss. 1, 2; 1971, c. 806, s. 1; 1983, c. 808, ss. 10, 11.)

§ 105-395. Application and effective date of Subchapter.

(a) The provisions of G.S. 105-333 through 105-344 (being Article 23 in this Subchapter) shall first be applicable to public service company property to be listed or reported for taxation as of January 1, 1972. Unless otherwise specifically provided herein, all other provisions of this Machinery Act (being Subchapter II of Chapter 105 of the General Statutes) shall become effective July 1, 1971, and shall apply to all taxes due and uncollected as of that date as well as to those that shall become due thereafter.

(b) Repealed by Session Laws 1998-98, s. 27.

(c) It is the intent of the General Assembly to make the provisions of this Subchapter uniformly applicable throughout the State, and to assure this objective all laws and clauses of laws, including private and local acts, other than local acts relating to the selection of tax collectors, in conflict with this Subchapter are repealed effective July 1, 1971. As used in this section, the term "local acts" means any acts of the General Assembly that apply to one or more counties by name, to one or more municipalities by name, or to all municipalities within one or more named counties. (1971, c. 806, s. 1; 1993, c. 485, s. 19; 1998-98, s. 27.)

§ 105-395.1. Applicable date when due date falls on weekend or holiday.

When the last day for doing an act required or permitted by this Subchapter falls on a Saturday, Sunday, or holiday, the act is considered to be done within the prescribed time limit if it is done on the next business day. (1987, c. 777, s. 5.)

§§ 105-396 through 105-398: Repealed by Session Laws 1971, c. 806, s. 1.

SUBCHAPTER III. COLLECTION OF TAXES.

Former Article 30.

General Provisions.

§§ 105-399 through 105-403: Repealed by Session Laws 1971, c. 806, s. 3.

§ 105-404: Transferred to G.S. 105-32 by Session Laws 1971, c. 806, s. 2.

§ 105-405: Repealed by Session Laws 1963, c. 548.

§§ 105-405.1 through 105-406: Repealed by Session Laws 1971, c. 806, s. 3.

§ 105-407: Transferred to G.S. 105-267.1 by Session Laws 1971, c. 806, s. 2.

Article 31.

Rights of Parties Adjusted.

§§ 105-408 through 105-411: Repealed by Session Laws 1971, c. 806, s. 3.

§ 105-412: Transferred to G.S. 105-207 by Session Laws 1971, c. 806, s. 2.

Article 32.

Tax Liens.

§§ 105-413 through 105-414: Repealed by Session Laws 1971, c. 806, s. 3.

Article 33.

Time and Manner of Collection.

§§ 105-415 through 105-417: Repealed by Session Laws 1971, c. 806, s. 3.

Article 33A.

Agreements with United States or Other States.

§§ 105-417.1 through 105-417.3: Transferred to G.S. 105-268.1 through 105-268.3 by Session Laws 1971, c. 806, s. 2.

Article 34.

Tax Sales.

Part 1. Sale of Realty.

§§ 105-418 through 105-421: Repealed by Session Laws 1971, c. 806, s. 3.

Part 2. Refund of Tax Sales Certificates.

§ 105-422: Repealed by Session Laws 1971, c. 806, s. 3.

§ 105-423. Repealed by Session Laws 1947, c. 1065, s. 2.

§ 105-423.1. Repealed by Session Laws 1971, c. 806, s. 3.

Article 35.

Sheriff's Settlement of Taxes.

§ 105-424. Repealed by Session Laws 1971, c. 806, s. 3.

SUBCHAPTER IV. LISTING OF AUTOMOBILES.

Article 35A.

Listing of Automobiles in Certain Counties.

§§ 105-425 through 105-429: Repealed by Session Laws 1971, c. 806, s. 3.

SUBCHAPTER V. MOTOR FUEL TAXES.

Article 36.

Gasoline Tax.

§§ 105-430 through 105-435: Repealed by Session Laws 1995, c. 390, s. 2.

§ 105-436: Repealed by Session Laws 1991, c. 193, s. 5.

§ 105-436.1. Repealed by Session Laws 1985, c. 261, s. 1.

§105-437. Repealed by Session Laws 1963, c. 1169, s. 6.

§§ 105-438 through 105-441.1: Repealed by Session Laws 1995, c. 390, s. 2.

§ 105-442: Repealed by Session Laws 1991 (Reg. Sess., 1992), c. 913, s. 3.

§ 105-443. Repealed by Session Laws 1963, c. 1169, s. 5.

§§ 105-444 through 105-446.3: Repealed by Session Laws 1995, c. 390, s. 2.

§ 105-446.3:1. Repealed by Session Laws 1985, c. 261, s. 1.

§ 105-446.4. Repealed by Session Laws 1977, c. 802, s. 50.10.

§§ 105-446.5 through 105-449A: Repealed by Session Laws 1995, c. 390, s. 2.

§ 105-449.01: Repealed by Session Laws 1983 (Regular Session, 1984), c. 1004, s. 1.

Article 36A.

Special Fuels Tax.

§§ 105-449.1 through 105-449.27: Repealed by Session Laws 1995, c. 390, s. 2.

§ 105-449.28. Repealed by Session Laws 1981, c. 105, s. 4.

§ 105-449.29: Repealed by Session Laws 1995, c. 390, s. 2.

§§ 105-449.30 through 105-449.31. Repealed by Session Laws 1985 (Reg. Sess., 1986), c. 937, s. 19.

§ 105-449.32: Repealed by Session Laws 1993 (Reg. Sess., 1994), c. 745, s. 27.

§§ 105-449.33 through 105-449.35: Repealed by Session Laws 1995, c. 390, s. 2.

§ 105-449.36: Repealed by Session Laws 1983 (Regular Session, 1984), c. 1004, s. 1.

Article 36B.

Tax on Carriers Using Fuel Purchased Outside State.

§ 105-449.37. Definitions; tax liability.

(a) Definitions. - The following definitions apply in this Article:

(1) International Fuel Tax Agreement. - The Articles of Agreement adopted by the International Fuel Tax Association, Inc., as amended as of June 1, 2010.

(2) Motor carrier. - A person who operates or causes to be operated on any highway in this State a motor vehicle that is a qualified motor vehicle. The term does not include the United States, a state, or a political subdivision of a state.

(3) Motor vehicle. - Defined in G.S. 20-4.01.

(4) Operations. - The movement of a qualified motor vehicle by a motor carrier, whether loaded or empty and whether or not operated for compensation.

(5) Person. - Defined in G.S. 105-228.90.

(6) Qualified motor vehicle. - Defined in the International Fuel Tax Agreement.

(7) Secretary. - Defined in G.S. 105-228.90.

(b) Liability. - A motor carrier who operates on one or more days of a reporting period is liable for the tax imposed by this Article for that reporting period and is entitled to the credits allowed for that reporting period. (1955, c. 823, s. 1; 1973, c. 476, s. 193; 1983, c. 713, s. 55; 1989, c. 7, s. 1; 1991, c. 182,

s. 2; c. 487, s. 2; 1991 (Reg. Sess., 1992), c. 913, s. 8; 1993, c. 354, s. 28; 1999-337, s. 36; 2000-140, s. 74; 2008-134, s. 16; 2010-95, s. 27.)

§ 105-449.38. Tax levied.

A road tax for the privilege of using the streets and highways of this State is imposed upon every motor carrier on the amount of motor fuel or alternative fuel used by the carrier in its operations within this State. The tax shall be at the rate established by the Secretary pursuant to G.S. 105-449.80 or G.S. 105-449.136, as appropriate. This tax is in addition to any other taxes imposed on motor carriers. (1955, c. 823, s. 2; 1969, c. 600, s. 22; 1981, c. 690, s. 3; 1985 (Reg. Sess., 1986), c. 982, s. 16; 1995, c. 390, s. 16; 2001-205, s. 2; 2008-134, s. 17.)

§ 105-449.39. Credit for payment of motor fuel tax.

Every motor carrier subject to the tax levied by this Article is entitled to a credit on its quarterly return for tax paid by the carrier on fuel purchased in the State. The amount of the credit is determined using the flat cents-per-gallon rate plus the variable cents-per-gallon rate of tax in effect during the quarter covered by the return. To obtain a credit, the motor carrier must furnish evidence satisfactory to the Secretary that the tax for which the credit is claimed has been paid.

If the amount of a credit to which a motor carrier is entitled for a quarter exceeds the motor carrier's liability for that quarter, the excess is refundable in accordance with G.S. 105-241.7. (1955, c. 823, s. 3; 1969, c. 600, s. 22; c. 1098; 1973, c. 476, s. 193; 1979, 2nd Sess., c. 1098; 1981, c. 690, s. 3; 1985 (Reg. Sess., 1986), c. 982, s. 17; 1987, c. 315; 1989, c. 692, s. 5.7; 1991, c. 182, s. 3; c. 487, s. 3; 1998-146, s. 1; 1999-337, s. 37; 2005-435, s. 3; 2007-491, s. 40; 2010-95, s. 26(a).)

§ 105-449.40. Secretary may require bond.

(a)   Authority. - The Secretary may require a motor carrier to furnish a bond when any of the following occurs:

(1) The motor carrier fails to file a return within the time required by this Article.

(2) The motor carrier fails to pay a tax when due under this Article.

(3) After auditing the motor carrier's records, the Secretary determines that a bond is needed to protect the State from loss in collecting the tax due under this Article.

(b) Amount. - A bond required of a motor carrier under this section may not be more than the larger of the following amounts:

(1) Five hundred dollars ($500.00).

(2) Four times the motor carrier's average tax liability or refund for a reporting period.

A bond must be in the form required by the Secretary. (1955, c. 823, s. 4; 1967, c. 1110, s. 15; 1973, c. 476, s. 193; 1991, c. 487, s. 4; 2010-95, s. 26(b).)

§ 105-449.41: Repealed by Session Laws 2002-108, s. 2, effective January 1, 2003.

§ 105-449.42. Payment of tax.

The tax levied by this Article is due when a motor carrier files a quarterly return under G.S. 105-449.45. The amount of tax due is calculated on the amount of motor fuel or alternative fuel used by the motor carrier in its operations within this State during the quarter covered by the return. (1955, c. 823, s. 6; 1973, c. 476, s. 193; 1979, 2nd Sess., c. 1086, s. 2; 1983, c. 29, s. 2; 1991, c. 182, s. 4; 1999-337, s. 38; 2010-95, s. 26(c).)

§ 105-449.42A. Leased motor vehicles.

(a) Lessor in Leasing Business. - A lessor who is regularly engaged in the business of leasing or renting motor vehicles without drivers for compensation is the motor carrier for a leased or rented motor vehicle unless the lessee of the leased or rented motor vehicle gives the Secretary written notice, by filing a return or otherwise, that the lessee is the motor carrier. In that circumstance, the lessee is the motor carrier for the leased or rented motor vehicle.

Before a lessee gives the Secretary written notice under this subsection that the lessee is the motor carrier, the lessee and lessor must make a written agreement for the lessee to be the motor carrier. Upon request of the Secretary, the lessee must give the Secretary a copy of the agreement.

(b) Independent Contractor. - The lessee of a motor vehicle that is leased from an independent contractor is the motor carrier for the leased motor vehicle unless one of the circumstances listed in this subsection applies. If either of these circumstances applies, the lessor is the motor carrier for the leased motor vehicle.

(1) The motor vehicle is leased for fewer than 30 days.

(2) The motor vehicle is leased for at least 30 days and the lessor gives the Secretary written notice, by filing a return or otherwise, that the lessor is the motor carrier. Before a lessor gives the Secretary written notice that the lessor is the motor carrier, the lessor and lessee must make a written agreement for the lessor to be the motor carrier. Upon request of the Secretary, the lessor must give the Secretary a copy of the agreement.

(c) Liability. - An independent contractor who leases a motor vehicle to another for fewer than 30 days is liable for compliance with this Article and the person to whom the motor vehicle is leased is not liable. Otherwise, both the lessor and lessee of a motor vehicle are jointly and severally liable for compliance with this Article. (1983, c. 29, s. 3; 1985 (Reg. Sess., 1986), c. 826, s. 11; 1991, c. 487, s. 5; 1991 (Reg. Sess., 1992), c. 913, s. 9; 2010-95, s. 26(d).)

§ 105-449.43. Application of tax proceeds.

Tax revenue collected under this Article and tax refunds or credits allowed under this Article shall be allocated among and charged to the funds and accounts listed in G.S. 105-449.125 in accordance with that section. (1955, c. 823, s. 7; 1981 (Reg. Sess., 1982), c. 1211, s. 3; 1989, c. 692, s. 1.16; 1995, c. 390, s. 17.)

§ 105-449.44. How to determine the amount of fuel used in the State; presumption of amount used.

(a) Calculation. - The amount of motor fuel or alternative fuel a motor carrier uses in its operations in this State for a reporting period is the number of miles the motor carrier travels in this State during that period divided by the calculated miles per gallon for the motor carrier for all qualified motor vehicles during that period.

(b) Presumption. - The Secretary must check returns filed under this Article against the weigh station records and other records of the Division of Motor Vehicles of the Department of Transportation and the State Highway Patrol of the Department of Public Safety concerning motor carriers to determine if motor carriers that are operating in this State are filing the returns required by this Article. If the records indicate that a motor carrier operated in this State in a quarter and either did not file a return for that quarter or understated its mileage in this State on a return filed for that quarter by at least twenty-five percent (25%), the Secretary may assess the motor carrier for an amount based on the motor carrier's presumed operations. The motor carrier is presumed to have mileage in this State equal to 10 trips of 450 miles each for each of the motor carrier's qualified motor vehicles and to have fuel usage of four miles per gallon.

(c) Vehicles. - The number of qualified motor vehicles of a motor carrier that is registered under this Article is the number of sets of decals issued to the carrier. The number of qualified motor vehicles of a carrier that is not registered under this Article is the number of qualified motor vehicles registered by the motor carrier in the carrier's base state under the International Registration Plan. (1955, c. 823, s. 8; 1995, c. 390, s. 35; 1999-337, s. 39; 2000-173, s. 12; 2005-435, s. 4; 2008-134, s. 18; 2010-95, s. 26(e); 2011-145, s. 19.1(g).)

§ 105-449.45. Returns of carriers.

(a) Return. - A motor carrier must report its operations to the Secretary on a quarterly basis unless subsection (b) of this section exempts the motor carrier from this requirement. A quarterly return covers a calendar quarter and is due by the last day in April, July, October, and January. A return must be filed in the form required by the Secretary.

(b) Exemptions. - A motor carrier is not required to file a quarterly return if any of the following applies:

(1) All the motor carrier's operations during the quarter were made under a temporary permit issued under G.S. 105-449.49.

(2) The motor carrier is an intrastate motor carrier, as indicated on the motor carrier's application for registration with the Secretary.

(c) Informational Returns. - A motor carrier must file with the Secretary any informational returns concerning its operations that the Secretary requires.

(d) Penalties. - A motor carrier that fails to file a return under this section by the required date is subject to a penalty of fifty dollars ($50.00). (1955, c. 823, s. 9; 1973, c. 476, s. 193; 1979, 2nd Sess., c. 1086, s. 2; 1981 (Reg. Sess., 1982), c. 1254, s. 2; 1989 (Reg. Sess., 1990), c. 1050, s. 1; 1991, c. 182, s. 5; 1995, c. 17, s. 13.1; 1998-212, s. 29A.14(q); 1999-337, s. 40; 2009-445, s. 31(a); 2010-95, s. 26(f).)

§ 105-449.46. Inspection of books and records.

The Secretary and his authorized agents and representatives shall have the right at any reasonable time to inspect the books and records of any motor carrier subject to the tax imposed by this Article or to the registration fee imposed by Article 3 of Chapter 20 of the General Statutes. (1955, c. 823, s. 10; 1973, c. 476, s. 193; 2005-435, s. 5.)

§ 105-449.47. Registration of vehicles.

(a) Requirement. - A motor carrier that is subject to the International Fuel Tax Agreement may not operate or cause to be operated in this State a qualified motor vehicle unless both the motor carrier and at least one qualified motor vehicle are registered with the motor carrier's base state jurisdiction. A motor carrier that is not subject to the International Fuel Tax Agreement may not operate or cause to be operated in this State a qualified motor vehicle unless both the motor carrier and at least one qualified motor vehicle are registered with the Secretary for purposes of the tax imposed by this Article. This subsection applies to a motor carrier that operates a recreational vehicle that is considered a qualified motor vehicle.

(a1) Registration and Decal. - When the Secretary registers a motor carrier, the Secretary must issue a registration card for the motor carrier and a set of decals for each qualified motor vehicle the motor carrier registers. A motor carrier must keep records of decals issued to it and must be able to account for all decals it receives from the Secretary. Registrations and decals issued by the Secretary are for a calendar year. All decals issued by the Secretary remain the property of the State. The Secretary may revoke a registration or a decal when a motor carrier fails to comply with this Article or Article 36C or 36D of this Subchapter.

A motor carrier must carry a copy of its registration in each motor vehicle operated by the motor carrier when the vehicle is in this State. A motor vehicle must clearly display one decal on each side of the vehicle at all times. A decal must be affixed to the qualified motor vehicle for which it was issued in the place and manner designated by the authority that issued it.

(b) Exemption. - This section does not apply to the operation of a qualified motor vehicle that is registered in another state and is operated temporarily in this State by a public utility, a governmental or cooperative provider of utility services, or a contractor for one of these entities for the purpose of restoring utility services in an emergency outage. (1955, c. 823, s. 11; 1973, c. 746, s. 193; 1983, c. 713, s. 56; 1985 (Reg. Sess., 1986), c. 937, s. 20; 1989, c. 692, s. 6.2; 1991, c. 487, s. 6; 1995, c. 50, s. 5; c. 390, s. 18; 1999-337, s. 41; 2002-108, s. 3; 2004-170, s. 24; 2005-435, s. 6; 2008-134, s. 19.)

§ 105-449.47A. Reasons why the Secretary can deny an application for a registration and decals.

The Secretary may refuse to register and issue a decal to an applicant that does not meet the requirements set out in G.S. 105-449.69(b) or that has done any of the following:

(1) Had a registration issued under Chapter 105 or Chapter 119 of the General Statutes cancelled by the Secretary for cause.

(2) Had a registration issued by another jurisdiction, pursuant to the International Fuel Tax Agreement, cancelled for cause.

(3) Been convicted of fraud or misrepresentation.

(4) Been convicted of any other offense that indicates that the applicant may not comply with this Article if registered and issued a decal.

(5) Failed to remit payment for a tax debt under Chapter 105 or Chapter 119 of the General Statutes. The term "tax debt" has the same meaning as defined in G.S. 105-243.1.

(6) Failed to file a return due under Chapter 105 or Chapter 119 of the General Statutes. (2005-435, s. 7; 2008-134, s. 20; 2009-445, s. 32; 2010-95, s. 28.)

§ 105-449.48: Repealed by Session Laws 2006-162, s. 12(c), effective July 24, 2006.

§ 105-449.49. Temporary permits.

(a) Issuance. - Upon application to the Secretary and payment of a fee of fifty dollars ($50.00), a motor carrier may obtain a temporary permit authorizing the carrier to operate a vehicle in the State for three days without registering the vehicle in accordance with G.S. 105-449.47. A motor carrier to whom a temporary permit has been issued may elect not to report its operation of the vehicle during the three-day period. Fees collected under this subsection are credited to the Highway Fund.

(b) Refusal. - The Secretary may refuse to issue a temporary permit to any of the following:

(1) A motor carrier whose registration has been withheld or revoked.

(2) A motor carrier who the Secretary determines is evading payment of tax through the successive purchase of temporary permits. (1955, c. 823, s. 13; 1973, c. 476, s. 193; 1979, c. 11; 1981 (Reg. Sess., 1982), c. 1254, s. 1; 1983, c. 713, s. 58; 1991, c. 182, s. 6; c. 487, s. 7; 1991 (Reg. Sess., 1992), c. 913, s. 10; 2003-349, s. 10.1; 2006-162, s. 12(d).)

§ 105-449.50. Repealed by Session Laws 2008-134, s. 21.

§ 105-449.51. Violations declared to be misdemeanors.

Any person who operates or causes to be operated on a highway in this State a qualified motor vehicle that does not carry a registration card as required by this Article, does not properly display a decal as required by this Article, or is not registered in accordance with this Article commits a Class 3 misdemeanor and is punishable by a fine of two hundred dollars ($200.00). Each day's operation in violation of this section constitutes a separate offense. (1955, c. 823, s. 15; 1973, c. 476, s. 193; 1983, c. 713, s. 59; 1993, c. 539, s. 734; 1994, Ex. Sess., c. 24, s. 14(c); 2005-435, s. 8; 2008-134, s. 22.)

§ 105-449.52. Civil penalties applicable to motor carriers.

(a) Penalty. - A motor carrier who does any of the following is subject to a civil penalty:

(1) Operates in this State or causes to be operated in this State a qualified motor vehicle that either fails to carry the registration card required by this Article or fails to display a decal in accordance with this Article. The amount of the penalty is one hundred dollars ($100.00).

(2) Is unable to account for a decal the Secretary issues the motor carrier, as required by G.S. 105-449.47. The amount of the penalty is one hundred dollars ($100.00) for each decal for which the carrier is unable to account.

(3) Displays a decal on a qualified motor vehicle operated by a motor carrier that was not issued to the carrier by the Secretary under G.S. 105-449.47. The amount of the penalty is one thousand dollars ($1,000) for each decal unlawfully obtained. Both the licensed motor carrier to whom the Secretary issued the decal and the motor carrier displaying the unlawfully obtained decal are jointly and severally liable for the penalty under this subdivision.

(a1) Payment. - A penalty imposed under this section is payable to the agency that assessed the penalty. When a qualified motor vehicle is found to be operating without a registration card or a decal or with a decal the Secretary did not issue for the vehicle, the qualified motor vehicle may not be driven for a purpose other than to park it until the penalty imposed under this section is paid unless the officer that imposes the penalty determines that operating it will not jeopardize collection of the penalty.

(b) Review. - The procedure set out in G.S. 105-449.119 for reviewing a penalty imposed under Article 36C, Part 6, of this Chapter applies to a penalty imposed under this section. (1955, c. 823, s. 16; 1957, c. 948; 1973, c. 476, s. 193; 1975, c. 716, s. 5; 1981, c. 690, s. 18; 1983, c. 713, s. 60; 1991, c. 42, s. 14; 1991 (Reg. Sess., 1992), c. 913, s. 11; 1998-146, s. 2; 1999-337, s. 43; 2002-108, s. 4; 2004-170, s. 25; 2007-527, s. 16(a); 2008-134, ss. 8, 23.)

§ 105-449.53. Repealed by Session Laws 1963, c. 1169, s. 6.

§ 105-449.54. Commissioner of Motor Vehicles made process agent of nonresident motor carriers.

By operating a motor vehicle on the highways of this State, a nonresident motor carrier consents to the appointment of the Commissioner of Motor Vehicles as its attorney in fact and process agent for all summonses or other lawful process or notice in any action, assessment, or other proceeding under this Chapter. (1955, c. 823, s. 18; 2004-170, s. 26.)

§§ 105-449.55 through 105-449.56: Repealed by Session Laws 1991, c. 42, s. 17.

§ 105-449.57. Cooperative agreements between jurisdictions.

(a) Authority. - The Secretary may enter into cooperative agreements with other jurisdictions for exchange of information in administering the tax imposed by this Article. No agreement, arrangement, declaration, or amendment to an agreement is effective until stated in writing and approved by the Secretary.

(b) Content. - An agreement may provide for determining the base state for motor carriers, records requirements, audit procedures, exchange of information, persons eligible for tax licensing, defining qualified motor vehicles, determining if bonding is required, specifying reporting requirements and periods, including defining uniform penalty and interest rates for late reporting, determining methods for collecting and forwarding of motor carrier taxes and penalties to another jurisdiction, and any other provisions that will facilitate the administration of the agreement.

(c) Disclosure. - In accordance with G.S. 105-259, the Secretary may, as required by the terms of an agreement, forward to officials of another jurisdiction any information in the Department's possession relative to the use of motor fuel or alternative fuel by any motor carrier. The Secretary may disclose to officials of another jurisdiction the location of offices, motor vehicles, and other real and personal property of motor carriers.

(d) Audits. - An agreement may provide for each jurisdiction to audit the records of motor carriers based in the jurisdiction to determine if the taxes due each jurisdiction are properly reported and paid. Each jurisdiction must forward the findings of the audits performed on motor carriers based in the jurisdiction to each jurisdiction in which the carrier has taxable use of motor fuel or alternative fuel. For motor carriers not based in this State, the Secretary may utilize the audit findings received from another jurisdiction as the basis upon which to propose assessments of taxes against the carrier as though the audit had been conducted by the Secretary. Penalties and interest must be assessed at the rates provided in the agreement.

No agreement entered into pursuant to this section may preclude the Department from auditing the records of any motor carrier covered by this Chapter.

The provisions of Article 9 of this Chapter apply to any assessment or order made under this section.

(e) Restriction. - The Secretary may not enter into any agreement that would increase or decrease taxes and fees imposed under Subchapter V of Chapter 105 of the General Statutes. Any provision to the contrary is void. (1989, c. 667, s. 1; 1993, c. 485, s. 36; 1995 (Reg. Sess., 1996), c. 647, s. 50; 1999-337, s. 42.)

§ 105-449.58. Reserved for future codification purposes.

§ 105-449.59. Reserved for future codification purposes.

Article 36C.

Gasoline, Diesel, and Blends.

Part 1. General Provisions.

§ 105-449.60. Definitions.

The following definitions apply in this Article:

(1) Additive. - A de minimus amount of product that is added or mixed with motor fuel. Examples of an additive include fuel system detergent, an oxidation inhibitor, gasoline antifreeze, or an octane enhancer.

(2) Aviation gasoline. - Fuel blended or produced specifically for use in an aircraft motor.

(3) Biodiesel. - Any fuel or mixture of fuels derived in whole or in part from agricultural products or animal fats or wastes from these products or fats.

(4) Biodiesel provider. - A person who does any of the following:

a. Produces an average of no more than 500,000 gallons of biodiesel per month during a calendar year. A person who produces more than this amount is a refiner.

b. Imports biodiesel outside the terminal transfer system by means of a transport truck, a railroad tank car, or a tank wagon.

(5) Blended fuel. - A mixture composed of gasoline or diesel fuel and another liquid, other than an additive, that can be used as a fuel in a highway vehicle.

(6) Blender. - A person who produces blended fuel outside the terminal transfer system.

(7) Bonded importer. - A person, other than a supplier, who imports by transport truck or another means of transfer outside the terminal transfer system motor fuel removed from a terminal located in another state in one or more of the following circumstances:

a. The state from which the fuel is imported does not require the seller of the fuel to collect motor fuel tax on the removal of the fuel at that state's rate or the rate of the destination state.

b. The supplier of the fuel is not an elective supplier.

c. The supplier of the fuel is not a permissive supplier.

(8) Bulk end-user. - A person who maintains storage facilities for motor fuel and uses part or all of the stored fuel to operate a highway vehicle.

(9) Bulk plant. - A motor fuel storage and distribution facility that is not a terminal and from which motor fuel may be removed at a rack.

(10) Code. - Defined in G.S. 105-228.90.

(11) Destination state. - The state, territory, or foreign country to which motor fuel is directed for delivery into a storage facility, a receptacle, a container, or a type of transportation equipment for the purpose of resale or use.

(12) Diesel fuel. - Any liquid, other than gasoline, that is suitable for use as a fuel in a diesel-powered highway vehicle. The term includes biodiesel, fuel oil, heating oil, high-sulfur dyed diesel fuel, and kerosene. The term does not include jet fuel.

(13) Distributor. - A person who does one or more of the activities listed in this subdivision. The term does not include a person who sells motor fuel only at retail.

a. Produces, refines, blends, compounds, or manufactures motor fuel.

b. Transports motor fuel into a state or exports motor fuel out of a state.

c. Engages in the distribution of motor fuel primarily by tank car or tank truck or both.

d. Operates a bulk plant where the person has active motor fuel bulk storage.

(14) Diversion. - The movement of motor fuel from a terminal to a state other than the destination state indicated on the original bill of lading.

(15) Dyed diesel fuel. - Diesel fuel that meets the dyeing and marking requirements as set out in 26 C.F.R. § 48.4082.1.

(16) Elective supplier. - A supplier that is required to be licensed in this State and that elects to collect the excise tax due this State on motor fuel that is removed by the supplier at a terminal located in another state and has this State as its destination state.

(17) Exempt card or code. - A credit card or an access code that enables the person to whom the card or code is issued to buy motor fuel at retail without paying the motor fuel excise tax on the fuel.

(18) Export. - To obtain motor fuel in this State for sale or other distribution in another state. In applying this definition, motor fuel delivered out-of-state by or

for the seller constitutes an export by the seller and motor fuel delivered out-of-state by or for the purchaser constitutes an export by the purchaser.

(19) Fuel alcohol. - Alcohol, methanol, or fuel grade ethanol.

(20) Fuel alcohol provider. - A person who does any of the following:

a. Produces an average of no more than 500,000 gallons of fuel alcohol per month during a calendar year. A person who produces more than this amount is a refiner.

b. Imports fuel alcohol outside the terminal transfer system by means of a transport truck, a railroad tank car, or a tank wagon.

(21) Gasohol. - A blended fuel composed of gasoline and fuel grade ethanol.

(22) Gasoline. - Any of the following:

a. All products that are commonly or commercially known or sold as gasoline and are suitable for use as a fuel in a highway vehicle, other than products that have an American Society for Testing Materials octane number of less than 75 as determined by the motor method. The term does not include aviation gasoline.

b. A petroleum product component of gasoline, such as naptha, reformate, or toluene.

c. Gasohol.

d. Fuel alcohol.

(23) Gross gallons. - The total amount of motor fuel measured in gallons, exclusive of any temperature, pressure, or other adjustments.

(24) Highway. - Defined in G.S. 20-4.01(13).

(25) Highway vehicle. - A self-propelled vehicle that is designed for use on a highway.

(26) Import. - To bring motor fuel into this State by any means of conveyance other than in the fuel supply tank of a highway vehicle. In applying this definition,

motor fuel delivered into this State from out-of-state by or for the seller constitutes an import by the seller, and motor fuel delivered into this State from out-of-state by or for the purchaser constitutes an import by the purchaser.

(27)   In-State supplier. - Either of the following:

a.   A supplier that is required to have a license and elects not to collect the excise tax due this State on motor fuel that is removed by the supplier at a terminal located in another state and has this State as its destination state.

b.   A supplier that does business only in this State.

(28)   Jet fuel. - Kerosene that meets all of the following requirements:

a.   Has a maximum distillation temperature of 400 degrees Fahrenheit at the ten percent (10%) recovery point and a final maximum boiling point of 572 degrees Fahrenheit.

b.   Meets American Society Testing Materials Specification D 1655 and Military Specifications MIL-T-5624P and MIL-T-83133D, Grades JP-5 and JP-8.

(29)   Kerosene. - Petroleum oil that is free from water, glue, and suspended matter and that meets the specifications and standards adopted under G.S. 119-26 by the Gasoline and Oil Inspection Board.

(30)   Marine vessel. - A ship, boat, or other watercraft used or capable of being used to move in or through a waterway.

(31)   Motor fuel. - Gasoline, diesel fuel, and blended fuel.

(32)   Motor fuel rate. - The rate of tax set in G.S. 105-449.80.

(33)   Motor fuel transporter. - A person who transports motor fuel by pipeline, transport truck, railroad tank car, or marine vessel.

(34)   Net gallons. - The amount of motor fuel measured in gallons when corrected to a temperature of 60 degrees Fahrenheit and a pressure of 14 7/10 pounds per square inch.

(35)   Occasional importer. - One or more of the following that imports motor fuel by any means outside the terminal transfer system:

a. A distributor that imports motor fuel on an average basis of no more than once a month during a calendar year.

b. A bulk end-user that acquires motor fuel for import from a bulk plant and is not required to be licensed as a bonded importer.

c. A distributor that imports motor fuel for use in a race car.

(36) Permissive supplier. - An out-of-state supplier that elects, but is not required, to have a supplier's license under this Article.

(37) Person. - Defined in G.S. 105-228.90.

(38) Pipeline. - A fuel distribution system that moves motor fuel, in bulk, through a pipe either from a refinery to a terminal or from a terminal to another terminal.

(39) Position holder. - The person who holds the inventory position on the motor fuel in a terminal, as reflected on the records of the terminal operator. A person holds the inventory position on the motor fuel when that person has a contract with the terminal operator for the use of storage facilities and terminaling services for fuel at the terminal. The term includes a terminal operator who owns fuel in the terminal.

(40) Rack. - A mechanism for delivering motor fuel from a refinery, a terminal, or a bulk plant into a transport truck, a railroad tank car, or another means of transfer that is outside the terminal transfer system.

(41) Refiner. - A person who owns, operates, or controls a refinery. The term includes a person who produces an average of more than 500,000 gallons of fuel alcohol or biodiesel a month during a calendar year.

(42) Refinery. - A facility used to process crude oil, unfinished oils, natural gas liquids, or other hydrocarbons into motor fuel and from which fuel may be removed by pipeline or vessel or at a rack. The term does not include a facility that produces only blended fuel or gasohol.

(43) Removal. - A physical transfer other than by evaporation, loss, or destruction. A physical transfer to a transport truck or another means of conveyance outside the terminal transfer system is complete upon delivery into the means of conveyance.

(44) Retailer. - A person who maintains storage facilities for motor fuel and who sells the fuel at retail or dispenses the fuel at a retail location.

(45) Secretary. - Defined in G.S. 105-228.90.

(46) Supplier. - Any of the following:

a. A position holder or a person who receives motor fuel pursuant to a two-party exchange.

b. A fuel alcohol provider.

c. A biodiesel provider.

d. A refiner.

(47) System transfer. - Either of the following:

a. A transfer of motor fuel within the terminal transfer system.

b. A transfer, by transport truck or railroad tank car, of fuel grade ethanol.

(48) Tank wagon. - A truck that is not a transport truck and is designed or used to carry at least 1,000 gallons of motor fuel.

(49) Tank wagon importer. - A person who imports only by means of a tank wagon motor fuel that is removed from a terminal or a bulk plant located in another state.

(50) Tax. - An inspection or other excise tax on motor fuel and any other fee or charge imposed on motor fuel on a per-gallon basis.

(51) Terminal. - A motor fuel storage and distribution facility that has been assigned a terminal control number by the Internal Revenue Service, is supplied by pipeline or marine vessel, and from which motor fuel, jet fuel, or aviation gasoline may be removed at a rack.

(52) Terminal operator. - A person who owns, operates, or otherwise controls a terminal.

(53)　Terminal transfer system. - The motor fuel distribution system consisting of refineries, pipelines, marine vessels, and terminals. The term has the same meaning as "bulk transfer/terminal system" under 26 C.F.R. § 48.4081-1.

(54)　Transmix. - Either of the following:

a.　The buffer or interface between two different products in a pipeline shipment.

b.　A mix of two different products within a refinery or terminal that results in an off-grade mixture.

(55)　Transport truck. - A tractor trailer designed or used to transport loads of motor fuel over a highway.

(56)　Trustee. - A person who is licensed as a supplier and who receives tax payments from and on behalf of a licensed distributor or licensed importer for remittance to the Secretary.

(57)　Two-party exchange. - A transaction in which motor fuel is transferred from one licensed supplier to another licensed supplier pursuant to an exchange agreement under which the supplier that is the position holder agrees to deliver motor fuel to the other supplier or the other supplier's customer at the rack of the terminal at which the delivering supplier is the position holder.

(58)　User. - A person who owns or operates a licensed highway vehicle that has a registered gross vehicle weight of at least 10,001 pounds and who does not maintain storage facilities for motor fuel. (1995, c. 390, s. 3; 1995 (Reg. Sess., 1996), c. 647, ss. 1, 2; 1998-146, s. 3; 2000-173, ss. 13(a), 14(a); 2001-414, s. 27; 2002-108, ss. 5, 6; 2003-349, s. 10.2; 2004-170, s. 27; 2006-162, s. 14(a); 2008-134, s. 24.)

§ 105-449.61. Tax restrictions; administration.

(a)　No Local Tax. - A county or city may not impose a tax on the sale, distribution, or use of motor fuel.

(b)　No Double Tax. - The tax imposed by this Chapter applies only once on the same motor fuel.

(c) Administration. - Article 9 of this Chapter applies to this Article. (1995, c. 390, s. 3.)

§ 105-449.62. Nature of tax.

This Article imposes a tax on motor fuel to provide revenue for the State's transportation needs and for the other purposes listed in Part 7 of this Article. The tax is collected from the supplier or importer of the fuel because this method is the most efficient way to collect the tax. The tax is designed, however, to be paid ultimately by the person who consumes the fuel. The tax becomes a part of the cost of the fuel and is consequently paid by those who subsequently purchase and consume the fuel. (1997-60, s. 1.)

§ 105-449.63. Reserved for future codification purposes.

§ 105-449.64. Reserved for future codification purposes.

Part 2. Licensing.

§ 105-449.65. List of persons who must have a license.

(a) License. - A person may not engage in business in this State as any of the following unless the person has a license issued by the Secretary authorizing the person to engage in that business:

(1) A refiner.

(2) A supplier.

(3) A terminal operator.

(4) An importer.

(5) An exporter.

(6) A blender.

(7) A motor fuel transporter who transports motor fuel for hire.

(8) Repealed by Session Laws 1999-438, s. 20, effective August 10, 1999.

(9) Repealed by Session Laws 1999-438, s. 21, effective August 10, 1999.

(10) A distributor who purchases motor fuel from an elective or permissive supplier at an out-of-state terminal for import into this State.

(b) Multiple Activity. - A person who is engaged in more than one activity for which a license is required must have a separate license for each activity, unless one of the following subdivisions provides otherwise.

(1) Supplier. - A person who is licensed as a supplier is considered to have a license as a distributor. A person who is licensed as a supplier and is a biodiesel provider is considered to have a license as a blender.

(2) Importer. - A person who is licensed as an occasional importer or a tank wagon importer is not required to obtain a separate license as a distributor unless the importer is also purchasing motor fuel, at the terminal rack, from an elective or permissive supplier who is authorized to collect and remit the tax to the State.

(3) Distributor. - A person who is licensed as a distributor is not required to obtain a separate license as an importer if the distributor acquires fuel for import only from an elective supplier or a permissive supplier and is not required to obtain a separate license as an exporter. (1995, c. 390, s. 3; 1995 (Reg. Sess., 1996), c. 647, s. 3; 1997-60, s. 2; 1999-438, ss. 20, 21; 2003-349, s. 10.3; 2005-435, s. 9; 2006-162, s. 13(a); 2008-134, s. 25.)

§ 105-449.66. Importer licensing.

An applicant for a license as an importer must indicate on the application the type of importer license sought. The types of importers are bonded importer, occasional importer, and tank wagon importer.

A person may not be licensed as more than one type of importer. A bulk end-user that imports motor fuel from a terminal of a supplier that is not an elective or a permissive supplier must be licensed as a bonded importer. A bulk end-user that imports motor fuel from a bulk plant and is not required to be licensed as a bonded importer must be licensed as an occasional importer. A bulk end-user that imports motor fuel only from a terminal of an elective or a permissive supplier is not required to be licensed as an importer. (1995, c. 390, s. 3; 1995 (Reg. Sess., 1996), c. 647, s. 4; 1997-60, s. 3; 2008-134, s. 26.)

§ 105-449.67. List of persons who may obtain a license.

A person who is engaged in business as any of the following may obtain a license issued by the Secretary for that business:

(1)　A distributor who is not required to be licensed under G.S. 105-449.65.

(2)　A permissive supplier. (1995, c. 390, s. 3; 1995 (Reg. Sess., 1996), c. 647, s. 5; 1997-60, s. 4; 2003-349, s. 10.4.)

§ 105-449.68. Restrictions on who can get a license as a distributor.

A bulk end-user of motor fuel may not be licensed as a distributor unless the bulk end-user also acquires motor fuel from a supplier or from another distributor for subsequent sale. This restriction does not apply to a bulk end-user that was licensed as a distributor on January 1, 1996. If a distributor license held by a bulk end-user on January 1, 1996, is subsequently cancelled, the bulk end-user is subject to the restriction set in this section. (1995, c. 390, s. 3; 2000-173, s. 14(b); 2008-134, s. 27.)

§ 105-449.69. How to apply for a license.

(a)　General. - To obtain a license, an applicant must file an application with the Secretary on a form provided by the Secretary. An application must include the applicant's name, address, federal employer identification number, and any other information required by the Secretary.

(b) Most Licenses. - An applicant for a license as a refiner, a supplier, a terminal operator, an importer, a blender, or a distributor must meet the following requirements:

(1) If the applicant is a corporation, the applicant must either be incorporated in this State or be authorized to transact business in this State.

(2) If the applicant is a limited liability company, the applicant must either be organized in this State or be authorized to transact business in this State.

(3) If the applicant is a limited partnership, the applicant must either be formed in this State or be authorized to transact business in this State.

(4) If the applicant is an individual or a general partnership, the applicant must designate an agent for service of process and give the agent's name and address.

(c) Federal Certificate. - An applicant for a license as a refiner, a supplier, a terminal operator, or a blender must have a federal Certificate of Registry that is issued under § 4101 of the Code and authorizes the applicant to enter into federal tax-free transactions in taxable motor fuel in the terminal transfer system. An applicant that is required to have a federal Certificate of Registry must include the registration number of the certificate on the application for a license under this section.

An applicant for a license as an importer, an exporter, or a distributor that has a federal Certificate of Registry issued under § 4101 of the Code must include the registration number of the certificate on the application for a license under this section.

(d) Import Activity. - An applicant for a license as an importer or as a distributor must list on the application each state from which the applicant intends to import motor fuel and, if required by a state listed, must be licensed or registered for motor fuel tax purposes in that state. If a state listed requires the applicant to be licensed or registered, the applicant must give the applicant's license or registration number in that state.

(e) Export Activity. - An applicant for a license as an exporter must designate an agent located in North Carolina for service of process and must give the agent's name and address. An applicant for a license as an exporter or as a distributor must list on the application each state to which the applicant intends to export motor fuel received in this State by means of a transfer that is outside the terminal transfer system and, if required by a state listed, must be licensed or registered for motor fuel tax purposes in that state. If a state listed requires the applicant to be licensed or registered, the applicant must give the applicant's license or registration number in that state. (1995, c. 390, s. 3; 1995 (Reg. Sess., 1996), c. 647, s. 6; 2003-349, s. 10.5; 2005-435, s. 10; 2008-134, s. 28.)

§ 105-449.70. Supplier election to collect tax on out-of-state removals.

(a) Election. - An applicant for a license as a supplier may elect on the application to collect the excise tax due this State on motor fuel that is removed by the supplier at a terminal located in another state and has this State as its destination state. The Secretary must provide for this election on the application form. A supplier that makes the election allowed by this section is an elective supplier. A supplier that does not make the election allowed by this section is an in-State supplier.

A supplier that does not make the election on the application for a supplier's license may make the election later by completing an election form provided by the Secretary. A supplier that does not make the election may not act as an elective supplier for motor fuel that is removed at a terminal in another state and has this State as its destination state.

(b) Effect. - A supplier that makes the election allowed by this section agrees to all of the following with respect to motor fuel that is removed by the supplier at a terminal located in another state and has this State as its destination state:

(1) To collect the excise tax due this State on the fuel and to waive any defense that the State lacks jurisdiction to require the supplier to collect the excise tax due this State under this Article on the fuel.

(2) To report and pay the tax due on the fuel in the same manner as if the removal had occurred at a terminal located in this State.

(3) To keep records of the removal of the fuel and submit to audits concerning the fuel as if the removal had occurred at a terminal located in this State.

(4) To report removals of fuel received by a person who is not licensed in the state where the removal occurred.

(c) Limited Jurisdiction. - A supplier that makes the election allowed by this section acknowledges that the State imposes the requirements listed in subsection (b) of this section on the supplier under its general police power set out in Article 3 of Chapter 119 of the General Statutes to regulate the quality of motor fuel and thereby promote public health and safety. A supplier that makes the election allowed by this section submits to the jurisdiction of the State only for the administration of this Article. (1995, c. 390, s. 3; 1995 (Reg. Sess., 1996), c. 647, ss. 7, 8; 2008-134, s. 29.)

§ 105-449.71. Permissive supplier election to collect tax on out-of-state removals.

(a) Election. - An out-of-state supplier that is not required to have a license under this Part may elect to have a license and thereby become a permissive supplier. An out-of-state supplier that does not make this election may not act as a permissive supplier for motor fuel that is removed at a terminal in another state and has this State as its destination state.

(b) Effect. - By obtaining a license as a permissive supplier, the permissive supplier agrees to be subject to the same requirements as a supplier and to all of the following with respect to motor fuel that is removed by the permissive supplier at a terminal located in another state and has this State as its destination state:

(1) To collect the excise tax due this State on the fuel and to waive any defense that the State lacks jurisdiction to require the supplier to collect the excise tax due this State under this Article on the fuel.

(2) To report and pay the tax due on the fuel in the same manner as if the removal had occurred at a terminal located in this State.

(3) To keep records of the removal of the fuel and submit to audits concerning the fuel as if the removal had occurred at a terminal located in this State.

(4) To report removals of fuel received by a person who is not licensed in the state where the removal occurred.

(c) Limited Jurisdiction. - A supplier that makes the election allowed by this section acknowledges that the State imposes the requirements listed in subsection (b) of this section on the supplier under its general police power set out in Article 3 of Chapter 119 of the General Statutes to regulate the quality of motor fuel and thereby promote public health and safety. A supplier that makes the election allowed by this section submits to the jurisdiction of the State only for the administration of this Article. (1995, c. 390, s. 3; 1995 (Reg. Sess., 1996), c. 647, s. 9.)

§ 105-449.72. Bond or letter of credit required as a condition of obtaining and keeping certain licenses or of applying for certain refunds.

(a) Initial Bond. - An applicant for a license as a refiner, a terminal operator, a supplier, an importer, a blender, a permissive supplier, or a distributor must file with the Secretary a bond or an irrevocable letter of credit. A bond or an irrevocable letter of credit must be conditioned upon compliance with the requirements of this Article, be payable to the State, and be in the form required by the Secretary. The amount of the bond or irrevocable letter of credit is determined as follows:

(1) For an applicant for a license as any of the following, the amount is two million dollars ($2,000,000):

a. A refiner.

b. A terminal operator.

c. A supplier that is a position holder or a person that receives motor fuel pursuant to a two-party exchange.

d. A bonded importer.

e. A permissive supplier.

(2) For an applicant for a license as any of the following, the amount is two times the applicant's average expected monthly tax liability under this Article, as

determined by the Secretary. The amount may not be less than two thousand dollars ($2,000) and may not be more than five hundred thousand dollars ($500,000):

    a.   Repealed by Session Laws 2007-527, s. 17(a), effective October 1, 2007.

    b.   An occasional importer.

    c.   A tank wagon importer.

    d.   A distributor.

    e.   Repealed by Session Laws 1997-60, s. 5, effective October 5, 1997.

(3)   For an applicant for a license as any of the following, a bond is required only if the applicant's average expected annual tax liability under this Article, as determined by the Secretary, is at least two thousand dollars ($2,000). When a bond is required, the bond amount is the same as under subdivision (2) of this subsection.

    a.   A blender.

    b.   A supplier that is a fuel alcohol provider or a biodiesel provider but is neither a position holder nor a person that receives motor fuel pursuant to a two-party exchange.

(b)   Multiple Activity. - An applicant for a license as a distributor and as a bonded importer must file only the bond required of a bonded importer. An applicant for two or more of the licenses listed in subdivision (a)(2) or (a)(3) of this section may file one bond that covers the combined liabilities of the applicant under all the activities. A bond for these combined activities may not exceed the maximum amount set in subdivision (a)(2) of this subsection.

(c)   Adjustment to Bond. - When notified to do so by the Secretary, a person that has filed a bond or an irrevocable letter of credit and that holds a license listed in subdivision (a)(2) of this section must file an additional bond or irrevocable letter of credit in the amount requested by the Secretary. The person must file the additional bond or irrevocable letter of credit within 30 days after receiving the notice from the Secretary. The amount of the initial bond or irrevocable letter of credit and any additional bond or irrevocable letter of credit filed by the license holder, however, may not exceed the limits set in subdivision (a)(2) of this section.

(d) Replacements. - When a license holder files a bond or an irrevocable letter of credit as a replacement for a previously filed bond or letter of credit and the license holder has paid all taxes and penalties due under this Article, the Secretary must take one of the following actions:

(1) Return the previously filed bond or letter of credit.

(2) Notify the person liable on the previously filed bond that the person is released from liability on the bond.

(e) Credit Card Companies. - The Secretary may require a credit card company to file with the Secretary a bond if the company applies for a refund under G.S. 105-449.105(a) and the Secretary determines after an audit that a bond is needed to protect the State from loss in collecting any additional tax due pursuant to the audit. The bond must be conditioned upon compliance with the requirements of this Article, be payable to the State, and be in the form required by the Secretary. The amount of a bond required under this subsection is two times the average monthly refund due, subject to the minimum and maximum amounts provided in subdivision (a)(2) of this section.

(f) Exemption. - The requirement to obtain a bond or an irrevocable letter of credit does not apply to a distributor, an importer, or a motor fuel transporter who supplies motor fuel when the market for motor fuel is disrupted and emergency supplies are needed, as identified by an executive order of the Governor. (1995, c. 390, s. 3; 1995 (Reg. Sess., 1996), c. 647, s. 10; 1997-60, s. 5; 1998-146, s. 4; 2001-205, s. 5; 2002-108, ss. 7, 8; 2003-349, s. 10.6; 2004-170, s. 28; 2007-527, s. 17(a); 2009-445, s. 33.)

§ 105-449.73. Reasons why the Secretary can deny an application for a license.

The Secretary may refuse to issue a license to an applicant that has done any of the following:

(1) Had a license or registration issued under this Article or former Article 36 or 36A of this Chapter cancelled by the Secretary for cause.

(1a) Had a motor fuel license or registration issued by another state cancelled for cause.

(2) Had a federal Certificate of Registry issued under § 4101 of the Code, or a similar federal authorization, revoked.

(3) Been convicted of fraud or misrepresentation.

(4) Been convicted of any other offense that indicates that the applicant may not comply with this Article if issued a license.

(5) Failed to remit payment for a tax debt under Chapter 105 or Chapter 119 of the General Statutes. The term "tax debt" has the same meaning as defined in G.S. 105-243.1.

(6) Failed to file a return due under Chapter 105 or Chapter 119 of the General Statutes. (1995, c. 390, s. 3; 1995 (Reg. Sess., 1996), c. 647, s. 11; 2003-349, s. 10.7; 2005-435, s. 11.)

§ 105-449.74. Issuance of license.

Upon approval of an application, the Secretary must issue a license to the applicant. A supplier's license must indicate the category of the supplier. An importer's license must indicate the category of the importer. A license holder must maintain and display a copy of the license issued under this Part in a conspicuous place at each place of business of the license holder. A license is not transferable and remains in effect until surrendered or cancelled. (1995, c. 390, s. 3; 2004-170, s. 29; 2008-134, s. 30.)

§ 105-449.75. License holder must notify the Secretary of discontinuance of business.

A license holder that stops engaging in this State in the business for which the license was issued must give the Secretary written notice of the change and must surrender the license to the Secretary. The notice must give the date the change takes effect and, if the license holder has transferred the business to another by sale or otherwise, the date of the transfer and the name and address of the person to whom the business is transferred.

The license holder is responsible for all taxes for which the license holder is liable under this Article but are not yet due. If the license holder has transferred the business to another and does not give the notice required by this section, the person to whom the license holder has transferred the business is liable for the amount of any tax the license holder owed the State on the date the business was transferred. The liability of the person to whom the business is transferred is limited to the value of the property acquired from the license holder. (1995, c. 390, s. 3; 2008-134, s. 31.)

§ 105-449.76. Reasons why the Secretary can cancel a license.

The Secretary may cancel a license issued under this Article upon the written request of the license holder. The Secretary may summarily cancel the license of a license holder when the Secretary finds that the license holder is incurring liability for the tax imposed under this Article after failing to pay a tax when due under this Article. In addition, the Secretary may cancel the license of a license holder that commits one or more of the acts listed in G.S. 105-449.120 after holding a hearing on whether the license should be cancelled.

The Secretary must send a person whose license is summarily cancelled a notice of the cancellation and must give the person an opportunity to have a hearing on the cancellation within 10 days after the cancellation. The Secretary must give a person whose license may be cancelled after a hearing at least 10 days' written notice of the date, time, and place of the hearing. A notice of a summary license cancellation and a notice of hearing must be sent by registered mail to the last known address of the license holder.

When the Secretary cancels a license and the license holder has paid all taxes and penalties due under this Article, the Secretary must take one of the following actions concerning a bond or an irrevocable letter of credit filed by the license holder:

(1)   Return an irrevocable letter of credit to the license holder.

(2) Return a bond to the license holder or notify the person liable on the bond and the license holder that the person is released from liability on the bond. (1995, c. 390, s. 3.)

§ 105-449.77. Records and lists of license applicants and license holders.

(a) Records. - The Secretary must keep a record of the following:

(1) Applicants for a license under this Article.

(2) Persons to whom a license has been issued under this Article.

(3) Persons that hold a current license issued under this Article, by license category.

(b) Lists. - The Secretary must annually give a list to each license holder of all the license holders under this Article. The list must state the name, account number, and business address of each license holder on the list. The Secretary must send a monthly update of the list to each licensed refiner or licensed supplier and to any other license holder that requests a copy of the list.

(c) Repealed by Session Laws 2002-108, s. 9, effective January 1, 2003. (1995, c. 390, s. 3; 1995 (Reg. Sess., 1996), c. 647, s. 12; 1997-60, s. 6; 2002-108, s. 9.)

§ 105-449.78. Reserved for future codification purposes.

§ 105-449.79. Reserved for future codification purposes.

Part 3. Tax and Liability.

§ 105-449.80. Tax rate.

(a) Rate. - The motor fuel excise tax rate is a flat rate of seventeen and one-half cents (17 1/2¢)a gallon plus a variable wholesale component. The variable wholesale component is either three and one-half cents (3 1/2¢) a gallon or seven percent (7%) of the average wholesale price of motor fuel for the applicable base period, whichever is greater.

The two base periods are six-month periods; one ends on September 30 and one ends on March 31. The Secretary must set the tax rate twice a year based on the wholesale price for each base period. A tax rate set by the Secretary using information for the base period that ends on September 30 applies to the six-month period that begins the following January 1. A tax rate set by the Secretary using information for the base period that ends on March 31 applies to the six-month period that begins the following July 1.

(b) Wholesale Price. - The Secretary must determine the average wholesale price of motor fuel for each base period. To do this, the Secretary must use information on refiner and gas plant operator sales prices of finished motor gasoline and No. 2 diesel fuel for resale, published by the United States Department of Energy in the "Monthly Energy Review", or equivalent data.

The Secretary must compute the average sales price of finished motor gasoline for the base period, compute the average sales price for No. 2 diesel fuel for the base period, and then compute a weighted average of the results of the first two computations based on the proportion of tax collected on each under this Article for the base period. The Secretary must then convert the weighted average price to a cents-per-gallon rate and round the rate to the nearest one-tenth of a cent (1/10¢). If the converted cents-per-gallon rate is exactly between two-tenths of a cent (2/10¢) the Secretary must round the rate up to the higher of the two.

(c) Notification. - The Secretary must notify affected taxpayers of the tax rate to be in effect for each six-month period beginning January 1 and July 1. (1995, c. 390, s. 3.)

§ 105-449.81. Excise tax on motor fuel.

An excise tax at the motor fuel rate is imposed on motor fuel that is:

(1)   Removed from a refinery or a terminal and, upon removal, is subject to the federal excise tax imposed by § 4081 of the Code.

(2)   Imported by a system transfer to a refinery or a terminal and, upon importation, is subject to the federal excise tax imposed by § 4081 of the Code.

(3)   Imported by a means of transfer outside the terminal transfer system for sale, use, or storage in this State and would have been subject to the federal excise tax imposed by § 4081 of the Code if it had been removed at a terminal or bulk plant rack in this State instead of imported.

(3a)   Repealed by Session Laws 2007-527, s. 38(a), effective January 1, 2008.

(3b)   Fuel grade ethanol that meets any of the following descriptions:

a.   Is produced in this State and is removed from the storage facility at the production location.

b.   Is imported to this State outside the terminal transfer system.

c.   Repealed by Session Laws 2009-445, s. 34(a), effective January 1, 2010.

(4)   Blended fuel made in this State or imported to this State.

(5)   Transferred within the terminal transfer system and is subject, upon transfer, to the federal excise tax imposed by section 4081 of the Code or is transferred to a person who is not licensed under this Article as a supplier. (1995, c. 390, s. 3; 1995 (Reg. Sess., 1996), c. 647, s. 13; 2004-170, s. 30; 2007-527, s. 38(a); 2008-134, s. 32; 2009-445, s. 34(a).)

§ 105-449.82. Liability for tax on removals from a refinery or terminal.

(a)   Refinery Removal. - The excise tax imposed by G.S. 105-449.81(1) on motor fuel removed from a refinery in this State is payable by the refiner.

(b)   Terminal System Removal. - The excise tax imposed by G.S. 105-449.81(1) on motor fuel removed by a system transfer from a terminal in this

State is payable by the position holder for the fuel. If the position holder is not the terminal operator, the terminal operator is jointly and severally liable for the tax.

(c) Terminal Rack Removal. - The excise tax imposed by G.S. 105-449.81(1) on motor fuel removed at a terminal rack in this State is payable by the person that first receives the fuel upon its removal from the terminal. If the motor fuel is removed by an unlicensed distributor, the supplier of the fuel is jointly and severally liable for the tax due on the fuel. If the motor fuel is sold by a person who is not licensed as a supplier, as required by this Article, the terminal operator, the person selling the fuel, and the person removing the fuel are jointly and severally liable for the tax due on the fuel. If the motor fuel removed is not dyed diesel fuel but the shipping document issued for the fuel states that the fuel is dyed diesel fuel, the terminal operator, the supplier, and the person removing the fuel are jointly and severally liable for the tax due on the fuel.

If the motor fuel is removed for export by an unlicensed exporter, the exporter is liable for tax on the fuel at the motor fuel rate and at the rate of the destination state. A supplier who sells motor fuel to a unlicensed exporter is jointly and severally liable for the tax due on the fuel at the motor fuel rate. (1995, c. 390, s. 3; 1995 (Reg. Sess., 1996), c. 647, s. 14; 1997-60, s. 7; 2008-134, s. 33.)

§ 105-449.83. Liability for tax on imports.

(a) By System Transfer. - The excise tax imposed by G.S. 105-449.81(2) on motor fuel imported by a system transfer to a refinery is payable by the refiner. The excise tax imposed by that subdivision on motor fuel imported by a system transfer to a terminal is payable by the person importing the fuel and by the terminal operator, both of which are jointly and severally liable for payment of the tax due on the fuel.

(b) From Out-of-State Terminal. - The excise tax imposed by G.S. 105-449.81(3) on motor fuel that is removed from a terminal rack located in another state and has this State as its destination state is payable by the importer of the fuel as follows:

(1)   If the importer of the fuel is a licensed supplier in this State and the fuel is removed for the supplier's own account for use in this State, the tax is payable by the supplier.

(2)   If the supplier of the fuel is licensed in this State as an elective supplier or a permissive supplier, the tax is payable to the supplier as trustee.

(3)   If no other subdivision of this subsection applies, the tax is payable by the importer when filing a return with the Secretary.

(c)   From Out-of-State Bulk Plant. - The excise tax imposed by G.S. 105-449.81(3) on motor fuel that is removed from a bulk plant located in another state is payable by the person that imports the fuel. (1995, c. 390, s. 3.)

§ 105-449.83A. Liability for tax on fuel grade ethanol.

The excise tax imposed by G.S. 105-449.81(3b) on fuel grade ethanol is payable by the refiner or fuel alcohol provider. (1995 (Reg. Sess., 1996), c. 647, s. 15; 2008-134, s. 34; 2009-445, s. 34(b).)

§ 105-449.84. Liability for tax on blended fuel.

(a)   On Blender. - The excise tax imposed by G.S. 105-449.81(4) on blended fuel made in this State is payable by the blender. The number of gallons of blended fuel on which the tax is payable is the difference between the number of gallons of blended fuel made and the number of gallons of previously taxed motor fuel used to make the blended fuel.

(b)   On Importer. - The excise tax imposed by G.S. 105-449.81(4) on blended fuel imported to this State is payable by the importer.

(c)   Blends Made at Terminal. - The following blended fuel is considered to have been made by the supplier of gasoline or undyed diesel fuel used in the blend:

(1) An in-line-blend made by combining a liquid with gasoline or undyed diesel fuel as the fuel is delivered at a terminal rack into the motor fuel storage compartment of a transport truck or a tank wagon.

(2) A kerosene splash-blend made when kerosene is delivered at a terminal into a motor fuel storage compartment of a transport truck or a tank wagon and undyed diesel fuel is also delivered at that terminal into the same storage compartment, if the buyer of the kerosene notified the supplier before or at the time of delivery that the kerosene would be used to make a splash-blend. (1995, c. 390, s. 3.)

§ 105-449.84A. Liability for tax on behind-the-rack transfers.

The excise tax imposed by G.S. 105-449.81(5) on motor fuel that is transferred within the terminal transfer system and is subject to the federal excise tax is payable by the supplier of the fuel, the person receiving the fuel, and the terminal operator of the terminal at which the fuel was transferred, all of whom are jointly and severally liable for the tax. The excise tax imposed by that subdivision on motor fuel that is transferred within the terminal transfer system by a person that is not licensed under this Article as a supplier is payable by the person transferring the motor fuel, the person receiving the motor fuel, and the terminal operation of the terminal at which the fuel was transferred, all of whom are jointly and severally liable for the tax. (1995 (Reg. Sess., 1996), c. 647, s. 17; 2008-134, s. 35.)

§ 105-449.85. Compensating tax on and liability for unaccounted for motor fuel losses at a terminal.

(a) Tax. - An excise tax at the motor fuel rate is imposed annually on unaccounted for motor fuel losses at a terminal that exceed one-half of one percent (0.5%) of the number of net gallons removed from the terminal during the year by a system transfer or at a terminal rack. To determine if this tax applies, the terminal operator of the terminal must determine the difference between the following:

(1) The amount of motor fuel in inventory at the terminal at the beginning of the year plus the amount of motor fuel received by the terminal during the year.

(2) The amount of motor fuel in inventory at the terminal at the end of the year plus the amount of motor fuel removed from the terminal during the year.

(b) Liability. - The terminal operator whose motor fuel is unaccounted for is liable for the tax imposed by this section and is liable for a penalty equal to the amount of tax payable. Motor fuel received by a terminal operator and not shown on an informational return filed by the terminal operator with the Secretary as having been removed from the terminal is presumed to be unaccounted for motor fuel. A terminal operator may establish that it can account for motor fuel received at a terminal but not shown on an informational return as having been removed from the terminal if the motor fuel was lost or part of a transmix. (1995, c. 390, s. 3; 1995 (Reg. Sess., 1996), c. 647, s. 18; 2008-134, s. 36.)

§ 105-449.86. Tax on and liability for dyed diesel fuel used to operate certain highway vehicles.

(a) Tax. - An excise tax at the motor fuel rate is imposed on dyed diesel fuel acquired to operate any of the following:

(1) Repealed by Session Laws 2003-349, s. 10.8, effective January 1, 2004.

(2) A local bus that is allowed by § 4082(b)(3) of the Code to use dyed diesel fuel.

(3) A highway vehicle that is owned by or leased to an educational organization that is not a public school and is allowed by § 4082(b)(1) or (b)(3) of the Code to use dyed diesel fuel.

(4) Repealed by Session Laws 2005-435, s. 12, effective September 27, 2005.

(b) Liability. - If the distributor of dyed diesel fuel that is taxable under this section is not liable for the tax imposed by this section, the person that acquires the fuel is liable for the tax. The distributor of dyed diesel fuel that is taxable under this section is liable for the tax imposed by this section in the following circumstances:

(1) When the person acquiring the dyed diesel fuel has storage facilities for the fuel and is therefore a bulk end-user of the fuel.

(2) When the person acquired the dyed diesel fuel from a retail outlet of the distributor by using an access card or code indicating that the person's use of the fuel is taxable under this section. (1995, c. 390, s. 3; 2003-349, s. 10.8; 2005-435, s. 12; 2008-134, s. 37.)

§ 105-449.87. Backup tax and liability for the tax.

(a) Tax. - An excise tax at the motor fuel rate is imposed on the following:

(1) Dyed diesel fuel that is used to operate a highway vehicle for a use that is not a nontaxable use under § 4082(b) of the Code.

(2) Motor fuel that was allowed an exemption from the motor fuel tax and was then used for a taxable purpose.

(3) Motor fuel that is used to operate a highway vehicle after an application for a refund of tax paid on the motor fuel is made or allowed under G.S. 105-449.107(a) on the basis that the motor fuel was used for an off-highway purpose.

(4) Repealed by Session Laws 1995 (Regular Session, 1996), c. 647, s. 19.

(5) Motor fuel that, based on its shipping document, is destined for delivery to another state and is then diverted and delivered in this State.

(b) General Liability. - The operator of a highway vehicle that uses motor fuel that is taxable under subdivisions (a)(1) through (a)(3) of this section is liable for the tax. If the highway vehicle that uses the fuel is owned by or leased to a motor carrier, the motor carrier is jointly and severally liable for the tax. If the end-seller of motor fuel taxable under this section knew or had reason to know that the motor fuel would be used for a purpose that is taxable under this section, the end-seller is jointly and severally liable for the tax. If the Secretary determines that a bulk end-user or retailer used or sold untaxed dyed diesel fuel to operate a highway vehicle when the fuel is dispensed from a storage facility or through a meter marked for nonhighway use, all fuel delivered into that storage facility is presumed to have been used to operate a highway vehicle. An end-seller of dyed diesel fuel is considered to have known or had reason to know that the fuel would be used for a purpose that is taxable under this section if the end-seller delivered the fuel into a storage facility that was not marked as required by G.S. 105-449.123.

(c) Diverted Fuel. - The person who authorizes a change in the destination state of motor fuel from the state given on the fuel's shipping document to North Carolina is liable for the tax due on the motor fuel. If motor fuel is diverted from North Carolina to another state, only the person who authorized the fuel to be diverted is eligible for a refund of the amount of tax paid on the fuel. (1995, c. 390, s. 3; 1995 (Reg. Sess., 1996), c. 647, s. 19; 1997-60, s. 8; 1998-146, s. 5; 1999-438, s. 22; 2002-108, s. 10; 2008-134, s. 38.)

§ 105-449.88. Exemptions from the excise tax.

The excise tax on motor fuel does not apply to the following:

(1) Motor fuel removed, by transport truck or another means of transfer outside the terminal transfer system, from a terminal for export, if the motor fuel is removed by a licensed distributor or a licensed exporter and the supplier of the motor fuel collects tax on it at the rate of the motor fuel's destination state.

(1a) Motor fuel removed by transport truck from a terminal for export if the motor fuel is removed by a licensed distributor or licensed exporter, the supplier that is the position holder for the motor fuel sells the motor fuel to another supplier as the motor fuel crosses the terminal rack, the purchasing supplier or its customer receives the motor fuel at the terminal rack for export, and the supplier that is the position holder collects tax on the motor fuel at the rate of the motor fuel's destination state.

(2) Motor fuel sold to the federal government for its use.

(3) Motor fuel sold to the State for its use.

(4) Motor fuel sold to a local board of education for use in the public school system.

(5) Diesel that is kerosene and is sold to an airport.

(6) Motor fuel sold to a charter school for use for charter school purposes.

(7) Motor fuel sold to a community college for use for community college purposes.

(8) Motor fuel sold to a county or a municipal corporation for its use.

(9) Biodiesel that is produced by an individual for use in a private passenger vehicle registered in that individual's name pursuant to Chapter 20 of the General Statutes. For the purposes of this subdivision, the term "private passenger vehicle" has the same meaning as in G.S. 20-4.01. (1995, c. 390, s. 3; 1995 (Reg. Sess., 1996), c. 647, ss. 20, 21; 1998-98, s. 28; 1998-146, s. 6; 2000-72, s. 2; 2000-173, ss. 13(b), 15; 2001-427, s. 9(a); 2002-108, s. 11; 2007-524, s. 1.)

§ 105-449.88A. Liability for tax due on motor fuel designated as exempt by the use of cards or codes.

(a) Repealed by Session Laws 2006-162, s. 14(b), effective January 1, 2007, and applicable to motor fuel purchased on or after that date.

(b) Exempt Card or Code. - An entity that issues an exempt card or code has a duty to determine if the person to whom it is issued is exempt from the motor fuel excise tax. An entity that issues an exempt card or code to a person who is not exempt from tax is liable for tax due on motor fuel the person purchases at retail by use of the exempt card or code. If a supplier authorizes another entity to issue an exempt card or code to a person who is not exempt from tax, the supplier and the entity that issued the card are jointly and severally liable for tax due on motor fuel the person purchases at retail by use of the exempt card or code.

(c) Card Holder. - A person to whom an exempt card or code is issued is liable for any tax due on fuel purchased with the card or code for a purpose that is not exempt. A person who misuses an exempt card or code by purchasing fuel with the card or code for a purpose that is not exempt is liable for the tax due on the fuel. (1997-60, s. 9; 2001-205, s. 4; 2006-162, s. 14(b).)

§ 105-449.89. Restrictions on removal of motor fuel from terminal.

(a) By Bulk End-User. - An out-of-state bulk end-user may not remove motor fuel from a terminal in this State for use in the state in which the bulk end-user is located unless the bulk end-user is licensed under this Article as an exporter. An out-of-state bulk end-user that is not licensed under this Article may remove motor fuel from a bulk plant in this State.

(b) To Marine Vessel. - A supplier may not transfer motor fuel from a terminal to a marine vessel unless the person to whom the supplier transfers the motor fuel is licensed as a supplier. (1995 (Reg. Sess., 1996), c. 647, s. 22; 1997-60, s. 10; 2008-134, s. 39.)

Part 4. Payment and Reporting.

§ 105-449.90. When tax return and payment are due.

(a) Filing Periods. - The excise tax imposed by this Article is payable when a return is due. A return is due annually or monthly, as specified in this section. A return must be filed with the Secretary and be in the form required by the Secretary.

An annual return is due within 45 days after the end of each calendar year. An annual return covers tax liabilities that accrue in the calendar year preceding the date the return is due.

A monthly return of a person other than an occasional importer is due within 22 days after the end of each month. A monthly return of an occasional importer is due by the 3rd of each month. A monthly return covers tax liabilities that accrue in the calendar month preceding the date the return is due.

(b) Annual Filers. - A terminal operator must file an annual return for the compensating tax imposed by G.S. 105-449.85.

(c) Repealed by Session Laws 2006-162, s. 14(c), effective January 1, 2007, and applicable to motor fuel purchased on or after that date.

(d) Monthly Filers on 22nd. - The following persons must file a monthly return by the 22nd of each month:

(1) A refiner.

(2) A supplier.

(3) A bonded importer.

(4) A blender.

(5) A tank wagon importer.

(6) A person that incurred a liability under G.S. 105-449.86 during the preceding month for the tax on dyed diesel fuel used to operate certain highway vehicles.

(7) A person that incurred a liability under G.S. 105-449.87 during the preceding month for the backup tax on motor fuel.

(e) Monthly Filers on 3rd. - An occasional importer must file a monthly return by the third day of each month. An occasional importer is not required to file a return, however, if all the motor fuel imported by the importer in a reporting period was removed at a terminal located in another state and the supplier of the fuel is an elective supplier or a permissive supplier. (1995, c. 390, s. 3; 1995 (Reg. Sess., 1996), c. 647, s. 23; 1997-60, s. 11; 2006-162, s. 14(c).)

§ 105-449.90A. Payment by supplier of destination state tax collected on exported motor fuel.

Tax collected by a supplier on exported motor fuel is payable by the supplier to the destination state. Payments of destination state tax are due to the destination state on the date set by the law of the destination state. (1995 (Reg. Sess., 1996), c. 647, s. 24; 2005-435, s. 13.)

§ 105-449.91. Remittance of tax to supplier.

(a) Distributor. - A distributor must remit tax due on motor fuel removed at a terminal rack to the supplier of the fuel. A licensed distributor has the right to defer the remittance of tax to the supplier, as trustee, until the date the trustee must pay the tax to this State or to another state. The time when an unlicensed distributor must remit tax to a supplier is governed by the terms of the contract between the supplier and the unlicensed distributor.

(b)   Exporter. - A licensed exporter must remit tax due on motor fuel removed at a terminal rack to the supplier of the fuel. The time when a licensed exporter must remit tax to a supplier is governed by the law of the destination state of the exported motor fuel.

(c)   Importer. - A licensed importer must remit tax due on motor fuel removed at a terminal rack of a permissive or an elective supplier to the supplier of the fuel. A licensed importer that removes fuel from a terminal rack of a permissive or an elective supplier has the right to defer the remittance of tax to the supplier until the date the supplier must pay the tax to this State.

(d)   General. - A person who removes motor fuel at a terminal rack and is not subject to another subsection in this section must remit tax due on the motor fuel to the supplier of the fuel. The time the person must remit tax to a supplier is governed by the terms of the contract between the supplier and the person.

The method by which a person must remit tax to a supplier under this section is governed by the terms of the contract between the supplier and that person. G.S. 105-449.76 governs the cancellation of a license of a distributor, an exporter, and an importer. (1995, c. 390, s. 3; 1995 (Reg. Sess., 1996), c. 647, s. 25; 1997-60, s. 12; 2008-134, s. 40.)

§ 105-449.92. Notice to suppliers of cancellation or reissuance of certain licenses; effect of notice.

(a)   Notice to Suppliers. - If the Secretary cancels a distributor's license, an exporter's license, or an importer's license, the Secretary must notify all suppliers of the cancellation. If the Secretary issues a license to a distributor, an exporter, or an importer whose license was cancelled, the Secretary must notify all suppliers of the issuance.

(b)   Effect of Notice. - A supplier that sells motor fuel to a distributor after receiving notice from the Secretary that the Secretary has cancelled the distributor's license is jointly and severally liable with the distributor for any tax due on motor fuel the supplier sells to the distributor after receiving the notice.

This joint and several liability does not apply to excise tax due on motor fuel sold to a previously unlicensed distributor after the supplier receives notice from the Secretary that the Secretary has issued another license to the distributor. (1995, c. 390, s. 3; 1995 (Reg. Sess., 1996), c. 647, s. 26; 1997-60, s. 13.)

§ 105-449.93. Percentage discount for licensed distributors and some licensed importers.

(a) Repealed by Session Laws 2006-162, s. 14(d), effective January 1, 2007, and applicable to motor fuel purchased on or after that date.

(b) Percentage Discount. - A licensed distributor that pays the tax due a supplier by the date the supplier must pay the tax to the State may deduct from the amount due a discount of one percent (1%) of the amount of tax payable. A licensed importer that removes motor fuel from a terminal rack of a permissive or an elective supplier and that pays the tax due the supplier by the date the supplier must pay the tax to the State may deduct from the amount due a discount of the same amount allowed a licensed distributor. The discount covers the expense of furnishing a bond and losses due to shrinkage or evaporation. A supplier may not directly or indirectly deny this discount to a licensed distributor or licensed importer that pays the tax due the supplier by the date the supplier must pay the tax to the State. (1995, c. 390, s. 3; 1995 (Reg. Sess., 1996), c. 647, s. 27; 2006-162, s. 14(d).)

§ 105-449.94: Repealed by Session Laws 2006-162, s. 14(e), effective January 1, 2007, and applicable to motor fuels purchased on or after that date.

§ 105-449.95: Recodified as G.S. 105-449.105B by Session Laws 2009-445, s. 35(a), effective January 1, 2010.

§ 105-449.96. Information required on return filed by supplier.

A return of a supplier must list all of the following information and any other information required by the Secretary:

(1) The number of gallons of tax-paid motor fuel received by the supplier during the month, sorted by type of fuel.

(2) The number of gallons of motor fuel removed at a terminal rack during the month from the account of the supplier, sorted by type of fuel.

(3) The number of gallons of motor fuel removed during the month for export, sorted by type of fuel.

(4) The number of gallons of motor fuel removed during the month at a terminal located in another state for destination to this State, as indicated on the shipping document for the fuel, sorted by type of fuel.

(5) The number of gallons of motor fuel the supplier sold during the month to a governmental unit whose use of fuel is exempt from tax, sorted by type of fuel.

(6) The amount of discounts allowed under G.S. 105-449.93(b) on motor fuel sold during the month to licensed distributors or licensed importers.

(7) The number of gallons of motor fuel the supplier exchanged during the month with another licensed supplier pursuant to a two-party exchange agreement, sorted by type of fuel. (1995, c. 390, s. 3; 1995 (Reg. Sess., 1996), c. 647, s. 30; 1997-60, s. 14; 2005-435, s. 14; 2008-134, s. 41.)

§ 105-449.97. Deductions and discounts allowed a supplier when filing a return.

(a) Taxes Not Remitted. - When a supplier files a return, the supplier may deduct from the amount of tax payable with the return the amount of tax any of the following license holders owes the supplier but failed to remit to the supplier:

(1) A licensed distributor.

(2) A licensed importer that removed the motor fuel on which the tax is due from a terminal of an elective or a permissive supplier.

(3) Repealed by Session Laws 1995, c. 647, s. 32.

A supplier is not liable for tax a license holder listed in this subsection owes the supplier but fails to pay. If a listed license holder pays tax owed to a supplier after the supplier deducts the amount on a return, the supplier must promptly remit the payment to the Secretary.

(b) Administrative Discount. - A supplier that files a timely return and sends a timely payment may deduct from the amount of tax payable with the return an administrative discount of one-tenth of one percent (0.1%) of the amount of tax payable to this State as the trustee, not to exceed eight thousand dollars ($8,000) a month. The discount covers expenses incurred in collecting taxes on motor fuel.

(c) Percentage Discount. - A supplier that sells motor fuel directly to an unlicensed distributor or to the bulk end-user, the retailer, or the user of the fuel may take the same percentage discount on the fuel that a licensed distributor may take under G.S. 105-449.93(b) when making deferred payments of tax to the supplier.

(d) Taxes Paid on Exempt Retail Sales. - When filing a return, a supplier that issues or authorizes the issuance of an exempt card or code to a person that enables the person to buy motor fuel without paying tax on the fuel may deduct the amount of excise tax imposed on fuel purchased with the exempt card or code. The amount of excise tax imposed on fuel purchased with an exempt card or code is the amount that was imposed on the fuel when it was delivered to the retailer of the fuel. (1995, c. 390, s. 3; 1995 (Reg. Sess., 1996), c. 647, ss. 31, 32; 1997-60, s. 15; 1999-438, s. 23; 2000-173, s. 14(c); 2006-162, s. 14(f); 2008-134, s. 42.)

§ 105-449.98. Duties of supplier concerning payments by distributors, exporters, and importers.

(a) As Fiduciary. - A supplier has a fiduciary duty to remit to the Secretary the amount of tax paid to the supplier by a licensed distributor, licensed exporter, or licensed importer. A supplier is liable for taxes paid to the supplier by a licensed distributor, licensed exporter, or licensed importer.

(b) Notice of Fuel Received. - A supplier must notify a licensed distributor, a licensed exporter, or a licensed importer that received motor fuel from the supplier during a reporting period of the number of taxable gallons received. The supplier must give this notice after the end of each reporting period and before the license holder must remit to the supplier the amount of tax due on the fuel.

(c) Notice to Department. - A supplier of motor fuel at a terminal must notify the Department within 10 business days after a return is due of any licensed distributors, licensed exporters, or licensed importers that did not pay the tax due the supplier when the supplier filed the return. The notice must be transmitted to the Department in the form required by the Department.

(d) Payment Application. - A supplier that receives a payment of tax from a licensed distributor, a licensed exporter, or a licensed importer may not apply the payment to a debt that person owes the supplier for motor fuel purchased from the supplier. (1995, c. 390, s. 3; 1995 (Reg. Sess., 1996), c. 647, s. 33; 1997-60, s. 16.)

§ 105-449.99. Returns and discounts of importers.

(a) Return. - A monthly return of a bonded importer, an occasional importer, or a tank wagon importer must contain the following information concerning motor fuel imported during the period covered by the return:

(1) The number of gallons of imported motor fuel acquired from a supplier that collected the excise tax due this State on the fuel.

(2) The number of gallons of imported motor fuel acquired from a supplier that did not collect the excise tax due this State on the fuel, listed by source state, supplier, and terminal.

(3) The import authorization number of each import that is reported under subdivision (2) of this subsection and was removed from a terminal.

(4) For an occasional importer or a tank wagon importer, the number of gallons of imported motor fuel acquired from a bulk plant, listed by bulk plant.

(b) Discounts. - An importer may not deduct an administrative discount from the amount remitted with a return. An importer that imports motor fuel received from an elective supplier or a permissive supplier may deduct the percentage discount allowed by G.S. 105-449.93(b) when remitting tax to the supplier, as trustee, for payment to the State. An importer that imports motor fuel received from a supplier that is not an elective supplier or a permissive supplier may not deduct the percentage discount allowed by G.S. 105-449.93(b) when filing a return for the tax due. (1995, c. 390, s. 3.)

§ 105-449.100. Terminal operator to file informational return showing changes in amount of motor fuel at the terminal.

(a) Requirement. - A terminal operator must file a monthly informational return with the Secretary that shows the amount of motor fuel received or removed from the terminal during the month. A terminal operator must report all motor fuel removed from an out-of-state terminal that has this State as its destination state.

(b) Content. - The return is due on the date a monthly return is due under G.S. 105-449.90. The return must contain the following information and any other information required by the Secretary:

(1) The number of gallons of motor fuel received in inventory at the terminal during the month and each position holder for the fuel, sorted by type of fuel.

(2) The number of gallons of motor fuel removed from inventory at the terminal during the month and, for each removal, the position holder for the fuel and the destination state of the fuel, sorted by type of fuel.

(3) The number of gallons of motor fuel gained or lost at the terminal during the month.

(4) The number of gallons of motor fuel in inventory at the beginning of each month and at the end of each month.

(c) Due Date. - The return is due on the date a monthly return is due under G.S. 105-449.90. (1995, c. 390, s. 3; 1995 (Reg. Sess., 1996), c. 647, s. 34; 2006-162, s. 15(a); 2008-134, s. 43.)

§ 105-449.101. Motor fuel transporter to file informational return showing deliveries of motor fuel.

(a) Requirement. - A motor fuel transporter that is required to be licensed under this Article must file a monthly informational return with the Secretary that shows motor fuel transported in this State by the transporter during the month.

(b) Content. - The return required by this section must contain the following information and any other information required by the Secretary:

(1) The name and address of each person from whom the transporter received motor fuel outside the State for delivery in the State, the amount of motor fuel received, the date the motor fuel was received, and the destination state of the fuel.

(2) The name and address of each person from whom the transporter received motor fuel in the State for delivery outside the State, the amount of motor fuel delivered, the date the motor fuel was delivered, and the destination state of the fuel.

(3) The name and address of each person from whom the transporter received motor fuel in the State for delivery in the State, the amount of motor fuel received, the date the motor fuel was received, and the destination state of the fuel.

(c) Due Date. - The return required by this section is due on the date a monthly return is due under G.S. 105-449.90. (1995, c. 390, s. 3; 1995 (Reg. Sess., 1996), c. 647, s. 35; 2002-108, s. 12; 2006-162, ss. 13(b), 15(b); 2008-134, s. 44.)

§ 105-449.102. Distributor to file return showing exports from a bulk plant.

(a) Requirement. - A distributor that exports motor fuel from a bulk plant located in this State must file a monthly return with the Secretary that shows the exports. The return serves as a claim for refund by the distributor for tax paid to this State on the exported motor fuel.

(b) Content. - The return must contain the following information and any other information required by the Secretary:

(1) The number of gallons of motor fuel exported during the month.

(2) The destination state of the motor fuel exported during the month.

(3) A certification that the distributor has paid to the destination state of the motor fuel exported during the month, or will pay on a timely basis, the amount of tax due that state on the fuel.

(c) Due Date. - The return is due on the date a monthly return is due under G.S. 105-449.90. (1995, c. 390, s. 3; 1995 (Reg. Sess., 1996), c. 647, s. 36; 2006-162, s. 15(c); 2008-134, s. 45.)

§ 105-449.103. Reserved for future codification purposes.

§ 105-449.104. Use of name and account number on return.

When a transaction with a person licensed under this Article is required to be reported on a return, the return must state the license holder's name and the account number used by the Department to identify the license holder. The name of a license holder and the license holder's account number is stated on the lists compiled under G.S. 105-449.77. (1995 (Reg. Sess., 1996), c. 647, s. 37.)

Part 5. Refunds.

§ 105-449.105. Monthly refunds for tax paid on exempt fuel, lost fuel, and accidental mixes that result in fuel unsuitable for highway use.

(a) Exempt Fuel. - An entity whose use of motor fuel is exempt from tax may obtain a monthly refund of any motor fuel excise tax the entity pays on its motor fuel. A person who sells motor fuel to an entity whose use of motor fuel is exempt from tax may obtain a monthly refund of any motor fuel excise tax the person pays on motor fuel it sells to the entity. A credit card company that issues a credit card to an entity whose use of motor fuel is exempt from tax may obtain a monthly refund of any motor fuel excise tax the company pays on motor fuel the entity purchases using the credit card.

A person may obtain a monthly refund of tax paid by the person on exported fuel, including fuel whose shipping document shows this State as the destination state but was diverted to another state in accordance with the diversion procedures established by the Secretary. An out-of-state bulk end-user is not allowed a refund on fuel exported from a bulk plant unless the bulk end-user is licensed as an exporter.

(b)   Lost Fuel. - A supplier, an importer, or a distributor that loses tax-paid motor fuel due to damage to a conveyance transporting the motor fuel, fire, a natural disaster, an act of war, or an accident may obtain a monthly refund for the tax paid on the fuel.

(c)   Accidental Mixes. - A person that accidentally combines any of the following may obtain a monthly refund for the amount of tax paid on the fuel:

(1)   Dyed diesel fuel with tax-paid motor fuel.

(2)   Gasoline with diesel fuel.

(3)   Undyed diesel fuel with dyed kerosene.

(d)   Repealed by Session Laws 1998-98, s. 29.

(e)   Refund Amount. - The amount of a refund allowed under this section is the amount of excise tax paid, less the amount of any discount allowed on the fuel under G.S. 105-449.93. (1995, c. 390, s. 3; c. 523, ss. 32.1, 32.2; 1995 (Reg. Sess., 1996), c. 647, s. 38; 1997-6, s. 12; 1997-60, s. 17; 1998-98, s. 29; 2000-173, s. 16; 2001-205, s. 3; 2008-134, s. 46.)

§ 105-449.105A. Monthly refunds for kerosene.

(a)   Refund for Undyed Kerosene Sold to an End User for Non-Highway Use. - A distributor who sells kerosene to an end user for one of the purposes listed in this subsection may obtain a monthly refund for the excise tax the distributor paid on the kerosene, less the amount of any discount allowed on the kerosene under G.S. 105-449.93, if the distributor dispenses the kerosene into a storage facility of the end user that contains fuel used only for one of those purposes and the storage facility is installed in a manner that makes use of the fuel for any other purpose improbable.

(1) Heating.

(2) Drying crops.

(3) A manufacturing process.

(b) Liability. - If the Secretary determines that the Department overpaid a distributor by refunding more tax to the distributor than is due under this section, the distributor is liable for the amount of the overpayment. (1998-146, s. 8; 2000-173, s. 17; 2001-205, s. 6; 2006-162, s. 14(g); 2008-134, ss. 47, 48; 2010-95, s. 29(a).)

§ 105-449.105B. Monthly hold harmless refunds for licensed distributors and some licensed importers.

If a licensed distributor or licensed importer purchases motor fuel from a licensed supplier during a month and the discount the distributor or importer receives under G.S. 105-449.93(b) on the motor fuel is less than the amount the distributor or importer would have received during that month if the distributor or importer had been allowed a discount on taxable gasoline purchased by the distributor or importer from a supplier under the following schedule, the distributor or importer is allowed a monthly refund of the difference:

Amount of Gasoline Purchased Each Month	Percentage Discount
First 150,000 gallons	2%
Next 100,000 gallons	1 1/2%
Amount over 250,000 gallons	1%.

In determining the amount of discounts a distributor or importer received under G.S. 105-449.93(b) for motor fuel purchased in a month, a distributor or importer is considered to have received the amount of any discounts the distributor or importer could have received under that subsection but did not receive because the distributor or importer failed to pay the tax due to the supplier by the date the supplier had to pay the tax to the State. (1995, c. 390, s. 3; 1995 (Reg. Sess., 1996), c. 647, s. 29; 1997-6, s. 11; 2009-445, s. 35(a); 2010-95, s. 30.)

§ 105-449.106. Quarterly refunds for nonprofit organizations, taxicabs, and special mobile equipment.

(a) Nonprofits. - A nonprofit organization listed below that purchases and uses motor fuel may receive a quarterly refund, for the excise tax paid during the preceding quarter, at a rate equal to the amount of the flat cents-per-gallon rate plus the variable cents-per-gallon rate in effect during the quarter for which the refund is claimed, less one cent (1¢) per gallon.

An application for a refund allowed under this subsection must be made in accordance with this Part and must be signed by the chief executive officer of the organization. The chief executive officer of a nonprofit organization is the president of the organization or another officer of the organization designated in the charter or bylaws of the organization.

Any of the following entities may receive a refund under this subsection:

(1) Repealed by Session Laws 2002-108, s. 13, effective January 1, 2003.

(2) A private, nonprofit organization that transports passengers under contract with or at the express designation of a unit of local government.

(3) A volunteer fire department.

(4) A volunteer rescue squad.

(5) A sheltered workshop recognized by the Department of Health and Human Services.

(b) Taxi. - A person who purchases and uses motor fuel in a taxicab while the taxicab is engaged in transporting passengers for hire, or in a bus operated as part of a city transit system that is exempt from regulation by the North Carolina Utilities Commission under G.S. 62-260(a)(8), may receive a quarterly refund, for the excise tax paid during the preceding quarter, at a rate equal to the flat cents-per-gallon rate plus the variable cents-per-gallon rate in effect during the quarter for which the refund is claimed, less one cent (1¢) per gallon. For purposes of this subsection, the term "taxicab" means a motor vehicle that seats no more than nine passengers, transports passengers for hire, operates on call or demand, and accepts and solicits passengers indiscriminately. An application for a refund must be made in accordance with this Part.

(c) Special Mobile Equipment. - A person who purchases and uses motor fuel for the off-highway operation of special mobile equipment registered under Chapter 20 of the General Statutes may receive a quarterly refund, for the excise tax paid during the preceding quarter, at a rate equal to the flat cents-per-gallon rate plus the variable cents-per-gallon rate in effect during the quarter for which the refund is claimed, less the amount of sales and use tax or privilege tax due on the fuel under this Chapter, as determined in accordance with G.S. 105-449.107(c). An application for a refund must be made in accordance with this Part. (1995, c. 390, s. 3; 1997-6, s. 13; 1997-443, s. 11A.118(a); 1999-438, s. 24; 2002-108, s. 13; 2005-435, s. 15; 2006-162, s. 16(a); 2010-95, s. 31(a), (b).)

§ 105-449.107. Annual refunds for off-highway use and use by certain vehicles with power attachments.

(a) Off-Highway. - A person who purchases and uses motor fuel for a purpose other than to operate a licensed highway vehicle may receive an annual refund for the excise tax the person paid on fuel used during the preceding calendar year. The amount of refund allowed is the amount of the flat cents-per-gallon rate in effect during the year for which the refund is claimed plus the average of the two variable cents-per-gallon rates in effect during that year, less the amount of sales and use tax or privilege tax due on the fuel under this Chapter. An application for a refund allowed under this section must be made in accordance with this Part.

(b) Certain Vehicles. - A person who purchases and uses motor fuel in one of the vehicles listed below may receive an annual refund for the amount of fuel consumed by the vehicle:

(1) A concrete mixing vehicle.

(2) A solid waste compacting vehicle.

(3) A bulk feed vehicle that delivers feed to poultry or livestock and uses a power takeoff to unload the feed.

(4) A vehicle that delivers lime or fertilizer in bulk to farms and uses a power takeoff to unload the lime or fertilizer.

(5) A tank wagon that delivers alternative fuel, as defined in G.S. 105-449.130, or motor fuel or another type of liquid fuel into storage tanks and uses a power takeoff to make the delivery.

(6) A commercial vehicle that delivers and spreads mulch, soils, composts, sand, sawdust, and similar materials and that uses a power takeoff to unload, blow, and spread the materials.

(7) A commercial vehicle that uses a power takeoff to remove and dispose of septage and for which an annual fee is required to be paid to the Department of Environment and Natural Resources under G.S. 130A-291.1.

(8) A sweeper.

The amount of refund allowed is thirty-three and one-third percent (33 1/3%) of the following: the sum of the flat cents-per-gallon rate in effect during the year for which the refund is claimed and the average of the two variable cents-per-gallon rates in effect during that year, less the amount of sales and use tax or privilege tax due on the fuel under this Chapter. An application for a refund allowed under this section must be made in accordance with this Part. This refund is allowed for the amount of fuel consumed by the vehicle in its mixing, compacting, or unloading operations, as distinguished from propelling the vehicle, which amount is considered to be one-third of the amount of fuel consumed by the vehicle.

(c) Sales Tax Amount. - Article 5 of this Chapter determines the amount of sales and use tax to be deducted under this section from a motor fuel excise tax refund. Article 5F of this Chapter determines the amount of privilege tax to be deducted under this section from a motor fuel excise tax refund. The sales price and the cost price of motor fuel to be used in determining the amount to deduct is the average of the wholesale prices used under G.S. 105-449.80 to determine the excise tax rates in effect for the two six-month periods of the year for which the refund is claimed. (1995, c. 390, s. 3; 1997-6, s. 14; 1997-423, s. 4; 2001-408, s. 1; 2005-377, s. 1; 2006-162, s. 16(b).)

§ 105-449.108. When an application for a refund is due.

(a) Due Dates. - The due dates of applications for refunds are as follows:

Refund Period	Due Date
Annual	April 15 after the end of the year
Quarterly	Last day of the month after the end of the quarter
Monthly	22nd day after the end of the month

(b) Requirements. - An application for a refund allowed under this Part must be filed with the Secretary and be in the form required by the Secretary. The application must state that the applicant has paid for the fuel for which a refund is claimed or that payment for the fuel has been secured to the seller's satisfaction. An application for an annual refund must state whether or not the applicant has filed a North Carolina income tax return for the preceding taxable year.

(c) Repealed by Session Laws 1998-146, s. 10, effective September 18, 1998.

(d) Late Application. - A refund applied for more than three years after the date the application is due is barred. (1995, c. 390, s. 3; 1997-6, s. 15; 1998-146, s. 10; 1998-212, s. 29A.14(r); 2008-134, s. 49; 2010-95, s. 32.)

§ 105-449.109: Repealed by Session Laws 1998-212, s. 29A.14(s).

§ 105-449.110. Review of refund application and payment of refund.

(a) Decision. - Upon determining that an application for refund is correct, the Secretary must issue the applicant a warrant upon the State Treasurer for the amount of the refund. If the Secretary determines that an application for refund is incorrect, the Secretary must send a written notice of the determination to the applicant. The notice must advise the applicant that the applicant may request a hearing on the matter in accordance with Article 9 of this Chapter.

(b) Interest. - The rate of interest payable on a refund is the rate set in G.S. 105-241.21. Interest accrues on a refund from the date that is 90 days after the later of the following:

(1) The date the application for refund was filed.

(2) The date the application for refund was due. (1995, c. 390, s. 3; 1998-98, s. 30; 2007-491, s. 44(1)a.)

§ 105-449.111. Reserved for future codification purposes.

§ 105-449.112. Reserved for future codification purposes.

§ 105-449.113. Reserved for future codification purposes.

§ 105-449.114. Authority for agreement with Eastern Band of Cherokee Indians.

(a) By virtue of an Act of June 4, 1924, Pub. L. No. 68-191, Ch. 253, 43 Stat. 370, Congress and the United States courts have recognized the Eastern Band of Cherokee Indians as possessing sovereign legal rights over their members and their trust lands.

(b) The following definitions apply in this act:

(1) Chief. - The Principal Chief of the Eastern Band of the Cherokee Indians.

(2) Council. - The Tribal Council of the Eastern Band of the Cherokee Indians.

(3) Tribe. - The Eastern Band of the Cherokee Indians.

(c) Notwithstanding any other provision of law concerning refunds of motor fuels and alternative fuels taxes, the Department of Revenue may enter into a memorandum of understanding or an agreement with the Eastern Band of Cherokee Indians to make refunds of motor fuels and alternative fuels taxes to the Tribe in its collective capacity on behalf of its members who reside on or engage in otherwise taxable transactions within Cherokee trust lands. The memorandum or agreement shall be approved by the Council and signed by the Chief on behalf of the Tribe and shall be signed by the Secretary of Revenue on behalf of Department of Revenue. The memorandum or agreement may not affect the right of an individual member of the Tribe to a refund and shall provide for deduction of amounts refunded to individual members of the Tribe from the amounts to be refunded to the Tribe on behalf of all members. The memorandum or agreement may be effective for a definite or indefinite period, as specified in the agreement. (1989, c. 753, ss. 1-3; 1991, c. 193, s. 6; 2002-108, s. 14.)

Part 6. Enforcement and Administration.

§ 105-449.115. Shipping document required to transport motor fuel by railroad tank car or transport truck.

(a) Issuance. - A person may not transport motor fuel by railroad tank car or transport truck unless the person has a shipping document for its transportation that complies with this section. A refiner, a terminal operator, a fuel alcohol provider, and the operator of a bulk plant must give a shipping document to the person who operates a railroad tank car or a transport truck into which motor fuel is loaded at the terminal rack or bulk plant rack.

(b) Content. - A shipping document issued by must contain the following information and any other information required by the Secretary:

(1) Identification, including address, of the terminal or bulk plant from which the motor fuel was received.

(1a) The type of motor fuel loaded.

(2) The date the motor fuel was loaded.

(3) The gross gallons loaded if the motor fuel is loaded onto a transport truck, and the gross pounds loaded if the motor fuel is loaded onto a railroad tank car.

(3a) The motor fuel transporter for the motor fuel.

(4) The destination state of the motor fuel, as represented by the purchaser of the motor fuel or the purchaser's agent.

(5) If the document is issued by a refiner or a terminal operator, the document must be machine printed. If the motor fuel is loaded onto a transport truck, the document must contain the following information:

a. The net gallons loaded.

b. A tax responsibility statement indicating the name of the supplier that is responsible for the tax due on the motor fuel.

(c) Reliance. - A person who issues a shipping document may rely on the representation made by the purchaser of motor fuel or the purchaser's agent concerning the destination state of the motor fuel. A purchaser is liable for any tax due as a result of the purchaser's diversion of fuel from the represented destination state.

(d) Duties of Transporter. - A person to whom a shipping document was issued must do all of the following:

(1) Carry the shipping document in the conveyance for which it was issued when transporting the motor fuel described in it.

(2) Show the shipping document to a law enforcement officer upon request when transporting the motor fuel described in it.

(3) Deliver motor fuel described in the shipping document to the destination state printed on it unless the person does all of the following:

a. Notifies the Secretary before transporting the motor fuel into a state other than the printed destination state that the person has received instructions since the shipping document was issued to deliver the motor fuel to a different destination state.

b. Receives from the Secretary a confirmation number authorizing the diversion.

c. Writes on the shipping document the change in destination state and the confirmation number for the diversion.

(4) Give a copy of the shipping document to the distributor or other person to whom the motor fuel is delivered.

(e) Duties of Person Receiving Shipment. - A person to whom motor fuel is delivered by railroad tank car or transport truck may not accept delivery of the motor fuel if the destination state shown on the shipping document for the motor fuel is a state other than North Carolina. To determine if the shipping document shows North Carolina as the destination state, the person to whom the fuel is delivered must examine the shipping document and must keep a copy of the shipping document. The person must keep a copy at the place of business where the motor fuel was delivered for 90 days from the date of delivery and must keep it at that place or another place for at least three years from the date of delivery. A person who accepts delivery of motor fuel in violation of this subsection is jointly and severally liable for any tax due on the fuel.

(f) Sanctions Against Transporter. - The acts listed in this subsection are grounds for a civil penalty. The penalty is payable to the agency that assessed the penalty and is payable by the person in whose name the conveyance is registered, if the conveyance is a transport truck, and is payable by the person responsible for the movement of motor fuel in the conveyance, if the conveyance is a railroad tank car. The amount of the penalty is five thousand dollars ($5,000). A penalty imposed under this subsection is in addition to any motor fuel tax assessed. The grounds for a civil penalty are:

(1) Transporting motor fuel in a railroad tank car or transport truck without a shipping document or with a false or an incomplete shipping document.

(2) Delivering motor fuel to a destination state other than that shown on the shipping document.

(g) Penalty Defense. - Compliance with the conditions set out in this subsection is a defense to a civil penalty imposed under subsection (f) of this section as a result of the delivery of fuel to a state other than the destination state printed on the shipping document for the fuel. The Secretary must waive a penalty imposed against a person under that subsection if the person establishes a defense under this subsection. The conditions for the defense are:

(1) The person notified the Secretary of the diversion and received a confirmation number for the diversion before the imposition of the penalty.

(2) Tax was timely paid on the diverted fuel, unless the person is a motor fuel transporter.

(h) Sanctions. - The Secretary may assess a civil penalty of five thousand dollars ($5,000) against a person who intentionally issues a shipping document that does not satisfy the requirements of subsection (b) of this section. (1995, c. 390, s. 3; 1995 (Reg. Sess., 1996), c. 647, ss. 39, 40; 2002-108, s. 15; 2003-349, s. 10.9; 2005-435, s. 16; 2007-527, ss. 16(b), 18(a); 2008-134, s. 50; 2009-445, s. 36(a).)

§ 105-449.115A. Shipping document required to transport fuel by tank wagon.

(a) Issuance. - A person who operates a tank wagon into which motor fuel is loaded at the terminal must comply with the document requirements in G.S. 105-449.115(b). A person who operates a tank wagon into which motor fuel is loaded from some other source must have an invoice, bill of sale, or shipping document containing the following information and any other information required by the Secretary:

(1) The name and address of the person from whom the motor fuel was received.

(2) The date the fuel was loaded.

(3) The type of fuel.

(4) The gross number of gallons loaded.

(b) Duties of Transporter. - A person to whom an invoice, bill of sale, or shipping document was issued must do all of the following:

(1) Carry the invoice, bill of sale, or shipping document in the conveyance for which it is issued when transporting the motor fuel described in it.

(2) Show the invoice, bill of sale, or shipping document upon request when transporting the motor fuel described in it.

(3) Keep a copy of the invoice, bill of sale, or shipping document at a centralized place of business for at least three years from the date of delivery.

(c) Sanctions. - Transporting motor fuel in a tank wagon without an invoice, bill of sale, or shipping document containing the information required by this section is grounds for a civil penalty. The penalty is payable to the agency that assessed the penalty and is payable by the person in whose name the tank wagon is registered. The amount of the penalty is one thousand dollars ($1,000). A penalty imposed under this subsection is in addition to any motor fuel tax assessed. (2002-108, s. 16; 2005-435, s. 17; 2007-527, s. 16(c).)

§ 105-449.116. Repealed by Session Laws 1999-438, s. 25.

§ 105-449.117. Penalties for highway use of dyed diesel or other non-tax-paid fuel.

(a) Violation. - It is unlawful to use dyed diesel fuel or other non-tax-paid fuel in a highway vehicle that is licensed or required to be licensed under Chapter 20 of the General Statutes unless that use is allowed under section 4082 of the Code. It is unlawful to use motor fuel or alternative fuel in a highway vehicle that is licensed or required to be licensed under Chapter 20 of the General Statutes unless the tax imposed by this Article or Article 36D of this Chapter and the tax imposed by Article 3 of Chapter 119 of the General Statutes have been paid. A person who violates this section is guilty of a Class 1 misdemeanor and is liable for a civil penalty.

(b) Civil Penalty. - The civil penalty is payable to the agency that assessed the penalty and is payable by the person in whose name the highway vehicle is registered. The amount of the penalty depends on the amount of fuel in the supply tank of the highway vehicle. The penalty is the greater of one thousand dollars ($1,000) or five times the amount of motor fuel tax payable on the fuel in the supply tank. A penalty imposed under this section is in addition to any motor fuel tax assessed.

(c) Enforcement. - The Secretary or a person designated by the Secretary may conduct investigations to identify violations of this Article. It is not a valid defense to a violation of this Article that the State is exempt from the tax imposed by this Article. (1995, c. 390, s. 3; 1997-60, s. 19; 2003-349, s. 10.10; 2007-527, s. 16(d); 2008-134, s. 51.)

§ 105-449.118. Civil penalty for buying or selling non-tax-paid motor fuel.

A person who dispenses non-tax-paid motor fuel into the supply tank of a highway vehicle or who allows non-tax-paid motor fuel to be dispensed into the supply tank of a highway vehicle is subject to a civil penalty of two hundred fifty dollars ($250.00) per occurrence.

The penalty is payable to the agency that assessed the penalty. Failure to pay a penalty imposed under this section is grounds under G.S. 20-88.01(b) to withhold or revoke the registration plate of the motor vehicle into which the motor fuel was dispensed. (1995, c. 390, s. 3; 2002-108, s. 17; 2007-527, s. 16(e).)

§ 105-449.118A. Civil penalty for refusing to allow the taking of a motor fuel sample.

A person who refuses to allow the taking of a motor fuel sample is subject to a civil penalty of one thousand dollars ($1,000). The penalty is payable to the agency that assessed the penalty. If the refusal is for a sample to be taken from a vehicle, the penalty is payable by the person in whose name the vehicle is registered. If the refusal is for a sample to be taken from any other storage tank or container, the penalty is payable by the owner of the container. (1995 (Reg. Sess., 1996), c. 647, s. 41; 2007-527, s. 16(f).)

§ 105-449.119. Review of civil penalty assessment.

A person who denies liability for a penalty imposed under this Part must pay the penalty and file a request for a Departmental review of the penalty. The request must be filed within the time set in G.S. 105-241.11 for requesting a

Departmental review of a proposed assessment. The procedures in Article 9 of this Chapter for review of a proposed assessment apply to the review of the penalty. The date the penalty was imposed is considered the date the notice of proposed assessment was delivered to the taxpayer. (1995, c. 390, s. 3; 1999-337, s. 44; 2007-491, s. 41.)

§ 105-449.120. Acts that are misdemeanors.

(a)   Class 1. - A person who commits any of the following acts is guilty of a Class 1 misdemeanor:

(1)   Fails to obtain a license required by this Article.

(2)   Willfully fails to file a return required by this Article.

(3)   Willfully fails to pay a tax when due under this Article or under former Article 36 or 36A of this Chapter. Failure to comply with a requirement of a supplier to remit tax payable to the supplier by electronic funds transfer is considered a failure to make a timely payment.

(3a)   Repealed by Session Laws 2006-162, s. 17, effective January 1, 2007, and applicable to motor fuel purchased on or after that date.

(4)   Makes a false statement in an application, a return, or a statement required under this Article.

(5)   Makes a false statement in an application for a refund.

(6)   Fails to keep records as required under this Article.

(7)   Refuses to allow the Secretary or a representative of the Secretary to examine the person's books and records concerning motor fuel.

(8)   Fails to disclose the correct amount of motor fuel sold or used in this State.

(9)   Fails to file a replacement bond or an additional bond as required under this Article.

(10)   Fails to show or give a shipping document as required under this Article.

(11)   Willfully refuses to allow a licensed distributor, a licensed exporter, or a licensed importer to defer payment of tax to the supplier, as required by G.S. 105-449.91.

(12)   Willfully refuses to allow a licensed distributor or a licensed importer to take the discount allowed by G.S. 105-449.93 when remitting tax to the supplier.

(b)   Class 2. - A person who commits any of the following acts is guilty of a Class 2 misdemeanor:

(1)   Knowingly dispenses non-tax-paid motor fuel into the supply tank of a highway vehicle.

(2)   Knowingly allows non-tax-paid fuel to be dispensed into the supply tank of a highway vehicle. (1995, c. 390, s. 3; 1995 (Reg. Sess., 1996), c. 647, s. 42; 1997-60, s. 20; 2006-162, s. 17.)

§ 105-449.121. Record-keeping requirements; inspection authority.

(a)   What Must Be Kept. - A person who is subject to audit under subsection (b) of this section must keep a record of all shipping documents or other documents used to determine information the person provides in a return or to determine the person's motor fuel transactions. The records must be kept for three years from the due date of the return to which the records apply or, if the records apply to a transaction not required to be reported in a return, for three years from the date of the transaction.

(b)   Inspection. - The Secretary or a person designated by the Secretary may do any of the following to determine tax liability under this Article:

(1)   Audit a person who is required to have or elects to have a license under this Article.

(2)   Audit a distributor, a retailer, a bulk end-user, or a motor fuel user that is not licensed under this Article.

(3) Examine a tank or other equipment used to make, store, or transport motor fuel, diesel dyes, or diesel markers.

(4) Take a sample of a product from a vehicle, a tank, or another container in a quantity sufficient to determine the composition of the product.

(5) Stop a vehicle for the purpose of taking a sample of motor fuel from the vehicle. (1995, c. 390, s. 3; 1995 (Reg. Sess., 1996), c. 647, s. 43; 2000-173, s. 18; 2008-134, s. 52; 2009-445, s. 37.)

§ 105-449.122. Equipment requirements.

(a) Metered Pumps. - All motor fuel dispensed at retail must be dispensed from metered pumps that indicate the total amount of fuel measured through the pumps. Each pump must be marked to indicate the type of motor fuel dispensed.

(b) Truck Equipment. - A highway vehicle that transports diesel fuel in a tank that is separate from the fuel supply tank of the vehicle may not have a connection from the transporting tank to the motor or to the supply tank of the vehicle. (1995, c. 390, s. 3; 1997-60, s. 21.)

§ 105-449.123. Marking requirements for dyed fuel storage facilities.

(a) Requirements. - A person who is a retailer of dyed motor fuel or who stores both dyed and undyed motor fuel for use by that person or another person must mark the storage facility for the dyed motor fuel as follows in a manner that clearly indicates the fuel is not to be used to operate a highway vehicle. The storage facility must be marked "Dyed Diesel, Nontaxable Use Only, Penalty For Taxable Use" or "Dyed Kerosene, Nontaxable Use Only, Penalty for Taxable Use" or a similar phrase that clearly indicates the fuel is not to be used to operate a highway vehicle. A person who intentionally fails to mark the storage facility as required by this section is subject to a civil penalty equal to the excise tax at the motor fuel rate on the inventory held in the storage tank at the time of the violation. If the inventory cannot be determined, then the penalty is calculated on the capacity of the storage tank.

(1) The storage tank of the storage facility must be marked if the storage tank is visible.

(2) The fillcap or spill containment box of the storage facility must be marked.

(3) The dispensing device that serves the storage facility must be marked.

(4) The retail pump or dispensing device at any level of the distribution system must comply with the marking requirements.

(b) Exception. - The marking requirements of this section do not apply to a storage facility that contains fuel used only for one of the purposes listed in G.S. 105-449.105A(a)(1) and is installed in a manner that makes use of the fuel for any other purpose improbable. (1997-60, s. 22; 2001-205, s. 7; 2003-349, s. 10.11; 2004-170, s. 31; 2005-435, s. 18.)

§ 105-449.124. Reserved for future codification purposes.

Part 7. Use of Revenue.

§ 105-449.125. Distribution of tax revenue among various funds and accounts.

The Secretary shall allocate the amount of revenue collected under this Article from an excise tax of one-half cent (1/2¢) a gallon to the following funds and accounts in the fraction indicated:

Fund or Account	Amount
Commercial Leaking Petroleum Underground Storage Tank Cleanup Fund	Nineteen thirty-seconds
Noncommercial Leaking Petroleum Underground Storage Tank Cleanup Fund	Three thirty-seconds

Water and Air Quality Account				Five-sixteenths.

The Secretary shall allocate seventy-five percent (75%) of the remaining excise tax revenue collected under this Article to the Highway Fund and shall allocate twenty-five percent (25%) to the Highway Trust Fund.

The Secretary shall charge a proportionate share of a refund allowed under this Article to each fund or account to which revenue collected under this Article is credited. The Secretary shall credit revenue or charge refunds to the appropriate funds or accounts on a monthly basis. (1995, c. 390, s. 3.)

§ 105-449.126. Distribution of part of Highway Fund allocation to Wildlife Resources Fund and Shallow Draft Navigation Channel and Lake Dredging Fund.

(a)	The Secretary shall credit to the Wildlife Resources Fund one-sixth of one percent (1/6 of 1%) of the amount that is allocated to the Highway Fund under G.S. 105-449.125 and is from the excise tax on motor fuel. Revenue credited to the Wildlife Resources Fund under this section may be used only for the boating and water safety activities described in G.S. 75A-3(c). The Secretary must credit revenue to the Wildlife Resources Fund on an annual basis.

(b)	The Secretary shall credit to the Shallow Draft Navigation Channel and Lake Dredging Fund one-sixth of one percent (1/6 of 1%) of the amount that is allocated to the Highway Fund under G.S. 105-449.125 and is from the excise tax on motor fuel. Revenue credited to the Shallow Draft Navigation Channel and Lake Dredging Fund under this section may be used only for the dredging activities described in G.S. 143-215.73F. The Secretary shall credit revenue to the Shallow Draft Navigation Channel and Lake Dredging Fund on an annual basis. (1995, c. 390, s. 3; c. 507, s. 18.16; 2013-360, s. 14.22(g).)

§ 105-449.127: Repealed by Session Laws 2006-162, s. 12(c), effective July 24, 2006.

§ 105-449.128. Reserved for future codification purposes.

§ 105-449.129. Reserved for future codification purposes.

Article 36D.

Alternative Fuel.

§ 105-449.130. Definitions.

The following definitions apply in this Article:

(1) Alternative fuel. - A combustible gas or liquid that can be used to generate power to operate a highway vehicle and that is not subject to tax under Article 36C of this Chapter.

(1a) Bulk end-user. - A person who maintains storage facilities for alternative fuel and uses part or all of the stored fuel to operate a highway vehicle.

(2) Highway. - Defined in G.S. 105-449.60.

(3) Highway vehicle. - Defined in G.S. 105-449.60.

(4) Motor fuel. - Defined in G.S. 105-449.60.

(5) Motor fuel rate. - Defined in G.S. 105-449.60.

(6) Provider of alternative fuel. - A person who does one or more of the following:

a. Acquires alternative fuel for sale or delivery to a bulk end-user or a retailer.

b. Maintains storage facilities for alternative fuel, part or all of which the person uses or sells to someone other than a bulk end-user or a retailer to operate a highway vehicle.

c. Sells alternative fuel and uses part of the fuel acquired for sale to operate a highway vehicle by means of a fuel supply line from the cargo tank of the vehicle to the engine of the vehicle.

d. Imports alternative fuel to this State, by a means other than the usual tank or receptacle connected with the engine of a highway vehicle, for use by that person to operate a highway vehicle.

(7) Retailer. - A person who maintains storage facilities for alternative fuel and who sells the fuel at retail or dispenses the fuel at a retail location to operate a highway vehicle. (1995, c. 390, s. 3; 1995 (Reg. Sess., 1996), c. 647, s. 44; 2008-134, s. 53.)

§ 105-449.131. List of persons who must have a license.

A person may not engage in business in this State as any of the following unless the person has a license issued by the Secretary authorizing the person to engage in that business:

(1) A provider of alternative fuel.

(2) A bulk end-user.

(3) A retailer. (1995, c. 390, s. 3; 1995 (Reg. Sess., 1996), c. 647, s. 45; 2008-134, s. 54.)

§ 105-449.132. How to apply for a license.

To obtain a license, an applicant must file an application with the Secretary on a form provided by the Secretary. An application must include the applicant's name, address, federal employer identification number, and any other information required by the Secretary. An applicant must meet the requirements for obtaining a license set out in G.S. 105-449.69(b). (1995, c. 390, s. 3; 1998-146, s. 11.)

§ 105-449.133. Bond or letter of credit required as a condition of obtaining and keeping certain licenses.

(a) Who Must Have Bond. - The following applicants for a license must file with the Secretary a bond or an irrevocable letter of credit:

(1) An alternative fuel provider.

(2) A retailer or a bulk end-user that intends to store highway and nonhighway alternative fuel in the same storage facility.

(b) Amount. - The amount of the bond is the amount that would be required if the fuel the applicant intended to provide or store was motor fuel rather than alternative fuel. An applicant that is also required to file a bond or an irrevocable letter of credit under G.S. 105-449.72 to obtain a license as a distributor of motor fuel may file a single bond or irrevocable letter of credit under that section for the combined amount.

A bond filed under this subsection must be conditioned upon compliance with this Article, be payable to the State, and be in the form required by the Secretary. The Secretary may require a bond issued under this subsection to be adjusted in accordance with the procedure set out in G.S. 105-449.72 for adjusting a bond filed by a distributor of motor fuel. (1995, c. 390, s. 3; 1997-60, s. 23; 2008-134, s. 55.)

§ 105-449.134. Denial or cancellation of license.

The Secretary may deny an application for a license or cancel a license under this Article for the same reasons that the Secretary may deny an application for a license or cancel a license under Article 36C of this Chapter. The procedure in Article 36C for cancelling a license applies to the cancellation of a license under this Article. (1995, c. 390, s. 3; 1995 (Reg. Sess., 1996), c. 647, s. 46.)

§ 105-449.135. Issuance of license; notification of changes.

(a) Issuance. - The Secretary must issue a license to each applicant whose application is approved. A license is not transferable and remains in effect until surrendered or cancelled.

(b) Notice. - A license holder that stops engaging in this State in the business for which the license was issued must give the Secretary written notice of the change and must surrender the license. The notice must give the date the change takes effect and, if the license holder has transferred the business to another by sale or otherwise, the date of the transfer and the name and address of the person to whom the business is transferred.

All taxes for which the license holder is liable under this Article but are not yet due become due on the date of the change. If the license holder transfers the business to another and does not give the notice required by this section, the person to whom the business was transferred is liable for the amount of any tax the license holder owed the State on the date the business was transferred. The liability of the person to whom the business is transferred is limited to the value of the property acquired from the license holder. (1995, c. 390, s. 3.)

§ 105-449.136. Tax on alternative fuel.

A tax at the motor fuel rate is imposed on liquid alternative fuel used to operate a highway vehicle by means of a vehicle supply tank that stores fuel only for the purpose of supplying fuel to operate the vehicle. A tax at the equivalent of the motor fuel rate is imposed on all other alternative fuel used to operate a highway vehicle. The Secretary must determine the equivalent rate. The exemptions from the tax on motor fuel in G.S. 105-449.88 apply to the tax imposed by this section. The refunds for motor fuel tax allowed by Part 5 of Article 36C of this Chapter apply to the tax imposed by this section, except that the refund allowed by G.S. 105-449.107(b) for certain vehicles that use power takeoffs does not apply to a vehicle whose use of alternative fuel is taxed on the basis of miles driven. The proceeds of the tax imposed by this section must be allocated in accordance with G.S. 105-449.125. (1995, c. 390, s. 3; 1995 (Reg. Sess., 1996), c. 647, s. 47; 2009-445, s. 38.)

§ 105-449.137. Liability for and payment of the tax.

(a) Liability. - A bulk end-user or retailer that stores highway and nonhighway alternative fuel in the same storage facility is liable for the tax imposed by this Article. The tax payable by a bulk end-user or retailer applies when fuel is withdrawn from the storage facility. The alternative fuel provider that sells or delivers alternative fuel is liable for the tax imposed by this Article on all other alternative fuel.

(b) Payment. - The tax imposed by this Article is payable when a return is due. A return is due on the same date as a monthly return due under G.S. 105-449.90. A monthly return covers liabilities that accrue in the calendar month preceding the date the return is due. A return must be filed with the Secretary and must be in the form and contain the information required by the Secretary. (1995, c. 390, s. 3; 1997-60, s. 24; 2006-162, s. 15(d); 2008-134, s. 56.)

§ 105-449.138. Requirements for bulk end-users and retailers.

(a) Informational Return. - A bulk end-user and a retailer must file a quarterly informational return with the Secretary. A quarterly return covers a calendar quarter and is due by the last day of the month that follows the quarter covered by the return.

The return must give the following information and any other information required by the Secretary:

(1) The amount of alternative fuel received during the quarter.

(2) The amount of alternative fuel sold or used during the quarter.

(b) Storage. - A bulk end-user or a retailer may store highway and nonhighway alternative fuel in separate storage facilities or in the same storage facility. If highway and nonhighway alternative fuel are stored in separate storage facilities, the facility for the nonhighway fuel must be marked in accordance with the requirements set by G.S. 105-449.123 for dyed diesel storage facilities. If highway and nonhighway alternative fuel are stored in the same storage facility, the storage facility must be equipped with separate metering devices for the highway fuel and the nonhighway fuel. If the Secretary determines that a bulk end-user or retailer used or sold alternative fuel to operate a highway vehicle when the fuel was dispensed from a storage facility or through a meter marked for nonhighway use, all fuel delivered into that storage facility is presumed to have been used to operate a highway vehicle. (1995, c. 390, s. 3; 1995 (Reg. Sess., 1996), c. 647, s. 48; 1997-60, s. 25; 2008-134, s. 57.)

§ 105-449.139. Miscellaneous provisions.

(a)   Records. - A license holder must keep a record of all documents used to determine the information provided in a return filed under this Article. The records must be kept for three years from the due date of the return to which the records apply. The records are open to inspection during business hours by the Secretary or a person designated by the Secretary.

(b)   Violations. - The offenses listed in subdivisions (1) through (9) of G.S. 105-449.120 apply to this Article. In applying those offenses to this Article, references to "this Article" are to be construed as references to Article 36D and references to "motor fuel" are to be construed as references to alternative fuel.

(c)   Lists. - The Secretary must give a list of licensed alternative fuel providers to each licensed bulk end-user and licensed retailer. The Secretary must also give a list of licensed bulk end-users and licensed retailers to each licensed alternative fuel provider. A list must state the name, account number, and business address of each license holder on the list. The Secretary must send an annual update of a list to each license holder, as appropriate. (1995, c. 390, s. 3; 1995 (Reg. Sess., 1996), c. 647, s. 49; 2008-134, s. 58.)

SUBCHAPTER VI. TAX RESEARCH.

Article 37.

Tax Research.

§§ 105-450 through 105-457: Repealed by Session Laws 1991, c. 10, s. 3.

SUBCHAPTER VII. PAYMENTS RECEIVED FROM TENNESSEE VALLEY AUTHORITY IN LIEU OF TAXES.

Article 38.

Equitable Distribution between Local Governments.

§ 105-458. Apportionment of payments in lieu of taxes between local units.

The payments received by the State and local governments from the Tennessee Valley Authority in lieu of taxes under section 13 of the Act of Congress creating it, and as amended, shall be apportioned between the local governments in which the property is owned or an operation is carried on, on the basis of each local government's percentage of the total value of the Authority's property in the State, determined as hereinafter provided: Provided, however, that the minimum annual payment to any local government from said fund, including the amounts paid direct to said local government by the Authority, shall not be less than the amount of annual actual tax loss to such local government based upon the two-year average on said property next prior to it being taken over by the Authority. (1941, c. 85, s. 1; 1959, c. 1060; 2009-569, s. 1.)

§ 105-459. Proration of T.V.A. funds.

The Department of Revenue shall determine each year, on the basis of current tax laws, the allocation of the Authority's valuation among the local governments in the same manner as if the property owned or operated by the Authority were owned or operated by a privately owned public utility. The Department of Revenue and the Treasurer of the State of North Carolina shall then prorate the funds received from the Authority by the State and local governments between the local governments upon the basis of the foregoing calculations. (1941, c. 85, s. 2; 1959, c. 1060; 1973, c. 476, s. 193; 2009-569, s. 2.)

§ 105-460. Distribution of funds by State Treasurer.

The Treasurer of the State of North Carolina shall then ascertain the payments to be made to the local governments upon the basis of the provisions of G.S. 105-459 and he is authorized and directed to distribute the same between the local governments in accordance with the foregoing provisions of G.S. 105-459. The Treasurer of the State of North Carolina is further authorized and directed to pay said sums to the local governments each month or so often as he shall receive payments from the Authority, but not more often than once each month, after first deducting from any sum to be paid a local government such amount as has theretofore been paid direct to said local government by the Authority for the same period: Provided, however, that the minimum annual payment to any local government from said fund shall not be less than the average annual tax on the property taken by the Authority for the two years next preceding the taking. (1941, c. 85, s. 3; 1959, c. 1060.)

§ 105-461. Duty of finance officer, etc.

The finance officer or other proper officer of each local government to which this Subchapter is applicable shall certify each month to the Treasurer of the State of North Carolina a statement of the amount received by the local government direct from the Authority.

No local government shall be entitled to receive its distributive share of said fund from the Treasurer of the State of North Carolina until the foregoing information has been properly furnished. If any such local government shall fail to furnish the information herein required within 10 days from and after receipt by it from the Department of Revenue of request for the same, forwarded by registered mail, then and in that event it shall be barred from participating in the benefits provided for the period for which the same is requested. (1941, c. 85, s. 4; 1973, c. 476, s. 193; 2009-569, s. 3.)

§ 105-462. Local units entitled to benefits; prerequisite for payments.

Any local governments within the State in which the Authority now or may hereafter own property or carry on an operation shall be entitled to the benefits arising under this Subchapter: Provided, however, that no payment shall be made to them by the Treasurer of the State of North Carolina until such time as such local governments shall have certified to the Department of Revenue and the Treasurer of the State of North Carolina the average annual tax loss it has sustained by the taking of said property for the two years immediately preceding the taking thereof: Provided, further, that in the event of any disagreement between said local governments and the Treasurer of the State of North Carolina as to such annual tax loss, then the same shall be determined by the Department of Revenue, and its decision thereon shall be final. (1941, c. 85, s. 5; 1973, c. 476, s. 193.)

SUBCHAPTER VIII. LOCAL GOVERNMENT SALES AND USE TAX.

Article 39.

First One-Cent (1¢) Local Government Sales and Use Tax.

§ 105-463. Short title.

This Article shall be known as the First One-Cent (1¢) Local Government Sales and Use Tax Act. (1971, c. 77, s. 2; 2002-123, s. 7(b).)

§ 105-464. Purpose and intent.

It is the purpose of this Article to afford the counties and municipalities of this State with opportunity to obtain an added source of revenue with which to meet their growing financial needs by providing all counties of the State with authority to levy a one percent (1%) sales and use tax as hereinafter provided. (1971, c. 77, s. 2.)

§ 105-465. County election as to adoption of local sales and use tax.

The board of elections of any county, upon the written request of the board of county commissioners, or upon receipt of a petition signed by qualified voters of the county equal in number to at least fifteen percent (15%) of the total number of votes cast in the county, at the last preceding election for the office of Governor, shall call a special election for the purpose of submitting to the voters of the county the question of whether a one percent (1%) sales and use tax will be levied.

The special election shall be held under the same rules applicable to the election of members of the General Assembly.

The county board of elections shall prepare ballots for the special election. The question presented on the ballot shall be "FOR one percent (1%) local sales and use tax on items subject to State sales and use tax at the general State rate and on food" or "AGAINST one percent (1%) local sales and use tax on items subject to State sales and use tax at the general State rate and on food".

The county board of elections shall fix the date of the special election on a date permitted by G.S. 163-287, except that the special election shall not be held within one year from the date of the last preceding special election under this section. (1971, c. 77, s. 2; 1981, c. 560, s. 2; 1991, c. 689, s. 315; 1996, 2nd Ex. Sess., c. 13, s. 1.2; 2013-381, s. 10.8.)

§ 105-466. Levy of tax.

(a)   In the event a majority of those voting in a special election held pursuant to G.S. 105-465 shall approve the levy of the local sales and use tax, the board of county commissioners may, by resolution, proceed to levy the tax.

(b)   In addition, the board of county commissioners may, in the event no election has been held within five years under the provisions of G.S. 105-465 in which the tax has been defeated, after not less than 10 days' public notice and after a public hearing held pursuant thereto, by resolution, impose and levy the local sales and use tax to the same extent and with the same effect as if the levy of the tax had been approved in an election held pursuant to G.S. 105-465.

(b1)   If the board of commissioners of a county has imposed the local sales and use tax authorized by this Article and any or all of the taxes authorized by Articles 40 and 42 of this Chapter, with or without a special election, and the county subsequently becomes part of a consolidated city-county, the taxes shall continue in effect unless and until repealed by the governing board of the consolidated city-county.

(c)   Collection of the tax, and liability therefor, must begin and continue only on and after the first day of a calendar quarter, as set by the board of county commissioners in the resolution levying the tax. In no event may the tax be imposed, or the tax rate changed, earlier than the first day of the second succeeding calendar month after the date of the adoption of the resolution. The county must give the Secretary at least 90 days advance notice of a new tax levy or tax rate change. The applicability of a new tax or a tax rate change to purchases from printed catalogs becomes effective on the first day of a calendar quarter after a minimum of 120 days from the date the Secretary notifies the seller that receives orders by means of a catalog or similar publication of the new tax or tax rate change.

(d)   Upon adoption of a resolution levying the tax, the board of county commissioners shall immediately deliver a certified copy of the resolution to the Secretary, accompanied by a certified statement from the county board of elections, if applicable, setting forth the results of any special election approving the tax in the county. Upon receipt of these documents, the Secretary shall collect and administer the tax as provided in this Article. (1971, c. 77, s. 2; 1973, c. 302; c. 476, s. 193; 1977, c. 372, s. 1; 1993, c. 485, s. 22; 1995, c. 461, s. 16; 2000-120, s. 12; 2001-414, s. 28; 2003-284, s. 45.10; 2010-95, s. 12.)

§ 105-467. Scope of sales tax.

(a)   Sales Tax. - The sales tax that may be imposed under this Article is limited to a tax at the rate of one percent (1%) of the following:

(1)   A retailer's net taxable sales and gross receipts that are subject to the general rate of sales tax imposed by the State under G.S. 105-164.4 except the tax does not apply to the sales price of a manufactured home or a modular home.

(2)   through (4) Repealed by Session Laws 2011-330, s. 45, effective June 27, 2011.

(5)   The sales price of food that is not otherwise exempt from tax pursuant to G.S. 105-164.13 but is exempt from the State sales and use tax pursuant to G.S. 105-164.13B.

(5a)   The sales price of a bundled transaction that includes food subject to tax under subdivision (5) of this subsection, if the price of the food exceeds ten percent (10%) of the price of the bundle. A retailer must determine the price of food in a bundled transaction in accordance with G.S. 105-164.4D.

(5b)   (See notes for delayed repeal of subdivision) The sales price of bread, rolls, and buns that are sold at a bakery thrift store and are exempt from State tax under G.S. 105-164.13(27a).

(6),   (7) Repealed by Session Laws 2011-330, s. 45, effective June 27, 2011.

(b)   (Effective until July 1, 2014) Exemptions and Refunds. - The State exemptions and exclusions contained in G.S. 105-164.13, the State sales and use tax holidays contained in G.S. 105-164.13C and G.S. 105-164.13D, and the State refund provisions contained in G.S. 105-164.14 through G.S. 105-164.14B apply to the local sales and use tax authorized to be levied and imposed under this Article. Except as provided in this subsection, a taxing county may not allow an exemption, exclusion, or refund that is not allowed under the State sales and use tax. A local school administrative unit and a joint agency created by interlocal agreement among local school administrative units pursuant to G.S. 160A-462 to jointly purchase food service-related materials, supplies, and equipment on their behalf is allowed an annual refund of sales and use taxes paid by it under this Article on direct purchases of tangible personal property and services, other than electricity, telecommunications service, and ancillary service. Sales and use tax liability indirectly incurred by the entity on building materials, supplies, fixtures, and equipment that become a part of or annexed to any building or structure that is owned or leased by the entity and is being erected, altered, or repaired for use by the entity is considered a sales or use tax liability incurred on direct purchases by the entity for the purpose of this subsection. A request for a refund shall be in writing and shall include any information and documentation required by the Secretary. A request for a refund is due within six months after the end of the entity's fiscal year. Refunds applied for more than three years after the due date are barred.

(b) (Effective July 1, 2014) Exemptions and Refunds. - The State exemptions and exclusions contained in G.S. 105-164.13 apply to the local sales and use tax authorized to be levied and imposed under this Article. The State refund provisions contained in G.S. 105-164.14 through G.S. 105-164.14B apply to the local sales and use tax authorized to be levied and imposed under this Article. The aggregate annual local refund amount allowed an entity under G.S. 105-164.14(b) for a fiscal year may not exceed thirteen million three hundred thousand dollars ($13,300,000).

Except as provided in this subsection, a taxing county may not allow an exemption, exclusion, or refund that is not allowed under the State sales and use tax. A local school administrative unit and a joint agency created by interlocal agreement among local school administrative units pursuant to G.S. 160A-462 to jointly purchase food service-related materials, supplies, and equipment on their behalf is allowed an annual refund of sales and use taxes paid by it under this Article on direct purchases of tangible personal property and services, other than electricity, telecommunications service, and ancillary service. Sales and use tax liability indirectly incurred by the entity on building materials, supplies, fixtures, and equipment that become a part of or annexed to any building or structure that is owned or leased by the entity and is being erected, altered, or repaired for use by the entity is considered a sales or use tax liability incurred on direct purchases by the entity for the purpose of this subsection. A request for a refund is due in the same time and manner as provided in G.S. 105-164.14. Refunds applied for more than three years after the due date are barred.

(c) Sourcing. - The sourcing principles in G.S. 105-164.4B apply in determining whether the local sales tax applies to a transaction. (1971, c. 77, s. 2; 1983 (Reg. Sess., 1984), c. 1097, s. 9; 1987, c. 557, s. 7; c. 832, s. 4; 1989, c. 692, s. 3.7; 1991, c. 689, s. 316; 1996, 2nd Ex. Sess., c. 13, s. 1.3; 1998-98, s. 30.1; 1998-171, s. 9; 2001-347, s. 2.15; 2001-414, s. 29; 2001-424, s. 34.16(b); 2001-430, s. 13; 2001-487, s. 67(e); 2002-16, s. 12; 2002-159, s. 61; 2005-276, s. 33.23; 2006-66, s. 7.20(a); 2006-162, s. 32; 2007-244, s. 6; 2007-368, s. 2; 2008-107, s. 28.12(c); 2010-166, s. 3.8; 2011-330, s. 45; 2013-316, ss. 3.1(c), 3.4(c), (d); 2013-414, s. 49(b).)

§ 105-468. Scope of use tax.

The use tax authorized by this Article is a tax at the rate of one percent (1%) of the cost price of each item or article of tangible personal property that is not sold in the taxing county but is used, consumed, or stored for use or consumption in the taxing county. The tax applies to the same items that are subject to tax under G.S. 105-467. The collection and administration of this tax shall be in accordance with Article 5 of Chapter 105 of the General Statutes.

Where a local sales or use tax was due and has been paid with respect to tangible personal property by the purchaser in another taxing county within the State, or where a local sales or use tax was due and has been paid in a taxing jurisdiction outside the State where the purpose of the tax is similar in purpose and intent to the tax which may be imposed pursuant to this Article, the tax paid may be credited against the tax imposed under this section by a taxing county upon the same property. If the amount of sales or use tax so paid is less than the amount of the use tax due the taxing county under this section, the purchaser shall pay to the Secretary an amount equal to the difference between the amount so paid in the other taxing county or jurisdiction and the amount due in the taxing county. The Secretary may require such proof of payment in another taxing county or jurisdiction as is deemed to be necessary. The use tax levied under this Article is not subject to credit for payment of any State sales or use tax not imposed for the benefit and use of counties and municipalities. No credit shall be given under this section for sales or use taxes paid in a taxing jurisdiction outside this State if that taxing jurisdiction does not grant similar credit for sales taxes paid under this Article. (1971, c. 77, s. 2; 1973, c. 476, s. 193; 1979, 2nd Sess., c. 1100, s. 2; 1989, c. 692, s. 3.8; 1991, c. 689, s. 317; 1996, 2nd Ex. Sess., c. 13, s. 1.4; 2012-79, s. 1.10; 2013-414, s. 49(a).)

§ 105-468.1. Certain building materials exempt from sales and use taxes.

The provisions of this Article shall not be applicable with respect to any building materials purchased for the purpose of fulfilling any lump sum or unit price contract entered into or awarded, or entered into or awarded pursuant to any bid made, before the effective date of the tax imposed by a taxing county when, absent the provisions of this section, such building materials would otherwise be subject to tax under the provisions of this Article. (1971, c. 77, s. 3.)

§ 105-469. Secretary to collect and administer local sales and use tax.

(a) The Secretary shall collect and administer a tax levied by a county pursuant to this Article. As directed by G.S. 105-164.13B, taxes levied by a county on food are administered as if they were levied by the State under Article 5 of this Chapter. The Secretary must, on a monthly basis, distribute local taxes levied on food to the taxing counties as follows:

(1) The Secretary must allocate one-half of the net proceeds on a per capita basis according to the most recent annual population estimates certified to the Secretary by the State Budget Officer. The Secretary must then adjust the amount allocated to each county as provided in G.S. 105-486(b). The Secretary must include one-half of the amount allocated under this subdivision in the distribution made under Article 40 of this Chapter and must include the remaining one-half in the distribution made under Article 42 of this Chapter.

(2) The Secretary must allocate the remaining net proceeds proportionately to each taxing county based upon the amount of sales tax on food collected in the taxing county in the 1997-1998 fiscal year under Article 39 of this Chapter or under Chapter 1096 of the 1967 Session Laws relative to the total amount of sales tax on food collected in all taxing counties in the 1997-1998 fiscal year under Article 39 of this Chapter and under Chapter 1096 of the 1967 Session

Laws. The Secretary must include the amount allocated under this subdivision in the distribution made under Article 39 of this Chapter.

(b) The Secretary shall require retailers who collect use tax on sales to North Carolina residents to ascertain the county of residence of each buyer and provide that information to the Secretary along with any other information necessary for the Secretary to allocate the use tax proceeds to the correct taxing county. (1971, c. 77, s. 2; 1973, c. 476, s. 193; 1993, c. 485, s. 23; 1996, 2nd Ex. Sess., c. 14, s. 12; 2003-284, s. 45.11(a); 2003-416, s. 27(a); 2004-170, s. 32; 2005-435, s. 41.)

§ 105-470: Repealed by Session Laws 1991, c. 689, s. 318.

§ 105-471. Retailer to collect sales tax.

Every retailer whose place of business is in a taxing county shall on and after the levy of the tax herein authorized collect the one percent (1%) local sales tax provided by this Article.

The tax to be collected under this Article shall be collected as a part of the sales price of the item of tangible personal property sold, the cost price of the item of tangible personal property used, or as a part of the charge for the rendering of any services, renting or leasing of tangible personal property, or the furnishing of any accommodation taxable hereunder. The tax shall be stated and charged separately from the sales price or cost price and shall be shown separately on the retailer's sales record and shall be paid by the purchaser to the retailer as trustee for and on account of the State or county wherein the tax is imposed. It is the intent and purpose of this Article that the local sales and use tax herein authorized to be imposed and levied by a taxing county shall be added to the sales price and that the tax shall be passed on to the purchaser instead of being borne by the retailer. The Secretary of Revenue shall design, print and furnish to all retailers in a taxing county in which he shall collect and administer the tax the necessary forms for filing returns and instructions to insure the full collection from retailers, and the Secretary may adapt the present form used for the reporting and collecting of the State sales and use tax to this purpose. (1971, c. 77, s. 2; 1973, c. 476, s. 193.)

§ 105-472. Disposition and distribution of taxes collected.

(a) County Allocation. - The Secretary shall, on a monthly basis, allocate to each taxing county for which the Secretary collects the tax the net proceeds of the tax collected in that county under this Article. For the purpose of this section, "net proceeds" means the gross proceeds of the tax collected in each county under this Article less taxes refunded, the cost to the State of collecting and administering the tax in the county as determined by the Secretary, and other deductions that may be charged to the county. If the Secretary collects local sales or use taxes in a month and the taxes cannot be identified as being attributable to a particular taxing county, the Secretary shall allocate the taxes among the taxing counties in proportion to the amount of taxes collected in each county under this Article during that month and shall include them in the monthly distribution. Amounts collected by electronic funds transfer payments are included in the distribution for the month in which the return that applies to the payment is received.

(b) Distribution Between Counties and Cities. - The Secretary shall divide the amount allocated to each taxing county among the county and its municipalities in accordance with the method determined by the county. The board of county commissioners shall, by resolution, choose one of the following methods of distribution:

(1) Per Capita Method. - The net proceeds of the tax collected in a taxing county shall be distributed to that county and to the municipalities in the county on a per capita basis according to the total population of the taxing county, plus the total population of the municipalities in the county. In the case of a municipality located in more than one county, only that part of its population living in the taxing county is considered its "total population". In order to make the distribution, the Secretary shall determine a per capita figure by dividing the amount allocated to each taxing county by the total population of that county plus the total population of all municipalities in the county. The Secretary shall then multiply this per capita figure by the population of the taxing county and by the population of each municipality in the county; each respective product shall be the amount to be distributed to the county and to each municipality in the county. To determine the population of each county and each municipality, the Secretary shall use the most recent annual estimate of population certified by the State Budget Officer.

(2) Ad Valorem Method. - The net proceeds of the tax collected in a taxing county shall be distributed to that county and the municipalities in the county in

proportion to the total amount of ad valorem taxes levied by each on property having a tax situs in the taxing county during the fiscal year next preceding the distribution. For purposes of this section, the amount of the ad valorem taxes levied by a county or municipality includes ad valorem taxes levied by the county or municipality in behalf of a taxing district and collected by the county or municipality. In addition, the amount of taxes levied by a county includes ad valorem taxes levied by a merged school administrative unit described in G.S. 115C-513 in the part of the unit located in the county. In computing the amount of tax proceeds to be distributed to each county and municipality, the amount of any ad valorem taxes levied but not substantially collected shall be ignored. Each county and municipality receiving a distribution of the proceeds of the tax levied under this Article shall in turn immediately share the proceeds with each district in behalf of which the county or municipality levied ad valorem taxes in the proportion that the district levy bears to the total levy of the county or municipality. Any county or municipality that fails to provide the Department of Revenue with information concerning ad valorem taxes levied by it adequate to permit a timely determination of its appropriate share of tax proceeds collected under this Article may be excluded by the Secretary from each monthly distribution with respect to which the information was not provided in a timely manner, and those tax proceeds shall then be distributed only to the remaining counties or municipalities, as appropriate. For the purpose of computing the distribution of the tax under this subsection to any county and the municipalities located in the county for any month with respect to which the property valuation of a public service company is the subject of an appeal and the Department of Revenue is restrained by law from certifying the valuation to the county and the municipalities in the county, the Department shall use the last property valuation of the public service company that has been certified.

The board of county commissioners in each taxing county shall, by resolution adopted during the month of April of each year, determine which of the two foregoing methods of distribution shall be in effect in the county during the next succeeding fiscal year. In order for the resolution to be effective, a certified copy of it must be delivered to the Secretary in Raleigh within 15 calendar days after its adoption. If the board fails to adopt a resolution choosing a method of distribution not then in effect in the county, or if a certified copy of the resolution is not timely delivered to the Secretary, the method of distribution then in effect in the county shall continue in effect for the following fiscal year. The method of distribution in effect on the first of July of each fiscal year shall apply to every distribution made during that fiscal year.

(b1)   Repealed by Session Laws 2008-134, s. 14(b), effective July 28, 2008.

(c) Municipality Defined. - As used in this Article, the term "municipality" means "city" as defined in G.S. 153A-1.

(d) No municipality may receive any funds under this section if it was incorporated with an effective date of on or after January 1, 2000, and is disqualified from receiving funds under G.S. 136-41.2. No municipality may receive any funds under this section, incorporated with an effective date on or after January 1, 2000, unless a majority of the mileage of its streets are open to the public. The previous sentence becomes effective with respect to distribution of funds on or after July 1, 1999. (1971, c. 77, s. 2; 1973, c. 476, s. 193; c. 752; 1979, c. 12, s. 1; 1979, 2nd Sess., c. 1137, s. 49; 1981, c. 4, s. 2; 1985 (Reg. Sess., 1986), c. 934, s. 2; 1991, c. 325, s. 8; 1993, c. 485, s. 24; 1999-458, s. 6; 2001-427, s. 13(a); 2001-487, s. 118(b); 2002-72, s. 5; 2003-349, s. 5; 2004-203, s. 5(j); 2007-323, s. 31.16.3(d); 2008-134, s. 14(b).)

§ 105-473. Repeal of levy.

(a) The board of elections of any county, upon the written request of the board of county commissioners thereof, or upon receipt of a petition signed by qualified voters of the county equal in number to at least fifteen percent (15%) of the total number of votes cast in the county at the last preceding election for the office of Governor, shall call a special election for the purpose of submitting to the voters of the county the question of whether the levy of a one percent (1%) sales and use tax theretofore levied should be repealed.

The special election shall be held under the same rules and regulations applicable to the election of members of the General Assembly.

The county board of elections shall prepare ballots for the special election which shall contain the words "FOR repeal of the one percent (1%) local sales and use tax levy," and the words "AGAINST repeal of the one percent (1%) local sales and use tax levy," with appropriate squares so that each voter may designate his vote by his cross (X) mark.

The county board of elections shall fix the date of the special election on a date permitted by G.S. 163-287; provided, however, that the special election shall not be held within one year from the date of the last preceding special election held under this section.

(b) In the event a majority of those voting in a special election held pursuant to this section shall approve the repeal of the levy, the board of county commissioners shall, by resolution, proceed to terminate the levy and the imposition of the tax in the taxing county unless and until the tax is levied again as provided in G.S. 105-466(a).

(c) In addition, the board of county commissioners may, by resolution and without the necessity of an election proceed to terminate the levy and the imposition of the tax in the taxing county if the tax was levied under the provisions of G.S. 105-466(b).

(d) No termination of taxes levied and imposed under this Article shall be effective until the end of the fiscal year in which the repeal election was held.

(e) The board of county commissioners, upon adoption of said resolution, shall cause a certified copy of the resolution to be delivered immediately to the Secretary of Revenue, accompanied by a certified statement from the county board of elections, if applicable, setting forth the results of any special election approving the repeal of the tax in the county.

(f) No liability for any tax levied under this Article which shall have attached prior to the effective date on which a levy is terminated shall be discharged as a result of such termination, and no right to a refund of tax or otherwise, which shall have accrued prior to the effective date on which a levy is terminated shall be denied as a result of such termination. (1971, c. 77, s. 2; 1973, c. 476, s. 193; 1981, c. 560, s. 2; 1995, c. 461, s. 17; 2013-381, s. 10.9.)

§ 105-474. Definitions; construction of Article; remedies and penalties.

The definitions set forth in G.S. 105-164.3 shall apply to this Article insofar as such definitions are not inconsistent with the provisions of this Article, and all other provisions of Article 5 and of Article 9 of Subchapter 1, Chapter 105 of the General Statutes, as the same relate to the North Carolina Sales and Use Tax Act shall be applicable to this Article unless such provisions are inconsistent with the provisions of this Article. The administrative interpretations made by the Secretary of Revenue with respect to the North Carolina Sales and Use Tax Act, to the extent not inconsistent with the provisions of this Article, may be uniformly applied in the construction and interpretation of this Article. It is the intention of this Article that the provisions of this Article and the provisions of the North Carolina Sales and Use Tax Act, insofar as practicable, shall be harmonized.

The provisions with respect to remedies and penalties applicable to the North Carolina Sales and Use Tax Act, as contained in Article 5 and Article 9, Subchapter 1, Chapter 105 of the General Statutes, shall be applicable in like manner to the tax authorized to be levied and collected under this Article, to the extent that the same are not inconsistent with the provisions of this Article. (1971, c. 77, s. 2; 1973, c. 476, s. 193.)

§§ 105-475 through 105-479. Reserved for future codification purposes.

Article 40.

First One-Half Cent (1/2¢) Local Government Sales and Use Tax.

§ 105-480. Short title.

This Article shall be known as the First One-Half Cent (1/2¢) Local Government Sales and Use Tax Act. (1983, c. 908, s. 1; 2002-123, s. 8(b).)

§ 105-481. Purpose and intent.

It is the purpose of this Article to afford the counties and cities of this State an opportunity to obtain an added source of revenue with which to meet their growing financial needs, and to reduce their reliance on other revenues, such as the property tax, by providing all counties of the State that are subject to this Article with authority to levy one-half percent (1/2%) sales and use taxes. (1983, c. 908, s. 1.)

§ 105-482. Limitations.

This Article applies only to counties that levy one percent (1%) sales and use taxes under Article 39 of this Chapter or under Chapter 1096 of the 1967 Session Laws. (1983, c. 908, s. 1; 1993, c. 485, s. 25.)

§ 105-483. Levy and collection of additional taxes.

Any county subject to this Article may levy one-half percent (1/2%) local sales and use taxes in addition to any other State and local sales and use taxes levied pursuant to law. Except as provided in this Article, the adoption, levy, collection, distribution, administration, and repeal of these additional taxes shall be in accordance with Article 39 of this Chapter. In applying the provisions of Article 39 of this Chapter to this Article, references to "this Article" mean Article 40 of this Chapter. The exemption for building materials in G.S. 105-468.1 does not apply to taxes levied under this Article. (1983, c. 908, s. 1; 1993, c. 485, s. 26.)

§ 105-484. Form of ballot.

(a)   The form of the question to be presented on a ballot for a special election concerning the additional taxes authorized by this Article shall be: "FOR additional one-half percent (1/2%) local sales and use taxes" or "AGAINST additional one-half percent (1/2%) local sales and use taxes."

(b)   The form of the question to be presented on a ballot for a special election concerning the repeal of any additional taxes levied pursuant to this Article shall be: "FOR repeal of the additional one-half percent (1/2%) local sales and use taxes" or "AGAINST repeal of the additional one-half percent (1/2%) local sales and use taxes." (1983, c. 908, s. 1.)

§ 105-485: Repealed by Session Laws 1991, c. 689, s. 318.

§ 105-486. Distribution of additional taxes.

(a) County Allocation. - The Secretary shall, on a monthly basis, allocate the net proceeds of the additional one-half percent (1/2%) sales and use taxes levied under this Article to the taxing counties on a per capita basis according to the most recent annual population estimates certified to the Secretary by the State Budget Officer.

(b) Adjustment. - The Secretary shall then adjust the amount allocated to each county under subsection (a) by multiplying the amount by the appropriate adjustment factor set out in the table below. If, after applying the adjustment factors, the resulting total of the amounts allocated is greater or lesser than the net proceeds to be distributed, the amount allocated to each county shall be proportionally adjusted to eliminate the excess or shortage.

County
Adjustment Factor

Dare
1.49

Brunswick
1.17

Orange
1.15

Carteret and Durham
1.14

Avery
1.12

Moore
1.11

Transylvania
1.10

Chowan, McDowell, and Richmond
1.09

Pitt and New Hanover
1.07

Beaufort, Perquimans, Buncombe, and Watauga
1.06

Cabarrus, Jackson, and Surry
1.05

Alleghany, Bladen, Robeson, Washington, Craven, Henderson,
1.04

    Onslow, and Vance

Gaston, Granville, and Martin
1.03

Alamance, Burke, Caldwell, Chatham, Duplin, Edgecombe,
1.02

    Haywood, Swain, and Wilkes

Hertford, Union, Stokes, Yancey, Halifax, Rockingham, and
1.01

    Cleveland

Alexander, Anson, Johnston, Northampton, Pasquotank, Person,
1.00

    Polk, and Yadkin

Catawba, Harnett, Iredell, Pamlico, Pender, Randolph, Stanly, and
0.99

    Tyrrell

Cherokee, Cumberland, Davidson, Graham, Hyde, Macon,
0.98

    Rutherford, Scotland, and Wilson

Ashe, Bertie, Franklin, Hoke, Lincoln, Montgomery, and Warren
0.97

Wayne, Clay, Madison, Sampson, Wake, Lee, and Forsyth
0.96

Caswell, Gates, Mitchell, and Greene
0.95

Currituck and Guilford
0.94

Davie and Nash
0.93

Rowan and Camden
0.92

Jones
0.90

Mecklenburg
0.89

Lenoir
0.88

Columbus
0.81

(c) Distribution Between Counties and Cities. - The amount allocated to each taxing county shall then be divided among the county and its municipalities in accordance with the method by which the one percent (1%) sales and use taxes levied in that county pursuant to Article 39 of this Chapter or Chapter 1096 of the 1967 Session Laws are distributed.

(d) No municipality may receive any funds under this section if it was incorporated with an effective date of on or after January 1, 2000, and is disqualified from receiving funds under G.S. 136-41.2. No municipality may receive any funds under this section, incorporated with an effective date on or after January 1, 2000, unless a majority of the mileage of its streets are open to the public. The previous sentence becomes effective with respect to distribution of funds on or after July 1, 1999. (1983, c. 908, s. 1; 1985 (Reg. Sess., 1986), c. 906, s. 2; 1987, c. 832, s. 6; 1987 (Reg. Sess., 1988), c. 1082, s. 2; 1999-458, s. 7; 2001-427, s. 13(b), (c).)

§ 105-487. Use of additional tax revenue by counties.

(a) Except as provided in subsection (c), forty percent (40%) of the revenue received by a county from additional one-half percent (1/2%) sales and use taxes levied under this Article during the first five fiscal years in which the additional taxes are in effect in the county and thirty percent (30%) of the revenue received by a county from these taxes after the first five fiscal years in which the taxes are in effect in the county may be used by the county only for public school capital outlay purposes as defined in G.S. 115C-426(f) or to retire any indebtedness incurred by the county for these purposes.

(b) Repealed by Session Laws 1998-98, s. 31, effective August 14, 1998.

(c) The Local Government Commission may, upon petition by a county, authorize the county to use part or all its tax revenue, otherwise required by subsection (a) of this section to be used for public school capital needs, for any lawful purpose. The petition shall be in the form of a resolution adopted by the Board of County Commissioners and transmitted to the Local Government Commission. The petition shall demonstrate that the county can provide for its public school capital needs without restricting the use of part or all of the designated amount of the additional one-half percent (½%) sales and use tax revenue for that purpose.

In making its decision, the Local Government Commission shall consider information contained in the petition concerning not only the public school capital needs, but also the other capital needs of the petitioning county. The Commission may also consider information from sources other than the petition. The Commission shall issue a written decision on each petition stating the findings of the Commission concerning the public school capital needs of the petitioning county and the percentage of revenue otherwise restricted by subsection (a) of this section that may be used by the petitioning county for any lawful purpose.

Decisions of the Commission allowing counties to use a percentage of their tax revenue that would otherwise be restricted under subsection (a) of this section for any lawful purpose are final and shall continue in effect until the restrictions imposed by that subsection expire. A county whose petition is denied, in whole or in part, by the Commission may subsequently submit a new petition to the Commission.

(d) For purposes of determining the number of fiscal years in which one-half percent (½%) sales and use taxes levied under this Article have been in effect in a county, these taxes are considered to be in effect only from the effective date of the levy of these taxes and are considered to be in effect for a full fiscal year during the first year in which these taxes were in effect, regardless of the number of months in that year in which the taxes were actually in effect.

(e) A county may expend part or all of the revenue restricted for public school capital needs pursuant to subsection (a) of this section in the fiscal year in which the revenue is received, or the county may place part or all of this revenue in a capital reserve fund and shall specifically identify this revenue in accordance with Chapter 159 of the General Statutes. (1983, c. 908, s. 1; 1993, c. 255, ss. 1, 3; 1998-98, s. 31; 1998-186, s. 1; 2009-395, s. 1.)

Article 41.

Alternative Local Government Sales and Use Taxes.

§§ 105-488 through 105-494: Repealed by Session Laws 1991, c. 689, s. 318.

Article 42.

Second One-Half Cent (1/2¢) Local Government Sales and Use Tax.

§ 105-495. Short title.

This Article shall be known as the Second One-Half Cent (1/2¢) Local Government Sales and Use Tax Act. (1985 (Reg. Sess., 1986), c. 906, s. 1; 2002-123, s. 9(b).)

§ 105-496. Purpose and intent.

It is the purpose of this Article to afford the counties and cities of this State an opportunity to obtain an added source of revenue with which to meet their growing financial needs, and to reduce their reliance on other revenues, such as the property tax and federal revenue sharing, by providing all counties of the State that are subject to this Article with authority to levy one-half percent (1/2%) sales and use taxes. (1985 (Reg. Sess., 1986), c. 906, s. 1.)

§ 105-497. Limitations.

This Article applies only to counties that levy one percent (1%) sales and use taxes under Article 39 of this Chapter or under Chapter 1096 of the 1967 Session Laws and also levy one-half percent (1/2%) local sales and use taxes under Article 40 of this Chapter. (1985 (Reg. Sess., 1986), c. 906, s. 1.)

§ 105-498. Levy and collection of additional taxes.

Any county subject to this Article may levy one-half percent (1/2%) local sales and use taxes in addition to any other State and local sales and use taxes levied pursuant to law. Except as provided in this Article, the adoption, levy, collection, distribution, administration, and repeal of these additional taxes shall be in accordance with Article 39 of this Chapter. In applying the provisions of Article 39 of this Chapter to this Article, references to "this Article" mean Article 42 of this Chapter. The exemption for building materials in G.S. 105-468.1 does not apply to taxes levied under this Article. (1985 (Reg. Sess., 1986), c. 906, s. 1; 1993, c. 485, s. 27.)

§ 105-499. Form of ballot.

(a) The form of the question to be presented on a ballot for a special election concerning the additional taxes authorized by this Article shall be: "FOR one-half percent (1/2%) local sales and use taxes in addition to the current one and one-half percent (1 1/2%) local sales and use taxes" or "AGAINST one-half percent (1/2%) local sales and use taxes in addition to the current one and one-half percent (1 1/2%) local sales and use taxes."

(b)   The form of the question to be presented on a ballot for a special election concerning the repeal of any additional taxes levied pursuant to this Article shall be: "FOR repeal of the additional one-half percent (1/2%) local sales and use taxes, thus reducing local sales and use taxes to one and one-half percent (1 1/2%)" or "AGAINST repeal of the additional one-half percent (1/2%) local sales and use taxes, thus reducing local sales and use taxes to one and one-half percent (1 1/2%)." (1985 (Reg. Sess., 1986), c. 906, s. 1.)

§ 105-500: Repealed by Session Laws 1991, c. 689, s. 318.

§ 105-501. Distribution of additional taxes.

(a)   Method. - The Secretary must, on a monthly basis, allocate to each taxing county the net proceeds of the additional one-half percent (1/2%) sales and use taxes collected in that county under this Article. If the Secretary collects taxes under this Article in a month and the taxes cannot be identified as being attributable to a particular taxing county, the Secretary must allocate the net proceeds of these taxes among the taxing counties in proportion to the amount of taxes collected in each county under this Article in that month.

The Secretary must divide and distribute the funds allocated to a taxing county each month under this section between the county and the municipalities located in the county in accordance with the method by which the one percent (1%) sales and use taxes levied in that county pursuant to Article 39 of this Chapter or Chapter 1096 of the 1967 Session Laws are distributed. No municipality may receive any funds under this section if it was incorporated with an effective date of on or after January 1, 2000, and is disqualified from receiving funds under G.S. 136-41.2. No municipality may receive any funds under this section, incorporated with an effective date on or after January 1, 2000, unless a majority of the mileage of its streets are open to the public.

(b)   Deductions. - The costs incurred by the State to provide the functions listed in this subsection that support local governments are deductible from the collections to be allocated each month for distribution.

(1)   The Department's cost of the following for the preceding month must be deducted and credited to the Department:

a.   The Local Government Division.

b.   The Property Tax Commission.

(1a)   The Department of State Treasurer's costs for personnel and operations of the Local Government Commission.

(2)   One-twelfth of the costs of the following for the preceding fiscal year must be deducted and credited to the General Fund:

a.   The School of Government at the University of North Carolina at Chapel Hill in operating a training program in property tax appraisal and assessment.

b.   (Repealed effective July 1, 2012) The personnel and operations provided by the Department of State Treasurer for the Local Government Commission.

c.   Seventy percent (70%) of the expenses of the Department of Revenue in performing the duties imposed by Article 2D of this Chapter. (1985 (Reg. Sess., 1986), c. 906, s. 1; 1987, c. 832, s. 8; 1987 (Reg. Sess., 1988), c. 1082, s. 4; 1995, c. 41, s. 4; c. 370, s. 1; 1999-458, s. 9; 2001-427, s. 13(d); 2002-126, s. 30D(a); 2006-264, s. 29(f); 2007-323, s. 31.16.4(b); 2010-31, s. 26.1(a); 2011-145, s. 27.1(a), (b).)

§ 105-502. Use of additional tax revenue by counties.

(a)   Restriction. - The county must use sixty percent (60%) of the amount of revenue specified in this subsection for public school capital outlay purposes as defined in G.S. 115C-426(f) or to retire any indebtedness incurred by the county for these purposes during the period beginning five years prior to the date the taxes took effect:

(1)   The amount of revenue the county receives under this Article.

(2) If the amount allocated to the county under G.S. 105-486 is greater than the amount allocated to the county under G.S. 105-501(a), the difference between the two amounts.

(b) Exception. - The Local Government Commission may, upon petition by a county, authorize a county to use part or all of the revenue, otherwise required by subsection (a) to be used for public school capital outlay purposes, for any lawful purpose. The petition must be in the form of a resolution adopted by the Board of County Commissioners and transmitted to the Local Government Commission. The petition must demonstrate that the county can provide for its public school capital needs without restricting the use of part or all of the specified revenue for these purposes.

In making its decision, the Local Government Commission must consider information in the petition concerning not only the public school capital needs but also the other capital needs of the petitioning county. The Commission may consider information from sources other than the petition. The Commission must issue a written decision on each petition stating the findings of the Commission concerning the public school capital needs of the petitioning county and the percentage of revenue otherwise restricted by subsection (a) that may be used by the petitioning county for any lawful purpose.

Decisions of the Commission allowing counties to use a percentage of the revenue that would otherwise be restricted under subsection (a) for any lawful purpose are final and continue in effect until the restrictions expire. A county whose petition is denied, in whole or in part, by the Commission may subsequently submit a new petition to the Commission.

(c) Reserve Fund. - A county may expend part or all of the revenue restricted for public school capital needs pursuant to subsection (a) in the fiscal year in which the revenue is received, or the county may place part or all of this revenue in a capital reserve fund. A county must specifically identify revenue placed in a reserve fund in accordance with Chapter 159 of the General Statutes.

(d) Taxes in Effect. - For purposes of this section in determining the number of fiscal years in which one-half percent (1/2%) sales and use taxes levied under this Article have been in effect in a county, these taxes are considered to be in effect only from the effective date of the levy of these taxes and are considered to be in effect for a full fiscal year during the first year in which these taxes were in effect, regardless of the number of months in that year in which the taxes were actually in effect. (1985 (Reg. Sess., 1986), c. 906, s. 1; 1987, c. 622, s. 11; 1993, c. 255, ss. 2, 4; 1998-186, s. 2; 2008-134, s. 13(a); 2009-395, s. 2.)

§ 105-503: Recodified as § 115C-440.1 by Session Laws 1995 (Regular Session, 1996), c. 666, s. 4.

§ 105-504: Repealed by Session Laws 1998-98, s. 32.

§ 105-505. Reserved for future codification purposes.

Article 43.

Local Government Sales and Use Taxes for Public Transportation.

Part 1. General.

§ 105-506. Short title; purpose.

This Article is the Local Government Public Transportation Sales Tax Act and may be cited by that name. This Article gives the counties and transportation authorities of this State an opportunity to obtain an additional source of revenue with which to meet their needs for financing local public transportation systems. It provides them with authority to levy sales and use taxes. All such taxes must be approved in a referendum. (1997-417, s. 1; 2009-527, s. 2(a), (b).)

§ 105-506.1. Definitions.

The definitions in G.S. 105-164.3 and the following definitions apply in this Article:

(1) Board of trustees. - The governing body of a transportation authority.

(2) Net proceeds. - Gross proceeds less the cost of administering and collecting the tax.

(3) Public transportation system. - Any combination of real and personal property established for purposes of public transportation. The systems may include one or more of the following: structures, improvements, buildings, equipment, vehicle parking or passenger transfer facilities, railroads and railroad rights-of-way, rights-of-way, bus services, shared-ride services, high-occupancy vehicle facilities, car-pool and vanpool programs, voucher programs, telecommunications and information systems, integrated fare systems, and the interconnected bicycle and pedestrian infrastructure that supports public transportation, bus lanes, and busways. The term does not include, however, streets, roads, or highways except to the extent they are dedicated to public transportation vehicles or to the extent they are necessary for access to vehicle parking or passenger transfer facilities.

(4) Transportation authority. - For the purposes of Parts 3 and 4 of this Article, a regional public transportation authority created pursuant to Article 26 of Chapter 160A of the General Statutes; and for the purposes of Parts 3 and 5 of this Article, a regional transportation authority created pursuant to Article 27 of Chapter 160A of the General Statutes. (1997-417, s. 1; 2009-527, s. 2(a), (b).)

§ 105-506.2. Exemption of food.

A tax levied under this Article does not apply to the sales price of food that is exempt from tax pursuant to G.S. 105-164.13B or to the sales price of a bundled transaction taxable pursuant to G.S. 105-467(a)(5a). (1997-417, s. 1; 2008-134, s. 74(a); 2009-527, s. 2(a), (b).)

Part 2. Mecklenburg County.

§ 105-507. Limitations.

A county may not levy a tax under this Part unless the county or at least one unit of local government in the county operates a public transportation system. In addition, a county may not levy a tax under this Part unless it has developed a financial plan and distributed it to each unit of local government in the county that operates a local public transportation system. The financial plan must provide for equitable allocation of the net proceeds distributed to the county in consideration of the identified needs of local public transportation systems in the county, countywide human service transportation systems, and expansion of public transportation service to unserved areas in the county. (1997-417, s. 1; 2009-527, s. 2(a), (b).)

§ 105-507.1. Local election on adoption of sales and use tax.

(a) Resolution. - The board of commissioners of a county may direct the county board of elections to conduct an advisory referendum within the county on the question of whether a local sales and use tax at the rate of one-half percent (1/2%) may be levied in accordance with this Part. The election shall be held in accordance with the procedures of G.S. 163-287. The board of commissioners shall hold a public hearing on the question at least 30 days before the date the election is to be held.

(b) Ballot Question. - The form of the question to be presented on a ballot for a special election concerning the levy of a tax authorized by this Article shall be:

"[ ] FOR   [ ] AGAINST

One-half percent (1/2%) local sales and use taxes, in addition to the current local sales and use taxes, to be used only for public transportation systems." (1997-417, s. 1; 2009-527, s. 2(a), (b); 2013-381, s. 10.10.)

§ 105-507.2. Levy and collection of sales and use tax.

If the majority of those voting in a referendum held pursuant to G.S. 105-507.1 vote for the levy of the tax, the board of commissioners of the county may, by resolution, levy one-half percent (½%) local sales and use taxes in addition to any other State and local sales and use taxes levied pursuant to law. Except as provided in this Part, the adoption, levy, collection, administration, and repeal of these additional taxes shall be in accordance with Article 39 of this Chapter. In applying the provisions of Article 39 of this Chapter to this Part, references to "this Article" mean "Part 1 of Article 43 of Chapter 105 of the General Statutes". (1997-417, s. 1; 2008-134, s. 74(b); 2009-527, s. 2(a), (b).)

§ 105-507.3. Distribution and use of taxes.

(a) Distribution. - The Secretary shall, on a monthly basis, allocate to each taxing county the net proceeds of the tax levied under this Part by that county. If the Secretary collects taxes under this Part in a month and the taxes cannot be identified as being attributable to a particular taxing county, the Secretary shall allocate these taxes among the taxing counties, in proportion to the amount of taxes collected in each county under this Part in that month and shall include them in the monthly distribution.

The Secretary shall distribute the net proceeds of the tax levied by a county on a per capita basis among the county and the units of local government in the county that operate public transportation systems. No proceeds shall be distributed to a county that does not operate a public transportation system or to a unit of local government that does not operate a public transportation system.

(b) Use. - A county must allocate the net proceeds distributed to it in accordance with its financial plan adopted pursuant to G.S. 105-507 and use the net proceeds only for financing, constructing, operating, and maintaining local public transportation systems. Any other unit of local government may use the net proceeds distributed to it under this Part only for financing, constructing, operating, and maintaining local public transportation systems. Every unit of government shall use the net proceeds to supplement and not to supplant or replace existing funds or other resources for public transportation systems. (1997-417, s. 1; 2001-427, s. 13(f); 2009-527, s. 2(a), (b).)

§ 105-507.4. Applicability.

This Part applies only to Mecklenburg County. (1997-417, s. 1; 2009-527, s. 2(a), (b).)

Part 3. Transportation Authorities.

§ 105-508. Special districts.

(a) Authority. - A transportation authority may create a special district as provided in Parts 4 and 5 of this Article. A special district is subject to the provisions of this Part as well as the Part under which it was created. A special district created under this Article is a local government body corporate and politic and has the power to carry out the purposes of the Part under which it is established.

(b) Governance. - The following entity shall serve ex officio as the governing board and be responsible for budget adoption and the operation and management of the transit services provided by the district:

(1) The board of trustees of the transportation authority, if the special district consists of multiple counties. If the special district is expanded under G.S. 105-509(d) or G.S. 105-510(d) to include more than one county, then the board of trustees of the transportation authority shall become the governing board of the district beginning on the first day of the next fiscal year after expansion of the district.

(2) The county board of commissioners, if the special district consists of one county. The board may contract with the transportation authority as needed.

(c) Filing Requirement. - The transportation authority creating a special district shall name it and file with the Secretary of State the documents creating the district, and shall also file notice of the addition to and removal from the district of any counties, or of the abolition of the special district. (2009-527, s. 2(b).)

§ 105-508.1. Limitations.

A transportation authority may not levy a tax under Part 4 or 5 of this Article unless:

(1) It operates a public transportation system.

(2) It has developed a financial plan and distributed it to each unit of local government located within its territorial jurisdiction. The plan must be approved by the board of commissioners of each county in the district prior to the levy of the tax. If the board of commissioners of a county in a multicounty district does not adopt the plan, the transportation authority may remove that county from the

district, and no tax may be levied in that county under this Part. The financial plan must provide for equitable use of the net proceeds within or to benefit the special district created under Part 4 or Part 5 of this Article and consider (i) the identified needs of local public transportation systems in the district, (ii) human service transportation systems within the district, and (iii) expansion of public transportation systems to underserved areas of the district. The financial plan must also be approved by all Metropolitan Planning Organizations under Article 16 of Chapter 136 of the General Statutes whose jurisdiction includes any of the area of the special district. The plan may be revised from time to time. An interlocal agreement between the transportation authority and all the counties in the special district may require periodic review and approval of the financial plan.

(3) The tax is approved by the voters. (2009-527, s. 2(b).)

§ 105-508.2. Distribution and use of taxes.

(a) Distribution. - The Secretary shall, on a monthly basis, allocate to each special district the net proceeds of the tax levied under this Part within the special tax district, to be used for the benefit of that district.

(b) Use. - A special district must expend the net proceeds distributed to it in accordance with its financial plan adopted pursuant to G.S. 105-508.1 and use the net proceeds only for financing, constructing, operating, and maintaining public transportation systems. The special district shall use the net proceeds to supplement and not to supplant or replace existing funds or other resources for public transportation systems. (2009-527, s. 2(b).)

Part 4. Regional Public Transportation Authority (Triangle).

§ 105-509. Local election on adoption of sales and use tax - regional public transportation authority.

(a) Special District. - A regional public transportation authority may create a special district that consists of the entire area of one or more counties within its territorial jurisdiction and may levy on behalf of the special district the tax authorized in this section. The proceeds of a tax levied under this section may be used only for the benefit of the special district and only for the purposes provided in this Article. If a referendum in a district fails in all the counties in the district, the transportation authority may abolish the special district.

(b) Resolution. - The board of trustees of the regional public transportation authority may, if all of the conditions listed in this subsection have been met, direct the respective county board or boards of elections to conduct an advisory referendum within the special district on the question of whether a local sales and use tax at the rate of one-half percent (1/2%) may be levied within the district in accordance with this Part. The tax may not be levied without voter approval. The election shall be held on a date jointly agreed upon by the authority, the county board or boards of commissioners, and the county board or boards of elections and shall be held on a date permitted by and in accordance with the procedures of G.S. 163-287. The conditions are as follows:

(1) The board of trustees has obtained approval to conduct a referendum by a vote of the following:

a. A majority vote of each of the county boards of commissioners within the special district, if it is a multicounty special district.

b. A majority of the county board of commissioners within the special district, if it is a single-county special district.

(2) A public hearing is held on the question by the board or boards of commissioners at least 30 days before the date the election is to be held.

(c) Ballot Question. - The form of the question to be presented on a ballot for a special election concerning the levy of a tax authorized by this Article shall be:

"[ ] FOR   [ ] AGAINST

One-half percent (1/2%) local sales and use taxes, in addition to the current local sales and use taxes, to be used only for public transportation systems."

(d) Expansion. - If a special district created under this Part does not include all the counties in the territorial jurisdiction of a transportation authority, it may be expanded to include an additional whole county or counties by joint action of the board of trustees of the transportation authority and the board of commissioners of the county or boards of commissioners of the counties to be added, with the approval of the voters in the county or counties to be added. The procedure for expansion of a district is the same as for the initial creation of the district, but the referendum shall be held separately within each of the counties to be added. (2009-527, s. 2(b); 2013-381, s. 10.11.)

§ 105-509.1. Levy and collection of sales and use tax - regional public transportation authority.

If the majority of those voting in a referendum held pursuant to G.S. 105-509 vote for the levy of the tax, the transportation authority may, by resolution, levy one-half percent (½%) local sales and use taxes within the special district, in addition to any other State and local sales and use taxes levied pursuant to law. In determining the results of the election in a multicounty district, all the counties of the district shall be considered to be one unit but also must receive a majority vote in each county, except that if the referendum is passed in one or more but not all of the counties, the counties in which the referendum was not approved are removed from the special district upon certification of the election result and the county or counties that approved the referendum shall remain in the special district. Except as provided in this Part, the adoption, levy, collection, administration, and repeal of these additional taxes shall be in accordance with Article 39 of this Chapter. In applying the provisions of Article 39 of this Chapter to this Article, references to "this Article" mean "Part 4 of Article 43 of Chapter 105 of the General Statutes." Any repeal of the tax shall be done by the same procedure as its enactment under this section, and in a multicounty district a petition for repeal under G.S. 105-473 shall be judged by the total votes in all the counties in the district. (2009-527, s. 2(b).)

Part 5. Regional Transportation Authority (Triad).

§ 105-510. Local election on adoption of sales and use tax - regional transportation authority.

(a)   Special District. - A regional transportation authority may create a special district that consists of the entire area of one or two counties within its territorial jurisdiction and may levy on behalf of the special district the tax authorized in this section. The special district may not include counties other than Forsyth and Guilford. The proceeds of a tax levied under this section may be used only for the benefit of the special district and only for the purposes provided in this Article. If a referendum in a district fails, the transportation authority may abolish the special district.

(b) Resolution. - The board of trustees of the regional transportation authority may, if all of the conditions listed in this subsection have been met, direct the respective county board or boards of elections to conduct an advisory referendum within the special district on the question of whether a local sales and use tax at the rate of one-half percent (1/2%) may be levied within the district in accordance with this Part. The tax may not be levied without voter approval. The election shall be held on a date jointly agreed upon by the authority, the county board or boards of commissioners, and the county board or boards of elections and shall be held on a date permitted by and in accordance with the procedures of G.S. 163-287. The conditions are as follows:

(1) The board of trustees has obtained approval to conduct a referendum by a vote of the following:

a. A majority vote of both of the county boards of commissioners within the special district, if it is a multicounty special district.

b. A majority of the county board of commissioners within the special district, if it is a single-county special district.

(2) A public hearing is held on the question by the board or boards of commissioners at least 30 days before the date the election is to be held.

(c) Ballot Question. - The form of the question to be presented on a ballot for a special election concerning the levy of a tax authorized by this Article shall be:

"[ ] FOR   [ ] AGAINST

One-half percent (1/2%) local sales and use taxes, in addition to the current local sales and use taxes, to be used only for public transportation systems."

(d) Expansion. - If a special district created under this Part does not include both of the eligible counties under subsection (a) of this section, it may be expanded to include the other county by joint action of the board of trustees of the transportation authority and the board of commissioners of the county to be added, with the approval of the voters in the county to be added. The procedure for expansion of the district is the same as for the initial creation of the district, but the referendum shall be held separately in the county to be added. (2009-527, s. 2(b); 2013-381, s. 10.12.)

§ 105-510.1. Levy and collection of sales and use tax - regional transportation authority.

If the majority of those voting in a referendum held pursuant to G.S. 105-510 vote for the levy of the tax, the transportation authority may, by resolution, levy one-half percent (1/2%) local sales and use taxes within the special district, in addition to any other State and local sales and use taxes levied pursuant to law. In determining the results of the election in a multicounty district, all the counties of the district shall be considered to be one unit but also must receive a majority vote in each county, except that if the referendum is passed in one but not both of the counties, the county in which the referendum was not approved is removed from the special district upon certification of the election result and the county that approved the referendum shall remain in the special district. Except as provided in this Part, the adoption, levy, collection, administration, and repeal of these additional taxes shall be in accordance with Article 39 of this Chapter. In applying the provisions of Article 39 of this Chapter to this Article, references to "this Article" mean "Part 5 of Article 43 of Chapter 105 of the General Statutes." Any repeal of the tax shall be done by the same procedure as its enactment under this section, and in a multicounty district a petition for repeal under G.S. 105-473 shall be judged by the total votes in all the counties in the district. (2009-527, s. 2(b).)

Part 6. Other Counties.

§ 105-511. Applicability.

This Part applies only in counties other than Durham, Forsyth, Guilford, Mecklenburg, Orange, or Wake. (2009-527, s. 2(b).)

§ 105-511.1. Limitations.

A county may not levy a tax under this Part unless the county or at least one unit of local government in the county operates a public transportation system. As used in this Part, operation of a public transportation system includes a contract or interlocal agreement for operation of the public transportation system by another county or municipality, or by a transportation authority created under (i) a municipal charter; or (ii) Article 25, 26, or 27 of Chapter 160A of the General Statutes. As used in this Part, operation of a public transportation system also includes a contract with a private entity for operation of the public transportation system. (2009-527, s. 2(b).)

§ 105-511.2. Local election on adoption of sales and use tax.

(a) Resolution. - The board of commissioners of a county may direct the county board of elections to conduct an advisory referendum within the county on the question of whether a local sales and use tax at the rate of one-quarter percent (1/4%) may be levied in accordance with this Part. The election shall be held on a date jointly agreed upon by the boards and shall be held on a date permitted by and in accordance with the procedures of G.S. 163-287. The board of commissioners shall hold a public hearing on the question at least 30 days before the date the election is to be held.

(b) Ballot Question. - The form of the question to be presented on a ballot for a special election concerning the levy of a tax authorized by this Article shall be:

"[ ] FOR   [ ] AGAINST

One-quarter percent (1/4%) local sales and use taxes, in addition to the current local sales and use taxes, to be used only for public transportation systems." (2009-527, s. 2(b); 2013-381, s. 10.13.)

§ 105-511.3. Levy and collection of sales and use tax.

If the majority of those voting in a referendum held pursuant to this Part vote for the levy of the tax, the board of commissioners of the county may, by resolution, levy one-quarter percent (1/4%) local sales and use taxes in addition to any other State and local sales and use taxes levied pursuant to law. Except as provided in this Part, the adoption, levy, collection, administration, and repeal of these additional taxes shall be in accordance with Article 39 of this Chapter. In applying the provisions of Article 39 of this Chapter to this Part, references to "this Article" mean "Part 6 of Article 43 of Chapter 105 of the General Statutes." (2009-527, s. 2(b).)

§ 105-511.4. Distribution and use of taxes.

(a)   Distribution. - The Secretary shall, on a monthly basis, allocate to each taxing county the net proceeds of the tax levied under this Part by that county. If the Secretary collects taxes under this Part in a month and the taxes cannot be identified as being attributable to a particular taxing county, the Secretary shall allocate these taxes among the taxing counties, in proportion to the amount of taxes collected in each county under this Part in that month and shall include them in the monthly distribution.

The Secretary shall distribute the net proceeds of the tax levied by a county on a per capita basis among the county and the units of local government in the county that operate a public transportation system as follows:

(1)   To the county based on the population of the county that is not in an incorporated area, and to the municipalities within the county based on the population of that municipality that is located within that county. To determine the population of each county and each municipality, the Secretary shall use the most recent annual estimate of population certified by the State Budget Officer.

(2)   Notwithstanding subdivision (1) of this subsection, if a municipality to which funds are to be allocated neither operates nor contracts for the operation of a public transportation system, the population of that municipality shall be excluded from the calculations of subdivision (1) of this subsection.

(3)   Notwithstanding subdivision (1) of this subsection, if a county to which funds are to be allocated neither operates nor contracts for the operation of a public transportation system, the population of that county not in an incorporated area shall be excluded from the calculations of subdivision (1) of this subsection.

If a county or a municipality that does not receive an allocation of funds on account of subdivision (2) or (3) of this subsection begins to operate or contract for the operation of a public transportation system, that county or municipality shall begin receiving funds beginning the first day of July that is more than 30 days thereafter.

(b) A county or municipality may use funds received under this Part only for financing, constructing, operating, and maintaining public transportation systems. Every unit of government shall use funds to supplement and not to supplant or replace existing funds or other resources for public transportation systems. (2009-527, s. 2(b).)

§ 105-512. Reserved for future codification purposes.

§ 105-513. Reserved for future codification purposes.

§ 105-514. Reserved for future codification purposes.

Article 44.

Local Government Hold Harmless Provisions.

§ 105-515: Repealed by Session Laws 2007-323, s. 31.16.4(a), effective October 1, 2009, and applicable to sales occurring on or after that date.

§ 105-516: Repealed by Session Laws 2007-323, s. 31.16.4(a), effective October 1, 2009, and applicable to sales occurring on or after that date.

§ 105-517: Repealed by Session Laws 2007-323, s. 31.16.4(a), effective October 1, 2009, and applicable to sales occurring on or after that date.

§ 105-518: Repealed by Session Laws 2007-323, s. 31.16.4(a), effective October 1, 2009, and applicable to sales occurring on or after that date.

§ 105-519: Repealed by Session Laws 2007-323, s. 31.16.4(a), effective October 1, 2009, and applicable to sales occurring on or after that date.

§ 105-520: Repealed by Session Laws 2007-323, s. 31.16.4(a), effective October 1, 2009, and applicable to sales occurring on or after that date.

§ 105-521. Transitional local government hold harmless for repealed reimbursements.

(a) Definitions. - The following definitions apply in this section:

(1) Local government. - A county or municipality that received a distribution of local sales taxes in the most recent fiscal year for which a local sales tax share has been calculated.

(2) Local sales tax share. - A local government's percentage share of the two-cent (2¢) sales taxes distributed during the most recent fiscal year for which data are available.

(3) Repealed reimbursement amount. - The total amount a local government would have been entitled to receive during the 2002-2003 fiscal year under G.S. 105-164.44C, 105-275.1, 105-275.2, 105-277.001, and 105-277.1A, if the Governor had not withheld any distributions under those sections.

(3a) Replacement revenue. - The sum of the following:

a. Fifty percent (50%) of the amount of sales and use tax revenue distributed under Article 40 of this Chapter, other than revenue from the sale of food that is subject to local tax but is exempt from State tax under G.S. 105-164.13B.

b. Twenty-five percent (25%) of the amount of sales and use tax revenue distributed under Article 39 of this Chapter or under Chapter 1096 of the 1967 Session Laws, other than revenue from the sale of food that is subject to local tax but is exempt from State tax under G.S. 105-164.13B.

(4) Two-cent (2¢) sales taxes. - The first one-cent (1¢) sales and use tax authorized in Article 39 of this Chapter and in Chapter 1096 of the 1967 Session Laws, the first one-half cent (1/2¢) local sales and use tax authorized in Article 40 of this Chapter, and the second one-half cent (1/2¢) local sales and use tax authorized in Article 42 of this Chapter.

(b) Distributions. - On or before September 15, 2013, the Secretary must multiply each local government's local sales tax share by the estimated amount of replacement revenue that all local governments are expected to receive during the current fiscal year. If the resulting amount is less than one hundred percent (100%) of the local government's repealed reimbursement amount, the

Secretary must pay the local government fifty percent (50%) of the difference, but not less than fifty dollars ($50.00).

On or before August 15, 2013, the Department of Revenue and the Fiscal Research Division of the General Assembly must each submit to the Secretary and to the General Assembly a final projection of the estimated amount of replacement revenue that all local governments would be expected to receive during the upcoming fiscal year. If, after May 1 and before a distribution is made, a law is enacted that would affect the projection, an updated projection must be submitted as soon as practicable. If the Secretary does not use the lower of the two final projections to make the calculation required by this subsection, the Secretary must report the reasons for this decision to the Joint Legislative Commission on Governmental Operations within 60 days after receiving the projections.

(c) Source of Funds. - The Secretary must draw the funds distributed under this section from sales and use tax collections under Article 5 of this Chapter.

(d) Reports. - The Secretary must report to the Revenue Laws Study Committee by January 31, 2014, the amount distributed under this section for the current fiscal year. (2001-424, s. 34.14(a); 2003-284, s. 37.1; 2003-349, s. 6; 2004-124, s. 6.3; 2007-323, s. 31.16.3(c); 2013-360, s. 6.17.)

§ 105-522. City hold harmless for repealed local taxes.

(a) Definitions. - The following definitions apply in this section:

(1) Eligible municipality. - A municipality that was incorporated on or before October 1, 2008, and receives a distribution of sales and use taxes under G.S. 105-472.

(2) Hold harmless amount. - The sum of the following amounts allocated for distribution to a municipality for a month:

a. The amount of sales and use tax revenue allocated under G.S. 105-486. This calculation determines the effect of repealing a one-half percent (1/2%) sales and use tax distributed on a per capita basis.

b. An amount determined by subtracting twenty-five percent (25%) of the amount of sales and use tax revenue allocated under G.S. 105-472 or Chapter 1096 of the 1967 Session Laws from fifty percent (50%) of the amount of sales and use tax revenue allocated under G.S. 105-486. This calculation determines the effect of distributing a one-quarter percent (.25%) tax on the basis of point of origin instead of on a per capita basis.

(b) Requirement. - A county is required to hold the eligible municipalities in the county harmless from the repeal of the local sales and use taxes formerly imposed under this Article. The Secretary must add an eligible municipality's hold harmless amount to the amount distributed to the municipality under this Subchapter. To obtain the revenue for the hold harmless distribution, the Secretary must reduce each county's monthly allocation under G.S. 105-472(b) or under Chapter 1096 of the 1967 Session Laws by the hold harmless amounts for the municipalities in that county. (2007-323, ss. 31.16.3(f), 31.16.4(c); 2007-345, s. 14.4(a); 2008-134, ss. 14(a), 15(c), (f), (g).)

§ 105-523. County hold harmless for repealed local taxes.

(a) Intent. - It is the intent of the General Assembly that each county benefit by at least five hundred thousand dollars ($500,000) annually from the exchange of a portion of the local sales and use taxes for the State's agreement to assume the responsibility for the non-administrative costs of Medicaid.

(b) Definitions. - The following definitions apply in this section:

(1) City hold harmless amount. - The hold harmless amount determined under G.S. 105-522 for the eligible municipalities in a county.

(2) Hold harmless threshold. - The amount of a county's Medicaid service costs and Medicare Part D clawback payments assumed by the State under G.S. 108A-54 for the fiscal year, less five hundred thousand dollars ($500,000). A county's Medicaid service costs for fiscal years 2008-2009, 2009-2010, and 2010-2011 are determined without regard to the changes made to the Federal Medical Assistance Percentage by section 5001 of the American Recovery and Reinvestment Act of 2009.

(3) Repealed sales tax amount. - The sum of the following amounts allocated for distribution to a county for a month:

a. The amount of sales and use tax revenue allocated under G.S. 105-486. This calculation determines the effect of repealing a one-half percent (1/2%) sales and use tax distributed on a per capita basis.

b. An amount determined by subtracting twenty-five percent (25%) of the amount of sales and use tax revenue allocated under G.S. 105-472 or Chapter 1096 of the 1967 Session Laws from fifty percent (50%) of the amount of sales and use tax revenue allocated under G.S. 105-486. This calculation determines the effect of distributing a one-quarter percent (.25%) tax on the basis of point of origin instead of on a per capita basis.

(c) Requirement. - If a county's repealed sales tax amount plus its city hold harmless amount for a fiscal year exceeds the county's hold harmless threshold for that fiscal year, the State is required to hold the county harmless for the difference by paying the amount of the difference to the county. The Secretary must withhold from sales and use tax collections under Article 5 of this Chapter the amount needed to make the county hold harmless payments required by this section.

(d) Method. - The Secretary must estimate a county's repealed sales tax amount, city hold harmless amount, and hold harmless threshold for a fiscal year to determine if the county is eligible for a hold harmless payment. The Secretary must send to an eligible county with the distribution made under G.S. 105-472 for March of that year an amount equal to ninety percent (90%) of its estimated hold harmless payment. At the end of each fiscal year, the Secretary must determine each county's hold harmless payment for that year. The Secretary must send by August 15 the remainder of the county's hold harmless payment for the fiscal year that ended on June 30. The Secretary of the Department of Health and Human Services must give the Secretary of Revenue the data needed to determine a county's hold harmless threshold by February 24th of each year, and the data needed for the final calculation of each county's hold harmless threshold by July 24th of each year. (2007-323, s. 31.16.4(d); 2007-345, s. 14.4(b); 2008-134, s. 15(a), (d), (f), (h); 2009-399, s. 4(a); 2010-95, s. 14.)

§§ 105-524 through 105-534: Reserved for future codification purposes.

§ 105-532: Reserved for future codification purposes.

§ 105-533: Reserved for future codification purposes.

§ 105-534: Reserved for future codification purposes.

Article 46.

One-Quarter Cent (1/4¢) County Sales and Use Tax.

§ 105-535. Short title.

This Article is the One-Quarter Cent (1/4¢) County Sales and Use Tax Act. (2007-323, s. 31.17(b).)

§ 105-536. Limitations.

This Article applies only to counties that levy the first one-cent (1¢) sales and use tax under Article 39 of this Chapter or under Chapter 1096 of the 1967 Session Laws, the first one-half cent (1/2¢) local sales and use tax under Article 40 of this Chapter, and the second one-half cent (1/2¢) local sales and use tax under Article 42 of this Chapter. (2007-323, s. 31.17(b).)

§ 105-537. Levy.

(a)   Authority. - If the majority of those voting in a referendum held pursuant to this Article vote for the levy of the tax, the board of county commissioners may, by resolution and after 10 days' public notice, levy a local sales and use tax at a rate of one-quarter percent (0.25%).

(b)   Vote. - The board of county commissioners may direct the county board of elections to conduct an advisory referendum on the question of whether to levy a local sales and use tax in the county as provided in this Article. The election shall be held in accordance with the procedures of G.S. 163-287.

(c)   Ballot Question. - The form of the question to be presented on a ballot for a special election concerning the levy of the tax authorized by this Article shall be:

"[ ] FOR   [ ] AGAINST

Local sales and use tax at the rate of one-quarter percent (0.25%) in addition to all other State and local sales and use taxes."

(d) Limitation. - A tax levied under this Article may not be in effect in a county at the same time as a tax levied under Article 60 of this Chapter. (2007-323, s. 31.17(b); 2013-381, s. 10.14.)

§ 105-538. Administration of taxes.

Except as provided in this Article, the adoption, levy, collection, administration, and repeal of these additional taxes must be in accordance with Article 39 of this Chapter. G.S. 105-468.1 is an administrative provision that applies to this Article. A tax levied under this Article does not apply to the sales price of food that is exempt from tax pursuant to G.S. 105-164.13B or to the sales price of a bundled transaction taxable pursuant to G.S. 105-467(a)(5a). The Secretary shall not divide the amount allocated to a county between the county and the municipalities within the county. (2007-323, s. 31.17(b); 2007-345, s. 14.5(a); 2008-134, s. 75; 2009-445, s. 18.)

§§ 105-539 through 105-549: Reserved for future codification purposes.

SUBCHAPTER IX. MULTICOUNTY TAXES.

Article 50.

Regional Transit Authority Vehicle Rental Tax.

§ 105-550. Definitions.

The definitions in G.S. 105-164.3 and the following definitions apply in this Article:

(1) Authority. - A regional public transportation authority or a regional transportation authority created pursuant to Article 26 or Article 27 of Chapter 160A of the General Statutes.

(2) Long-term lease or rental. - Defined in G.S. 105-187.1.

(3) Motorcycle. - Defined in G.S. 20-4.01.

(4) Repealed by Session Laws 1998-98, s. 33.

(5) Public transportation system. - Any combination of real and personal property established for purposes of public transportation. The systems may include one or more of the following: structures, improvements, buildings, equipment, vehicle parking or passenger transfer facilities, railroads and railroad rights-of-way, rights-of-way, bus services, shared-ride services, high-occupancy vehicle facilities, carpool and vanpool programs, voucher programs, telecommunications and information systems, integrated fare systems, bus lanes, and busways. The term does not include, however, streets, roads, or highways except to the extent they are dedicated to public transportation vehicles or to the extent they are necessary for access to vehicle parking or passenger transfer facilities.

(6) Short-term lease or rental. - A lease or rental that is not a long-term lease or rental.

(7) U-drive-it vehicle. - Defined in G.S. 20-4.01. (1997-417, s. 3; 1998-98, s. 33; 1999-452, s. 26.)

§ 105-551. Tax on gross receipts authorized.

(a) Tax. - The board of trustees of an Authority may levy a privilege tax on a retailer who is engaged in the business of leasing or renting U-drive-it vehicles or motorcycles based on the gross receipts derived by the retailer from the short-term lease or rental of these vehicles. The tax rate must be a percentage and may not exceed five percent (5%). A tax levied under this section applies to short-term leases or rentals made by a retailer whose place of business or inventory is located within the territorial jurisdiction of the Authority. This tax is in addition to all other taxes.

(b) Restrictions. - The board of trustees of an Authority may not levy a tax under this section or increase the tax rate of a tax levied under this section until all of the following requirements have been met:

(1) The board of trustees has held a public hearing on the tax or the increase in the tax rate after giving at least 10 days' notice of the hearing.

(2) If the Authority has a special tax board, the special tax board has adopted a resolution approving the levy of the tax or the increase in the tax rate.

(3) The board of commissioners of each county included in the territorial jurisdiction of the Authority has adopted a resolution approving the levy of the tax or the increase in the tax rate.

(c) Special Tax District. - If a regional transportation authority created under Article 27 of Chapter 160A of the General Statutes has not levied the tax under this section or has levied the tax at a rate of less than five percent (5%), it may create a special district that consists of the entire area of one or more counties within its territorial jurisdiction and may levy on behalf of the special district the tax authorized in this section. The rate of tax levied within the special district may not, when combined with the rate levied within the entire territorial jurisdiction of the authority, exceed five percent (5%). The regional transportation authority may not levy or increase a tax within the special district unless the board of commissioners of each county in the special district has adopted a resolution approving the levy or increase.

A special district created pursuant to this subsection is a body corporate and politic and has the power to carry out the purposes of this subsection. The board of trustees of the regional transportation authority created under Article 27 of Chapter 160A of the General Statutes shall serve, ex officio, as the governing body of a special district it creates pursuant to this subsection. The proceeds of a tax levied under this subsection may be used only for the benefit of the special district and only for the purposes provided in G.S. 105-554. Except as provided in this subsection, a tax levied under this subsection is governed by the provisions of this Article. (1997-417, s. 3; 1998-98, s. 34; 1999-445, s. 3; 1999-452, s. 27.)

§ 105-552. Collection and administration of gross receipts tax.

(a) Effective Date. - A tax or a tax increase levied under this Article becomes effective on the date set by the board of trustees in the resolution levying the tax or the tax increase. The effective date must be the first day of a month and may not be earlier than the first day of the second month after the board of trustees adopts the resolution.

(b) Collection. - A tax levied by an Authority under this Article shall be collected by the Authority but shall otherwise be administered in the same manner as the optional gross receipts tax levied by G.S. 105-187.5. Like the optional gross receipts tax, a tax levied under this Article is to be added to the lease or rental price of a U-drive-it vehicle or motorcycle and thereby be paid by the person to whom it is leased or rented.

A tax levied under this Article applies regardless of whether the retailer who leases or rents the U-drive-it vehicle or motorcycle has elected to pay the optional gross receipts tax on the lease or rental receipts from the vehicle. A tax levied under this Article must be paid to the Authority that levied the tax by the date an optional gross receipts tax would be payable to the Secretary of Revenue under G.S. 105-187.5 if the retailer who leases or rents the U-drive-it vehicle or motorcycle had elected to pay the optional gross receipts tax.

(c) Penalties and Remedies. - The penalties and remedies that apply to local sales and use taxes levied under Subchapter VIII of this Chapter apply to a tax levied under this Article. The board of trustees of an Authority may exercise any power the Secretary of Revenue or a board of county commissioners may exercise in collecting local sales and use taxes. (1997-417, s. 3; 1998-98, s. 35; 1999-452, s. 28.)

§ 105-553. Exemptions and refunds.

No exemptions are allowed from a tax levied under this Article. No refunds are allowed for a tax lawfully levied under this Article. (1997-417, s. 3.)

§ 105-554. Use of tax proceeds.

An Authority that levies a tax under this Article may use the proceeds of the tax for any purpose for which the Authority is authorized to use funds. An Authority shall use the tax proceeds to supplement and not to supplant or replace existing funds or other resources for public transportation systems. Authorized purposes for which an Authority may use funds include the following:

(1) Pledging funds in connection with the financing of a public transportation system or any part of a public transportation system.

(2) Paying a note, bond, or other obligation entered into by the Authority pursuant to Article 26 or Article 27 of Chapter 160A of the General Statutes. (1997-417, s. 3.)

§ 105-555. Repeal of tax or decrease in tax rate.

The board of trustees of an Authority may repeal a tax levied under this Article or decrease the tax rate of a tax levied under this Article. The same restrictions that apply to the levy of a tax or an increase in a tax rate under this Article apply to the repeal of the tax or a decrease in the tax rate.

A tax repeal or a tax decrease becomes effective on the date set by the board of trustees in the resolution repealing or decreasing the tax. The effective date must be on the first day of a month and may not be earlier than the first day of the second month after the board of trustees adopts the resolution. Repeal or decrease of a tax levied under this Article does not affect the rights or liabilities of an Authority, a taxpayer, or another person arising before the repeal or decrease. (1997-417, s. 3.)

§§ 105-556 through 105-559. Reserved for future codification purposes.

Article 51.

Regional Transit Authority Registration Tax.

§ 105-560. Definitions.

(1) Authority. - Any of the following:

a. A public transportation authority created pursuant to Article 25 of Chapter 160A of the General Statutes that includes two or more counties.

b. A regional public transportation authority created pursuant to Article 26 of Chapter 160A of the General Statutes.

c. A regional transportation authority created pursuant to Article 27 of Chapter 160A of the General Statutes.

(2) Board of trustees. - The governing body of an Authority.

(3) Public transportation system. - Defined in G.S. 105-550. (1997-417, s. 4.)

§ 105-561. Authority registration tax authorized.

(a) Tax Authorized. - The board of trustees of an Authority may, by resolution, levy an annual license tax in accordance with this Article upon any motor vehicle with a tax situs within its territorial jurisdiction. The purpose of the tax levied under this Article is to raise revenue for capital and operating expenses of an Authority in providing public transportation systems. The rate of tax levied under this Article must be a full dollar amount, but may not exceed eight dollars ($8.00) a year.

(b) Restrictions. - The board of trustees of an Authority may not levy a tax under this Article or increase the tax rate until all of the following requirements have been met:

(1) The board of trustees has held a public hearing on the tax or the increase in the tax rate after giving at least 10 days' notice of the hearing.

(2) If the Authority has a special tax board, the special tax board has adopted a resolution approving the levy of the tax or the increase in the tax rate.

(3) Except where the levy or increase in tax is necessary for debt service on bonds or notes that each of the boards of county commissioners had previously approved under G.S. 159-51, the board of commissioners of each county included in the territorial jurisdiction of the Authority has adopted a resolution approving the levy of the tax or the increase in the tax rate.

(c)   Resolutions. - The board of trustees and the board of county commissioners, upon adoption of a resolution pursuant to this section, shall cause a certified copy of the resolution to be delivered immediately to the Authority and to the Division of Motor Vehicles.

(d)   Special Tax District. - If a regional transportation authority created under Article 27 of Chapter 160A of the General Statutes or a regional public transportation authority created under Article 26 of Chapter 160A of the General Statutes has not levied the tax under this section or has levied the tax at a rate of less than eight dollars ($8.00), it may create a special district that consists of the entire area of one or more counties within its territorial jurisdiction and may levy on behalf of the special district the tax authorized in this section. The rate of tax levied within the special district may not, when combined with the rate levied within the entire territorial jurisdiction of the authority; exceed eight dollars ($8.00). The regional transportation authority may not levy or increase a tax within the special district unless the board of commissioners of each county in the special district has adopted a resolution approving the levy or increase.

A special district created pursuant to this subsection is a body corporate and politic and has the power to carry out the purposes of this subsection. The board of trustees of the regional transportation authority created under Article 27 of Chapter 160A of the General Statutes or a regional public transportation authority created under Article 26 of Chapter 160A of the General Statutes shall serve, ex officio, as the governing body of a special district it creates pursuant to this subsection. The proceeds of a tax levied under this subsection may be used only for the benefit of the special district and only for the purposes provided in G.S. 105-564. Except as provided in this subsection, a tax levied under this subsection is governed by the provisions of this Article. (1997-417, s. 4; 1999-445, s. 4; 2009-527, s. 3(a)-(d); 2013-414, s. 50.)

§ 105-562. Collection and scope.

(a)   Collection. - A tax or a tax increase levied under this Article becomes effective on the date set by the board of trustees in the resolution levying the tax or the tax increase. The effective date must be the first day of a month and may not be earlier than the first day of the sixth calendar month after the board of trustees adopts the resolution. To the extent the tax applies to vehicles whose tax situs is in a county the entire area of which is within the jurisdiction of the Authority, the Division of Motor Vehicles shall collect and administer the tax. To the extent the tax applies to vehicles whose tax situs is in a county that is only partially within the jurisdiction of the county, the Authority shall collect and administer the tax. The Authority may contract with one or more local governments in its jurisdiction to collect the tax on its behalf.

Upon receipt of the resolutions under G.S. 105-561, the Division of Motor Vehicles shall proceed to collect and administer the tax as provided in this Article. The tax is due at the same time and subject to the same restrictions as in G.S. 20-87(1), (2), (4), (5), (6), and (7) and G.S. 20-88. The Division of Motor Vehicles may adopt rules to carry out its responsibilities under this Article.

(b)   Scope. - Only vehicles required to pay a tax under G.S. 20-87(1), (2), (4), (5), (6), and (7) and G.S. 20-88 shall be subject to the tax provided by this Article. Taxes shall be prorated in accordance with G.S. 20-95.

(c)   Tax Situs. - The tax situs of a motor vehicle for the purpose of this Article is its ad valorem tax situs. If the vehicle is exempt from ad valorem tax, its tax situs for the purpose of this Article is the ad valorem tax situs it would have if it were not exempt from ad valorem tax. (1997-417, s. 4; 2009-527, s. 5(a).)

§ 105-563. Modification or repeal of tax.

The Board of Trustees may, by resolution, repeal the levy of the tax under this Article or decrease the amount of the tax, under the same procedures and subject to the same limitations as provided in G.S. 105-561. A tax repeal or a tax decrease becomes effective on the date set by the board of trustees in the resolution repealing or decreasing the tax. The effective date must be on the first day of a month and may not be earlier than the first day of the sixth calendar month after the board of trustees adopts the resolution. Repeal or decrease of a tax levied under this Article does not affect the rights or liabilities of an Authority, a taxpayer, or another person arising before the repeal or decrease. (1997-417, s. 4; 2009-527, s. 5(b).)

§ 105-564. Distribution and use of proceeds.

The Authority shall retain the net proceeds of taxes it collects under this Article. Taxes collected by the Division of Motor Vehicles under this Article shall be credited to a special fund and the net proceeds disbursed quarterly to the appropriate Authority. Interest credited to the fund shall be disbursed quarterly to the Highway Fund to reimburse the Division of Motor Vehicles for the cost of collecting and administering the tax.

An Authority that levies a tax under this Article may use the proceeds of the tax for any purpose for which the Authority is authorized to use funds. An Authority shall use the tax proceeds to supplement and not to supplant or replace existing funds or other resources for public transportation systems. (1997-417, s. 4.)

§ 105-565. Reserved for future codification purposes.

§ 105-566. Reserved for future codification purposes.

§ 105-567. Reserved for future codification purposes.

§ 105-568. Reserved for future codification purposes.

§ 105-569. Reserved for future codification purposes.

Article 52.

County Vehicle Registration Tax.

§ 105-570. County Vehicle Registration Tax; shared with municipalities.

(a)   A county is considered an authority under Article 51 of this Chapter, and the board of commissioners of that county is considered the board of trustees of the authority under Article 51, except that the maximum tax that may be levied by a county under this Article is seven dollars ($7.00) per year.

(b)   A county may not levy a tax under this Article unless the county or at least one unit of local government in the county operates a public transportation system.

(c) Any tax levied under this Article shall, after the receipt of those funds from the Division of Motor Vehicles, be retained or distributed by the county on a per capita basis as it receives those funds as follows:

(1) Pro rata (i) retained by the county based on the population of the county that is not in an incorporated area, and (ii) distributed to the municipalities within the county based on the population of that municipality that is located within that county. To determine the population of each county and municipality, the county shall use the most recent annual estimate of population certified by the State Budget Officer.

(2) Notwithstanding subdivision (1) of this subsection, if a municipality to which funds are to be distributed does not operate a public transportation system, the population of that municipality shall be excluded from the calculations of subdivision (1) of this subsection and no distribution shall be made to that municipality.

(3) Notwithstanding subdivision (1) of this subsection, if a county for which funds are to be retained does not operate a public transportation system, the population of that county not in an incorporated area shall be excluded from the calculations of subdivision (1) of this subsection, and the county shall not retain any funds.

If a county that does not retain funds or a municipality that does not receive an allocation of funds on account of subdivision (2) or (3) of this subsection begins to operate a public transportation system, that county or municipality shall begin retaining or receiving funds beginning the first day of July that is more than 30 days thereafter.

(d) The proceeds of a tax imposed under this Article may be used by that county or municipality only to operate a public transportation system, including financing, constructing, operating, and maintaining that public transportation system. The term "public transportation system" has the same meaning as defined in G.S. 105-506.1.

(e) As used in this section, operation of a public transportation system includes a contract or interlocal agreement for operation of the public transportation system by another county or municipality, or by a transportation authority created under (i) a municipal charter; or (ii) Article 25, 26, or 27 of Chapter 160A of the General Statutes. As used in this section, operation of a public transportation system also includes a contract with a private entity for operation of the public transportation system.

(f) An interlocal agreement under this section may also deal with allocation of funds between a municipality and county for operation by the county of a human services public transportation system within the municipality when the municipality also operates a public transportation system.

(g) This Article is supplemental to Article 51 of this Chapter. (2009-527, s. 4.)

§ 105-571: Reserved for future codification purposes.

§ 105-572: Reserved for future codification purposes.

§ 105-573: Reserved for future codification purposes.

§ 105-574: Reserved for future codification purposes.

§ 105-575: Reserved for future codification purposes.

§ 105-576: Reserved for future codification purposes.

§ 105-577: Reserved for future codification purposes.

§ 105-578: Reserved for future codification purposes.

§ 105-579: Reserved for future codification purposes.

§ 105-580: Reserved for future codification purposes.

§ 105-581: Reserved for future codification purposes.

§ 105-582: Reserved for future codification purposes.

§ 105-583: Reserved for future codification purposes.

§ 105-584: Reserved for future codification purposes.

§ 105-585: Reserved for future codification purposes.

§ 105-586: Reserved for future codification purposes.

§ 105-587: Reserved for future codification purposes.

§ 105-588: Reserved for future codification purposes.

§ 105-589: Reserved for future codification purposes.

§ 105-590: Reserved for future codification purposes.

§ 105-591: Reserved for future codification purposes.

§ 105-592: Reserved for future codification purposes.

§ 105-593: Reserved for future codification purposes.

§ 105-594: Reserved for future codification purposes.

§ 105-595: Reserved for future codification purposes.

§ 105-596: Reserved for future codification purposes.

§ 105-597: Reserved for future codification purposes.

§ 105-598: Reserved for future codification purposes.

§ 105-599: Reserved for future codification purposes.

SUBCHAPTER X. LOCAL OPTION COUNTY TAXES.

Article 60.

Land Transfer Tax.

§ 105-600: Repealed by Session Laws 2011-18, s. 1, effective March 31, 2011.

§ 105-601: Repealed by Session Laws 2011-18, s. 1, effective March 31, 2011.

§ 105-602: Repealed by Session Laws 2011-18, s. 1, effective March 31, 2011.

§ 105-603: Repealed by Session Laws 2011-18, s. 1, effective March 31, 2011.

§ 105-604: Repealed by Session Laws 2011-18, s. 1, effective March 31, 2011.

Vision Books Order Form

Fax Orders: 1-980-299-5965

Phone Orders: 1-704-898-0770

E-mail Orders: www.visionbooks.org

Mail Orders: Vision Books, LLC
P.O. Box 42406
Charlotte, NC 28215

Shipp To:
Name_____
Address_____
City_____State_____Zip_____
Phone_____Fax_____
Email_____@_____

Bill To: We can bill a third party on your behalf.
Name_____
Address_____
City_____State_____Zip_____
Phone___(_____)_____Fax_____
Email_____@_____

Pamphlet Number ($15.00 Each)	Qty	Total Cost
_____	_____	_____
_____	_____	_____
_____	_____	_____
_____	_____	_____
_____	_____	_____
_____	_____	_____
_____	_____	_____
_____	_____	_____
<u>Full Volume Set 1-92</u>	<u>92 Pamphlets</u>	<u>1,380.00</u>

Free Shipping Shipping & Handling on Full Volume Orders
Add $1.00 Shipping & Handling per pamphlet $_____

Total Cost $_____

Thank you for your support. Management!

DID YOU ENJOY THIS BOOK?

Vision Books, LLC would like to hear from you! If you or someone you know has been fasely imprisoned, we would like to hear your story. If the 'North Carolina Criminal Law and Procedure' has had an effect in your life or if you have suggestions, we would like to hear from you. Send your letters to:

Vision Books, LLC
Attn: Staff Writers
P.O. Box 42406
Charlotte, NC 28215
Email: staff@visionbooks.org

Order Additional Copies:

Fax Orders:	1-980-299-5965
Phone Orders:	1-704-898-0770
E-mail Orders:	www.visionbooks.org
Mail Orders:	Vision Books, LLC P.O. Box 42406 Charlotte, NC 28215

www.ingramcontent.com/pod-product-compliance
Lightning Source LLC
Chambersburg PA
CBHW051626170526
45167CB00001B/71